D1391720

To School Through The Fields

A Country Childhood

To School Through The Fields

A Country Childhood

Alice Taylor

BRANDON

Copyright *To School Through The Fields* © Alice Taylor 1988
Quench The Lamp © Alice Taylor 1990

First published in two separate volumes by Brandon Book Publishers Ltd,
Dingle, Co. Kerry, Ireland

This edition published in Ireland in 1991 by Brandon
Brandon Book Publishers Ltd, Dingle, Co. Kerry

Alice Taylor's right to be identified as the author of this work has been
asserted by her in accordance with the Copyright, Designs and
Patents Act, 1988.

Set in Linotronic Palatino by SX Composing Ltd, Rayleigh, Essex
Printed and bound in U.K. by Mackays of Chatham PLC,
Chatham, Kent

British Library Cataloguing in Publication Data

Taylor, Alice
To school through the fields; and Quench the lamp.
1. Ireland (Republic). Social life, 1922-1969 –
Biographies
I. Title
941.70822092

ISBN 0-7126-4873-9

Contents

Different Times

This is the story of a childhood. In its day it was an ordinary childhood but, with the changing winds of time, now it could never be.

Ours was a large family in a close-knit rural community that was an extension of our home. Neighbours came to our house and we went to theirs as freely as the birds flew across the sky; invitations were unheard of and welcomes unquestioned.

The old were never alone as the neighbours joined hands around them and the young, too, were included in the circle. As in every group of individuals, all had their own idiosyncracies, and we as children were educated in human awareness by the close association with many people.

Sharing was taken for granted, from the milk in the winter when some cows went dry, to the pork steak and puddings when the pig was killed. Work was also shared from the saving of the hay to the cutting of the corn and preparing for the Stations. It was an interlaced community and its structure helped those within it to support each other.

So please come back with me, to where we had time to be children and life moved at a different pace.

A Child's Nest

Lisnasheoga was the nest from which we learned to fly. An ivy-clad farmhouse surrounded by trees, it stood on the sunny side of a sloping hill at the foot of which the Darigle river curved its way through gold-furzed inches to disappear under a stone bridge into the woods beyond.

In the summers we swam in the river and caught minnows with jam pots; on Sunday evenings my father fished in it, bringing home each time a bag of trout. In winter salmon came up to this quiet backwater to spawn and, of course, there was a certain amount of poaching, to which my father objected strongly. Once, when a generous neighbour gave us a present of a poached salmon, he lined us all up around the kitchen table and proceeded to open up the fish. As the eggs poured out he explained about the huge loss of fish life due to the poaching of this one salmon. In my father's world nature possessed a balance and man had no right to upset that balance to satisfy his own greed; killing this fish was going against the laws of nature.

The river showed us two different faces of nature: in summer it was our friend but in winter it burst into brown torrents of anger that overflowed its banks and swept down our valley with a menacing roar. From the river valley the land rose and stretched away into rolling countryside, climbing into misty mountains at the horizon. This was farming country, where the farmers and nature changed the face of the landscape with the seasons.

Our parents were a blend of opposites. My mother was kind and gentle, with a far-seeing wisdom, and she expected only the best from her fellow human beings. My father was a man with a high level of intelligence and a low threshold of tolerance; patience was not one of his virtues. He loved trees, birds and all his farm animals: nature he appreciated to the full, but he viewed his fellow human beings with a jaundiced eye and never expected too much from them.

With seven children in the family, we were reared as free as birds, growing up in a world of simplicity untouched by outside influences. Our farm was our world and nature as an educator gave free rein to our imaginations; unconsciously we absorbed the natural order of things and observed the facts of life unfolding daily before our eyes. We were free to be children and to grow up at our own pace in a quiet place close to the earth.

Preparing For The Stations

In our townland our turn for the Stations came around every six years and then it was like three Christ-mases rolled into one. The preparations might start as much as twelve months in advance as they provided an opportunity to get everything done in the house that needed to be done. The reason, of course, for this big clean-up was that Mass was going to be said in the house and all the neighbours for miles around were going to descend on us.

Broken walls in the yard were repaired and any gate pillar that had lost its balance suddenly found itself standing erect. Gates that had sagged previously now swung with free aban-don. Loose sheets of galvanised were nailed down and mis-sing slates replaced. Muddy grey walls became virgin white overnight and dunghills disappeared out of sight. The cows could be forgiven for thinking that they were in a strange farmyard and we almost expected them not to do what they always did.

The outside clean-up was insignificant compared to what went on inside: nothing from the roof down was safe. Mice and spiders that had nested comfortably for months suddenly found themselves in need of boating facilities as soapy water gushed around them. Broken panes of glass that had been patched up with bits of timber were replaced, sometimes a whole new window was installed. Bags of rubbish were burned indiscriminately and many a family treasure was re-duced to ashes. Rooms that were full of clutter before, now doubled in size: we wandered around in a house full of hollow sounds.

When the burning and washing had finished the painting

4

began and nothing escaped the paint brush. Ceilings, walls, tables and chairs all took on a new, bright look. It was the era of the slow drying paint and if you forgot to watch your step you could end up with a multi-coloured look yourself. The Stations only affected the downstairs rooms fully, but if a nosy visitor strayed off the main thoroughfare we were not going to be caught with our pants down.

Cleaning and painting finished, the next target was the big ware press in the parlour. Out came delicate china which had been in the family for years. My mother's respect for the Stations weighed against her fear of breakage, but the Stations won every time. Once when a precious jug was broken she mourned it for days, telling us how long it had been in the family. Finally, Dan, our part-time travelling farm worker, said: 'Missus, if it was here that long it was time to break it'. And that was the end of that.

On the day before the Stations everything started to come together. The house was full of women polishing and setting tables. White linen table-cloths saw the light of day for the first time in years and moth balls rolled from between their creases. A strict eye was kept on the children, and for good reason. One year on the day before a neighbour's Stations all the good furniture was out in the yard while a new floor was being laid. The adults were busy in the house while the children, discovering a bucket of whitewash, proceeded to paint the dark mahogany furniture a brilliant white. Such potential catastrophes had to be borne in mind.

The night before the Stations had a special atmosphere filled with a sense of expectancy. The whole house lay in readiness, with fires set in all the downstairs rooms. Tables were laid with fine china and shining silver while bowls of lump sugar and dishes of butter rolls lay covered in the kitchen. In front of the fire was a row of polished shoes graduating from tiny tots upwards. We were all bathed in a big timber tub in front of the bedroom fire and we young ones were the last to be washed because our chances of getting dirty again were the greatest.

I doubt that my mother went to bed at all that night and if she did it was for a very short period. The cows got an early awakening in the morning and the milk was carried off to the creamery bright and early. Dirty jobs finished, everybody put on their finery. The large kitchen table was raised with a chair under each end to act as the altar. My mother was very particular about the altar, as for her this was what it was all about. She was a deeply religious person and the honour of having Mass said in her house was something which she appreciated to the full; on the morning of the Stations she had about her a special aura of peace. All the fuss of preparation was over and now, surrounded by her family and friends, because all her neighbours were her friends, she was going to welcome the Lord into her home. They were the two most important things in her life: her family and her God.

My father, dressed in his best black suit and shining soft boots – he never wore shoes – waited outside the door to welcome his neighbours and the priests when they came. It was grand to see the neighbours arriving, some having worked late with us the night before, but now all dressed up for the occasion.

Finally the priests arrived to a flurry of handshakes all around. One priest said Mass in the kitchen while the other heard confessions by the fire in the parlour; it always tickled my fancy going to confession by our own parlour fire. There was a warm feeling about this Mass and communion, with all the neighbours gathered around the kitchen table. We had worked and played together and now we were sharing something much greater which formed a different bond between us. It was like the Last Supper.

After Mass the confession priest joined the other and dues were collected. A volunteer was sought for the next Stations, which posed no problem as every house took its turn and everybody knew who was next. Then the flurry started: feeding the multitudes, but instead of loaves and fishes there was usually an abundance of goodies. Everybody helped so there was no panic, only organized confusion, and all were fed in the end. When breakfast was over the priests left and that was the official end of the Stations, but in reality it carried on all day and far into the night. Neighbours who could not come in the morning and maybe were not in our Stations area came in the evening or even that night. Relations of varying degrees turned up and as ours was a long-tailed family this meant half the parish.

As well as a religious event it was also a social occasion. People came together who normally only worked together and visitors met old neighbours. Great talking was done. An impromptu concert often started up and anybody who could sing, and indeed some who could not, entertained the light-hearted gathering. This evolved into a dance with a neighbour providing music on a melodeon. There was no shortage of energy and you would think that we had been resting up for a week beforehand.

After the Stations nothing could be found for weeks. Caps had disappeared and wellingtons were reported missing and many a man was left without his favourite old jacket. But who cared? We had had a great day and the house was fit to receive visitors from America for months afterwards.

Beneath God's Altar

Old Nell carried her false teeth around in her pocket. Our most eccentric neighbour, Nell was often in trouble. Once my mother took her to Cork to visit a doctor and afterwards they went into the old Savoy for a meal. As soon as the waitress had placed the meal on the table out came Nell's false teeth and into the ashtray. My mother never batted an eyelid and nobody would ever have known of this occurrence but for the fact that my sister, who was working in Cork at the time, had joined them, much to her regret. Why Nell bothered with the teeth at all was difficult to understand: she did not use them for eating and you had only to see her to know that, for her, appearance did not have a high priority. The truth of the matter was that she had paid good money for the teeth and regarded them rather like the new hat which she wore for special occasions. The fact that she ever acquired them in the first place was entirely due to the considerable persuasive powers of the dentist, because making Nell part with her money was like prising a stubborn barnacle from a rock. She was not short of money. She was the youngest of a large family who had all gone to America and done well and, as they did not have marrying blood in their veins, when they died Nell was the beneficiary.

She lived in a little house with a sagging thatched roof where birds nested and swallows gathered every year. The house itself was like a birds' nest and so overgrown with greenery that it was always dark inside. My father often tried to coax her to build a new house but to her that was out of the question, and she would not disturb the birds by repairing the old one. While things remained unchanged my father often said that he hoped the house would last longer than Nell herself and, indeed, it did.

Few of the neighbours called on her, not because they did not want to but because she did not want them to; she did not trust many people and preferred to keep to herself. Even when she called to our house she would start screeching about a field away: we heard her before we saw her. My father would raise his eyes to heaven and say, 'Nell is beagling again'. She had a high-pitched, quarrelsome voice and she shouted to you whether you were in the same room as her or a field away. When she came she was usually in a panic: the cows were after breaking out, or the donkey was stuck in a hole, or some other disaster had befallen her. And no matter what we were doing at the time we had to drop everything to go to her rescue. Nevertheless, she was not in the least bit grateful for anything that was done for her: as far as she was concerned virtue was its own reward. One day my father spent a few particularly tough hours trying to repair her thatched roof without disturbing her birds or falling through it himself. When he had finished she shouted out the door at him, 'You are dressing a bed in heaven for yourself'. The implication was that he should be grateful to her for affording his soul such a golden opportunity.

If you met Nell without being prepared for the shock she would frighten the wits out of you. She had long black hair which she never washed and which was stiff with a combination of grease and soot. She had a straight black fringe, a little like Cleopatra's, except that Nell's was perfumed with smoke. A strange combination of dress and overall covered her from neck to ankles and down to her wrists. Her virgin skin never saw the light of day. She wore black knitted stockings and black leather boots laced above her ankles. Her face was almost as black as her hair and if she happened to have her teeth in they emphasised her overall blackness because from lack of use they were as pearly as the day the dentist gave them to her. When they were not in her mouth or her pocket they were soaking in a jam pot on the dresser, the only bright spot grinning in the semi-darkness of the kitchen.

I thought that Nell was a kindred spirit. Every day I called to her house and stayed there for hours. With that strange affinity which often develops between the very old and the very young we were in perfect accord. She did not comply with normal acceptable adult behaviour and in my eyes that brought her almost into my world, for to me she was more a child like me than an adult. We went to town in the donkey and cart and I was allowed to guide the donkey who had a mind of his own so we sometimes ended up in places far from where we had intended going.

With Nell I saw my first corpse. Some old woman who had gone to school with Nell had died many miles away, so we tackled up the donkey and set out. It was a lovely warm day and as the donkey stopped for a feed of grass whenever he got the notion it took half the day to go and the other half to come back. When we arrived at the wake house we were ushered into the room where the corpse was laid out; I had never before seen anybody dead and it scared the daylights out of me. Whatever she had been like in life, in death this old lady looked forbidding and aggressive. She was propped up in bed wearing a blue, high-necked frilled gown and her abundant hair was swept high on her head. Her face was grey and rigid. She looked as if she had spent her life giving out and that at any minute she might start again. I was glad when we made a hasty exit. Nell did not go in for social niceties and so, without exchanging any formalities with the other mourners, we boarded our donkey and cart for the return journey. I was half nervous that the old lady might be coming after us. I looked back. Everybody at the wake was out in the road looking in our direction. Nell had not bothered to say who she was and, as this was in a different parish, they had never seen her before. They probably thought she was the devil.

The only other regular caller to Nell's house was an old half-blind man called Tim Joe. He lived further back the valley and brought her any news that he thought she should hear; it was he who had brought her the news of the old lady's death.

Despite her lack of visitors, Nell decided that she would have the Stations when her turn came. She was not expected to have them but, contrary as she was, that was sufficient reason for Nell to do so. She sent word to all the neighbours via Tim Joe that she did not want them eating her out of house and home when they came, however. Undoubtedly they got the message, for there was none of her neighbours involved in Nell's Stations or the preparations apart from Tim Joe and me. And, compared with what went on in other houses, there were almost no preparations at all. My mother worried more about Nell's Stations than did Nell herself, but she was powerless to do anything as Nell, when she put her mind to it, was as unyielding as steel. The colour of Nell's altar cloths and the lack of anything for the priest to eat caused my mother sleepless nights, but they did not cost Nell a thought.

The day before the Stations Nell and I brushed the kitchen and threw out the ashes that sometimes accumulated if Nell did not get the urge to shift them. We whitewashed the inside walls and any parts of the outside not covered by ivy and, having washed out the floor and cleaned the windows, we thought the little place was a palace. Indeed, the cats and dogs that I had put out for the clean-up were nearly afraid to come back in. After our strenuous efforts Nell made tea and to my delight produced a currant cake, but while we were having our tea-party she saw through the window a curious neighbour approaching and straight away hid the cake behind a bucket of milk on the table. It was Nell's belief that it was more blessed to receive than to give.

After the tea, down from the smoky rafters she took a timber box. Before we had time to open it a brown mouse shot out between our fingers; his ancestors had probably moved in years previously and generations of his kin had been reared in the box. They were, of course, forced to live in such high places because of Nell's collection of cats which now gave chase and put a sudden end to the long, undisturbed tenancy. There was plenty of evidence of the mouse family in the box but apart from that and a few gigantic spiders the box was a store of treasures. It contained some lovely old lace cloths and brass candlesticks. We shook out the cloths and discovered that they had some gaping holes; these, however, did not bother

Nell and she selected the two best ones to act as altar cloths. She had two hens hatching in boxes under the table but she decided not to disturb them; anyway, when it was covered by the white cloth the hens disappeared from view. And though the cloth was not perfectly white after long years in the box we thought that it was perfect, and we also used the candlesticks feeling no need to polish them.

On the morning of the Stations I arrived before the priests to find that Nell had no fire lighting: she refused to light it because the birds were not used to such an early fire and she would not upset them. Such reasoning could not be argued with: the priests would be there for only one morning, the birds were always there.

The parish priest was a kind, wise old man who, after evicting a few of Nell's cats from their warm bed, sat himself down on the chair beside where the fire should have been. The curate, Fr Kelly, knew Nell well and had a good working relationship with her: he agreed with everything she said. As he set up his altar I prayed that the hens would stay put and that he would not stand too close to the table as one of them was very cross and could stick out her neck and bite.

It was a peaceful sunny morning and the dogs lay asleep around the floor and the cats were curled up in the pool of sunlight on the doorstep. We had a heavenly choir as the birds chirped from their nests in the thatch and sang in the bushes and trees that grew wild and free close to the door. God smiled on us all that morning: it was a beautiful Mass and I saw a tear slip down the face of the old priest.

Suddenly, in the middle of the last blessing, the curate exclaimed, with extra vehemence, 'Christ!' The old priest nodded kindly but I knew that the hatching hen had struck when I saw her head disappearing back through the folds of the altar cloth.

Mass over, the problem of breakfast reared its ugly head. In order to boil the kettle we had to light a fire, and lighting this fire was something of an ordeal. There was a hole under the open fire to create a draught and the bellows lay just beside to blow air into it. The problem was that ashes got into this hole and it had to be cleaned regularly, but Nell never cleaned it at all. Fr Kelly decided to tackle the problem. He lit bits of newspaper and pushed them in under Nell's black turf; they flickered feebly and, in order to encourage them, he went down on his hands and knees to blow at them. Unfortunately, Tim Joe chose that precise moment to turn the bellows, sending a shower of ashes over the head of the kneeling curate. Nell, who was chatting with the parish priest – or rather, shouting at him – then solved the whole problem in two seconds by pouring a jam pot of paraffin oil on the fire and set it roaring up the chimney. In no time the kettle was singing and Nell made tea as strong as porter. We boiled eggs in a black tin saucepan over the open fire, which was now glowing red and ideal for toasting bread. At last the five of us sat down and had a companionable breakfast, during which the hatching hens decided that it was time to stretch their legs and trotted out the door leaving evidence of their passage on the floor behind them. When Fr Kelly saw them a look of understanding came over his face and he smiled in amusement. Perhaps he had thought until then that forces other than divine were under Nell's altar.

When breakfast was over and we were relaxing in the sunny kitchen Nell retired to her usual chair by the fire and after a few minutes sent out a loud snore. The priests took the hint: their time was up. Nell was not accustomed to visitors and she had had enough for one day. I went to the gate with the two priests. The parish priest put his hand on my head and said, 'Little girl, God is found in strange places. Try not to forget this morning'. I never did.

Animal Nanny

In the farmyard the gift of new life came with the spring. After Christmas, when we had celebrated the birth of the child Jesus, the baby calves were the first to arrive in the animal kingdom. We had watched the cows heavy with calf trample daily through the winter mud; indeed, I had sometimes witnessed the commencement of this saga in the coming together of the bull and cow.

At night the cows were tied up in the warm stalls on beds of yellow straw and every night before going to sleep my father lit the storm lantern to go and see them. The lantern was filled with oil and had a lighted wick surrounded by a glass globe which protected it from the weather; this lamp hung from a long handle so that it could be carried comfortably by hand. In checking the cows nightly he had to be able to ascertain if any of them were going to calve during the night. He needed to be a bit of a gynaecologist as an unattended cow could get into difficulty calving and the result might be a dead calf in the morning. Many a night he went out in the cold of winter to check.

I loved to watch the baby calves arrive though I hated to hear the cows groan in pain; however, like all mothers, they recovered quickly once it was over. The new-born calf was put under the mother's head and she licked it dry. Soon it stood on its spindly legs and wobbled around before being picked up and carried to the calf house where it was put in a section by itself. The cow, after a feed of warm bran, would be milked and the beastings, as this milk was called, fed to the calf. At this stage he was not quite sure how to drink, so you put your fingers into his mouth and he sucked the milk off them. The cow never again saw her calf, which seemed cruel to me though it did not appear to bother her.

The calves were kept in their house during the cold weather where they were fed morning and evening with buckets of milk warm from the cows. It was one of the first signs of summer when the calves were left out and they were so accustomed to the limitations of house life that it took a lot of gentle persuasion to coax them into the bright sunlight. When we brought them through the haggard into a big green field they could not believe their eyes: they spread their legs and put out their noses expecting to meet a barrier; then took a couple of steps and tested with their noses again. They did this a few times until gradually it dawned on them that there were no more barriers: this was freedom. Then they took off, whipping their tails high into the air and galloping around the field with sheer abandon.

Each night they were brought back to the farmyard to be fed. They drank from a communal trough and had to be watched closely or they would drink too much as, like most teenagers, they still had to learn when to put the brakes on. One night I was supervising the feeding when one strong whiteheaded bull would not take his head from the trough despite all my efforts. Later on, while milking the cows, we heard a low bellow of pain coming from the haggard. My stubborn whitehead was prone on the ground with a swollen belly, his tongue hanging out and his eyes rolling in his head. Quick action was needed and my father pulled out his penknife and lanced the exact spot in the whitehead's belly. It receded like a balloon deflating and within minutes he was back on his legs. He had gone almost past the point of no return and I viewed his recovery as if he were Lazarus rising from the dead. My father took on a new dimension in my eyes.

As these calves grew older they did not need to return to the farmyard for feeding as they were able to eat sufficient grass for themselves. They were then kept in the fields, known as the inches, along by the river where they grew strong and during the winter cold when grass was scarce hay was carried down to them. However, if the snow came they had to be brought back up to the stalls for shelter. It was strange to see these calves, who but a few months previously had been nervous of open spaces, now terrified of the constraint of the stalls.

When spring came the large dunghills which had risen outside the cowhouses, stables and piggery during the winter were drawn by horse and butt to the fields, tilted out in heaps, and spread to make the grass grow. This was the only fertilizer used on the land and on the drills of potatoes, mangles, turnips and cabbage. The land which had been ploughed in winter or early spring was now harrowed and drills made ready for setting.

Setting the spuds was a big job. First my father sorted out the seed potatoes and cut them into *sciolláns*, a section with an 'eye' from which the new growth would sprout. On the day of setting we would each have a bucket of *sciolláns* – or a gallon if you were very small – and started setting at one end of the field. The drills stretched the whole length of a three- or four-acre field and if you looked too far ahead you could face that mental wall which long-distance runners meet. We had a cheery character called Mick working with us on the farm, and he shortened many a long drill with his stories. His advice in these or indeed many other circumstances was to 'Keep your head down, your arse to the wind, and keep going'.

If we were after having some wet weather the earth would be damp and clammy, clinging to boots, knees and hands. We went on our knees to set potatoes, wrapping jute bags tied with binder twine around them, and as the day wore on we were often weighed down with mud, which clung in lumps to boots and knees, and to add to the discomfort our hands got colder and colder while our noses were chilled enough to hang icicles.

If we all got fed up at the same time, which could happen coming on evening, we would all sit down and Mick would sing a song. We learned many songs while setting spuds and many a story was told, imaginary or otherwise. We understood well the story of the Gobán Saor, an old Irish legend.

The Gobán Saor ruled a large kingdom which he wanted to

leave to the cleverest of his three sons. One day, he took his eldest son on a long journey and after some time walking said: 'Son, shorten the road for me.'

The son was totally at a loss as to how to help his father, so they returned home. The following day the Gobán Saor took his second son, and again the same thing happened. On the third day he took his youngest son and after they had travelled some distance he said once more: 'Son, shorten the road for me'.

The youngest son immediately began to tell his father a story that was long and interesting, and they became so engrossed in the tale that they never noticed the length of the journey. In our lives, Mick was the Gobán Saor's youngest son.

When all the spuds were set they were covered over with the dark brown earth and, even though we had suffered setting them, we felt a great sense of achievement the day the last drill was filled in. They stretched away into the distance, holding their secret growth within, and we knew every inch of that soft earth with the hidden stones that caused sharp pain when they came in contact with tender kneecaps. It would be difficult to be closer to the earth than we were.

We grew our own wheat, barley and oats. After ploughing and harrowing the land the corn drill was used to sow the grain. The drill was a long timber box with a hinged cover and into this the bag of seed was emptied. Underneath the box were long slender pipes that fed the seeds into the earth in regular rows as the horse drew the corn drill along.

When everything was planted it was in the hands of nature to provide the growth, and it was wonderful to see the earth returning our trust when the bright green growth burst forth. In spring the land wakes up from its winter rest, the grass emerges, the buds begin to appear on the trees and the whole countryside loses its threadbare coat. The birds start to sing again, telling us all that winter is over.

The spring also brought the young lambs. If there is anything that puts the 'closed' sign on the door of winter it is the sight of frisky lambs playing in the fields. Sometimes, if the ewe decided that she was not designed for motherhood, a baby lamb would find its way into a box by the kitchen fire where it was bottle fed. Once I had such a pet and I called him Sam. He was cared for lovingly and by early summer he had grown to be a big fellow, able to follow me everywhere. One day, while I was stooped forward playing in the garden, he came from behind and butted me with his head. I was very offended by this ingratitude but it was evidence that Sam was ready to return to the flock; his pet days were over and he was letting me know in no uncertain terms.

On the poultry side of the farm the production cycle stretched across the summer months. In order to hatch chickens a hen had to get the hatching urge which motivated her to sit on a nest of eggs for three weeks. We had an old stone house at the end of the yard where rows of hatching hens sat in state in their boxes. They had to be fed and watered daily in the house because they all but refused to leave the nest. At the end of the three weeks the chickens chipped their way out of the shells and when they emerged they were soft and beautiful. The mother hen, or clucker as she was called, looked after her chicks with loving care and paraded around the farmyard leading her brood proudly. Sometimes, too, a hen might lay her eggs in a remote corner of the haggard and hatch them unknown to anybody; then one day she would march her chicks into the yard as if to say, 'Look at me; aren't I clever?'

The turkeys, ducks and geese also hatched their eggs but took a week longer than the hens to do so. The goose liked to make her own nest and line it inside with soft down. The gander for his part was a most responsible father and guarded his goose on the nest; if you came too close he flapped his wings and stretched out his long neck to bite you. The young goslings were fluffy and yellow as butter and the goose and gander led them daily to the water where they all washed and swam around happily. But the males in the turkey and hen families were irresponsible fathers: once they had made their original contribution they disclaimed all responsibility for the consequences.

Great care had to be taken of the baby turkeys as they were a bit stupid and unlike the chickens and goslings had a tendency to get lost. The goose was a very good mother and she had a strong family unit working for her; the ordinary hen was the head of a one-parent family but her mothering instinct was fantastic. The turkey on the other hand had neither factor going for her: she was on her own and she was not unduly concerned about the well-being of her young. She needed a strong social welfare system to back her up and, of course, we provided that. Minding the turkeys was one of the chores of my young days. When they were set loose in a grassy field which was supposed to be good for them I was the social welfare officer who saw that none of them fell by the wayside. They had endless ways of going wrong. If they fell on their backs they could not right themselves; they could ramble off through the long grass and, with no sense of direction, get totally lost, and their mother would never bother to answer their plaintive 'peep-peep'. I liked this job because it was leisurely and did not require a great deal of concentration, so I could take a book along with me. Sitting on the warm grass on a sunny day reading was a pleasant way to while away the time, though occasionally I would forget what I was actually there for and would have to make a mad scramble to collect lost turkeys from all over the field.

A common enemy of all the young chicks was the hawk. He would circle around in the sky, observing, and then he would make a sudden dive, swooping down on the chicks, and soar off with one grasped in his taloned feet. He was accurate and deadly. The old hens were wise to his ways and if they saw him circling they cackled and set up a loud noise to alert us to the danger. We always came running to the rescue and clapped our hands at the hawk but sometimes it took my father's shot-gun to frighten him away. When I was very young I dreaded the hawk because I had visions of soaring skywards myself, caught in his fearsome talons.

The farmyard was a symphony of colour and sound. The hens were multi-coloured because they consisted of many breeds: there were Rhode Island Reds, the black Minorca with the golden beak, the white Leghorn and the frilly Sussex with her two white aprons giving her the appearance of a head nurse. Once they had produced their eggs they did not believe in hiding their light under a bushel, so they came out of the door of the henhouse emitting a high-pitched cackling noise telling everybody about their good deed for the day. The black turkeys gave off a continuous yodelling sound, the grey guinea fowl a single high-pitched clucking noise. We had the brown duck with their ringed necks and the soft-bosomed, voluptuous white ducks with their constant quack, quack. The geese seldom stayed around the yard as they preferred the open fields and waterways, but they came back at night to their own house; if they had stayed out the fox would have had a Christmas dinner every night.

There was seldom a fight between the different families on the farmyard as each one went its own way. If there was a fight it would be between the sow and the gander. The sow was not averse to thinking that a soft yellow gosling made a tasty mouthful, but before she could put her bad thoughts into action the gander, with outstretched flapping wings and with his sharp beak aimed at the sow's delicate snout and eyes, drove her squealing in the opposite direction.

Most of the new life on the farm arrived in the spring and early summer and almost all the births fitted into the ordinary farm proceedings. But the pig was not tied to any calendar month and her bonhams' arrival disrupted the normal routine. She was the one mother who required round-the-clock surveillance because she was quite capable of lying down on her baby bonhams and crushing them to death. This sounds as if the mother pig was a monster but how many mothers could cope with twenty babies at one go? It was enough to stretch even the strongest maternal instincts. The hen was the only other to come near her in number and she had just about a dozen. As well as that the hen hatched while sitting in comfort on her eggs for three weeks, while the poor old sow had the ordeal of labour pains and the messy job of physical production, and then finished up with twenty squealing bonhams which she was expected to breast-feed. It was a tough job and it was no wonder if sometimes she felt like sitting on them.

When the bonhams were due the sow started to make a bed wherever she happened to be. She was put into a little house by herself with plenty of straw or hay and proceeded to chop up the straw with her mouth and tease it out with her crubeens. She kept working on the bed until she had everything settled and her nesting instinct satisfied. Finally she settled down and got on with the real business of the day. The litter of pretty, pink bonhams could vary from twelve to twenty in number and if there were more than the sow could cater for they had to be bottle fed. When it was feeding time the sow grunted with a loud, regular rhythm and all her little ones got the message straight away. Between feeds they lay cuddled up together against the mother. The need for supervision came when the sow got up and had to be let out for a walk or just wanted to stretch her legs, for when she returned to lie down she never checked to see where her bonhams were. She just flopped down and if they were in the wrong place she lay on them and killed them. In fairness to the sow, with the best intentions in the world it was impossible to keep her big brood out from under her legs. This was where we came in, using a brush to get the bonhams out of the way quickly.

The bonhams learned fast and after a few days they could look out for themselves, but while they were very small somebody had to stay up at night to mind them. The first time I was ever allowed up with an older sister to mind the bonhams was of a Friday night as we had no school on Saturday. I was delighted because I was curious to know what a night up was like. At that time we had a big open fireplace in the kitchen and we banked it up with turf for the night. The sow only required checking at regular intervals so, apart from that, our time was our own. We played cards and made an apple tart. At about two o'clock I sat on the old sofa by the blazing fire and must have dozed off because the next time I heard the clock strike it was four in the morning.

It was midsummer and the dawn was breaking when I went out into the garden. It was bathed in a pink translucent light and a soft mist lay along the river valley. I was mesmerized by the absolute beauty of the morning and the dawn chorus in full volume from the trees around the house. It was one of those rare moments of perfection that are imprinted in the memory forever.

A Touch of Spring

Spring came today
And walked with me
Up the hill
Breathing softness in the air
Opening gates within my head
The birds felt his presence
Pouring forth symphonies
Of unrestrained welcome
It was mid-January
And he just came
To have a peep
Trailing behind him
Along the valley
Wisps of purple veils.

Forever Young

As children we all loved Bill. Though of our father's generation he had not closed the gate of childhood behind him, and we knew this instinctively. He did not talk down to us but met us at eye level. He lived on the top of the hill beside our home; part of the hill was an ancient fort and at the foot of it was a fairy well. At that time farmers' houses lacked piped water so all drinking water was drawn by bucket from the local well, and every night without fail Bill brought a bucket to our house. So regular was this bucket that when calculating our fresh water requirements we automatically counted in Bill's contribution.

When he arrived after supper his first task was to teach us our lessons. His patience was endless. Maths, catechism and Irish were all done diligently but English was his favourite; he read profusely and his reading took precedence over all other activities in his life. I remember one sunny day coming on him sitting on a grassy bank reading Shakespeare when every other farmer in the neighbourhood was busy saving hay.

My father often despaired of Bill's farming methods and was constantly urging him to be more efficient. At that time artificial insemination had not come to the bovine world and some farmers kept a bull to provide the necessary service; Bill availed of our facilities for his cows. One summer morning my father met him coming across one of our fields trailing a rope behind him; he was, he told my father, bringing a cow to our bull. When my father enquired as to the whereabouts of the cow Bill turned to discover that there was nothing at the end of his rope! His thoughts, no doubt, had been on less mundane matters.

24

Bill had a stone cowhouse with a thatched roof mellowed to a soft creamy white by years of sun and rain, while the cows had fashioned their own windows by gently butting their heads through the thatch. Milking time presented a pleasant picture with each cow's head protruding through the low roof, contentedly chewing the cud and looking out over the farmyard. The yard was always spotlessly clean, though some of it through lack of use was covered with soft green moss and the timber gates were weather-beaten to an almost grey-white smoothness that had a silken texture beneath your hand. An old grey donkey completed this peaceful scene.

As a child this was my retreat corner. Being the youngest of a large, noisy household this hilltop haven often provided a welcome escape when older sisters proved too much to handle. Here there was nobody to boss or annoy me or to make me move any faster than I wanted to; Bill and his two old sisters had all the time in the world and were delighted to see me.

His two sisters were the bane of his life. They ran the house with clockwork efficiency and expected him to run the farm in the same manner. But though they were of the same family Bill was cast in a different mould to his sisters. He never believed in doing today what he could put off until tomorrow, and they pursued him relentlessly in order to make sure that nothing was put off. He devised many ploys to outmanoeuvre them so that he could enjoy his reading in comfort. At the far end of the haggard was Bill's rick of hay and into this, on the side facing away from the house, he cut a large hole with the hay knife, and the fact that it faced the sun was an added bonus. In his sunny seat Bill sat, totally oblivious to the world around him and safe from the pursuing sisters. This plan worked for a long time until one day the dog and the gander had a fight and chased each other around the rick of hay. Eventually, the gander got a reeling in his head and collapsed. One of the sisters, who had watched the fight, came running to investigate the condition of the gander. Bill had also watched the fight and, thinking it hilariously funny, roared with laughter, which his sister on hearing traced to his retreat

25

corner, where all his books told their own story. That was the end of that hideout.

Bill lived close to nature and if the summer was very warm he swam nude in our river, in a pool that was clean and fresh and full of brown trout. This gentle giant of a man – he was a splendid figure standing over six feet – would dive from the cliff into the pool and swim like a giant fish. I found his knees very impressive: male knees were rarely seen in rural Ireland at the time, shorts being an unknown mode of apparel. Other, more intimate details of his form did not provide the same interest as specimens of male reproductive organs were part of the animal survival pattern of everyday life on the farm.

During the long summer holidays the plague of lessons did not exist, so Bill joined in our many games. One of our pretend games was shop, which we played under the trees in the grove. We nailed rough planks between the trees to display our goods – empty cartons collected from the kitchen and from neighbours – which we arranged along the shelves, and we erected a makeshift counter in front. Here we traded for hours using pebbles collected from a nearby stream as currency, and though the rate of exchange posed no problem, the price of each item was open to long and complicated negotiations. It was up to the shopkeeper to sell the goods, with a convincing argument as to their value, and it was up to the customer to buy as cheaply as possible. Bill always joined the row of customers when he came after supper, and he brought new and colourful arguments to bear on the shopkeeper. Everybody wanted to be the shopkeeper as we felt that this was the leading role, but Bill turned the tide in favour of the shopper.

During the winter holidays card playing and dancing replaced the lessons, and we were often joined by other neighbours who came visiting. Playing cards was the only occasion on which Bill could lose his temper: if anybody cheated he put his head down like an angry bull, threw his cards on the table and tore out the door. Being completely honest himself, he would not tolerate the slightest deviation from the straight and narrow path of right. The dancing, however, posed no problems. We all lined out around the kitchen while somebody wound up the old gramophone, and then we hopped off the stone floor, ranging in age from seven to seventy. The fairy reel, set dances and barn dances were executed with more gusto than skill until everybody was exhausted and collapsed into the *súgán* chairs that had been pushed back against the walls. My mother then put the kettle on over the open fire and when we had recovered our breath and cooled down we all gathered around the fire for cups of cocoa.

Bill and my father had gone to school together and were friends all their lives. There existed between them perfect understanding, though they were very different types of people. To Bill my mother was a welcome extension to his own life and he loved all of us unquestioningly; indeed, in some ways we were a three-parent family, and Bill was a plus in our lives which we took for granted. When he died quite suddenly it came as a hard, sharp blow. He died at home and the wake took the usual form of the time with all the neighbours rallying round to give help and support, but for some reason I did not go anywhere near the house. On the day of the removal I went to the highest field in our farm, overlooking Bill's home, and from here I watched the hearse leave the house, and tried to come to terms with the concept of a world without Bill.

After the funeral one of the sisters came and asked my mother if one of us children would go and stay with them for a while. It was Easter holiday time, so we were all at home. There was no great rush on the invitation but to me the idea of trying to ease their loss of Bill was strangely appealing so, putting my night-dress under my arm, I set out happily back through the field behind the house. Coming to the fairy well I lay on the large mossy stone in front of it and gazed into its dark green depths. Then I ran up the steep hill, stopping to sit on all Bill's resting places which he had made during his lifetime.

I do not remember how long I spent with the sisters but it was a whole new experience. Here life was lived at a defined pace. The amount of water to go into the kettle was measured, the number of slices of bread needed for the tea was calculated. Nothing was left to chance, everything was ordered and regulated. One of the sisters was in a wheelchair and from there she ran the house down to the very last detail. To me it was fascinating because it was such a complete contrast to our house.

Not everything had changed, though. I would walk around the grey stone yard, into the white-thatched cowhouse, and rub my hand along the silken timber of the weather-beaten gates. Here was a timeless existence. Below the house was a long narrow garden shadowed by overhanging trees and filled with daffodils. I lay among the green and yellow rows and gazed up into the sky through the soft green leaves. I saw Bill smiling down between the clouds, which was no great surprise as heaven was just above them and Bill was sure to be there.

The Long-Tailed Family

We children were very attached to the farm animals. Some of them were older than ourselves and very much part of our home life; not alone were some of our animals born and reared on the farm but so also were some of their mothers and grandmothers, and a lot of them died of old age and were buried there. Our burial ground was at the bottom of the orchard and here the jennet, when he decided that he had had enough and lay down and died, was laid to rest. All our pals, including cats and dogs, got an official burial and at times we marked the graves with little timber crosses.

The horses held a special status on our farm. We had a red bay called Paddy and a grey mare named Jerry and the jennet who, because he was the only one of his species on the farm – or indeed in the parish – was just called the jennet. He was a strange animal, smaller than a horse, bigger than a pony, and with the face of a donkey. I once heard John Dillon say on radio that the jennet 'did not have pride of ancestry or hope of succession; he was, in other words, a non starter'. It was a harsh pronouncement, giving the jennet nothing to look back at and even less to look forward to. However, it did not seem to bother our particular fellow: black and long-tailed, he brayed like a donkey and kicked like a devil and if you stood too close to him he might decide to sink his long yellow teeth into you to see if you tasted good. One of his jobs, which he did every day, was to go to the creamery; he could find his own way to town and stopped along the route at houses where my father regularly gave in gallons of milk. He was a real loner and he did not fraternise with the horses or the pony. However, he had one thing in his favour: in the morning, when my father went to the gate of the field and whistled, he came willingly, not needing to be called a second time or coaxed on his way.

Catching the horses, on the other hand, was a job that had to be done most mornings and sometimes they were very un-cooperative. Some people are reluctant to get out of bed early to face a day's work, and likewise horses are loath to be rounded up to face their day's labour. My eldest sister, Frances, was the one who loved the horses most and she usually went out to catch them early in the morning; if she got close enough she would swing off Paddy's mane and jump on his back for a gallop. One morning she had on a pair of loose wooden clogs that were a fashionable necessity during the war, but when she had Paddy galloping the clogs fell off under his belly and frightened him. He bolted. He raced up the fields like a steak of red lightning, but the effort of coming up the steep incline to the yard slowed him. He arrived in the farm-yard frothing from the mouth and covered in sweat, Frances clinging to him like a leech. She had enjoyed the challenge of holding on, while I watched with my heart in my mouth.

Of all the animals that belonged on the farm, it was Paddy's death that caused most trauma in our house. He was older than I and was a horse with great class. In animals you get as much individual variation as in humans: there are the mean, sly, stupid, intelligent and honest ones just the same as us. Paddy was the cream of the animal world. He would neither kick nor bite and was hard-working. He was also an honest animal – if you think there is no such thing as a dishonest animal then you have never heard of a thieving cow. Some cows always have their heads up to see if there is something better in the next field and if there is, up and over they go to get it. We have that much in common with the cows. With horses, when they worked in pairs there was the one who pulled hardest and did the most work; there was also the horse who had no mean traits and was loved and respected by his owner. Such a horse was Paddy.

At the top of our farm was a wild area known as the Glen. It was bushy and rocky and the horses seldom went there. One spring morning, however, when my father went out to bring them in from the fields Paddy was not with the others. After a long search he was found lying in a deep hollow in the Glen. My father's heart must have stood still when he saw him: Paddy made an effort to rise but was not able. When the news got back to the house we were shattered and all made a bee-line for the Glen. There he lay, unable to rise, whimpering in distress because he could not follow us home. That day in school, instead of the blackboard I saw Paddy lying in that hollow. I was completely distracted for lesson after lesson and got many slaps, but it felt as if they were hitting someone else. The clock dragged slowly around to three.

When I got home I learned that the vet had come during the day and had pronounced that Paddy had broken his back and would have to be put down. It was like a death in the family. We all knew that my father would do the needful; a shot would be quick and merciful, but it would be so terrible for my father who had worked with Paddy for years and loved him dearly.

I went by myself to say goodbye. Going up to the Glen in the dusk on that late spring evening was a sorrowful journey. There was a soft mist falling and I felt that even the leaves were crying. I climbed down over the rocks to where Paddy lay in the grassy hollow; he whimpered when he heard me coming and turned his dark, moist eyes in my direction. Sitting beside him I stroked his silken face with its white star. He nuzzled me gently and, as I put my arms around him, my tears ran down his neck. He neighed softly and looking up I saw my father silhouetted against the darkening sky. He had his shot-gun with him. It was time to go.

Walking home through the soft wet grass I waited to hear the shot break the silence of the evening. When it did not come I knew that my father was waiting for me to get home first. I sat on a stone to wait and at last it came like an explosion in the quietness of the Glen. After a while my father came down the rocky path. There was no need to say anything when he saw me. I put my hand into his pocket and we walked home together.

Close To The Earth

Come to a quiet place,
A place so quiet
That you can hear
The grass grow.
Lie on the soft grass,
Run your fingers
Through the softness
Of its petals,
And listen:
Listen to the earth.
The warm earth,
The life pulse
Of us all.
Rest your body
Against its warmth;
Feel its greatness,
The pulse and throb,
The foundation
Of the world.
Look up into the sky,
The all-embracing sky,
The canopy of heaven.
How small
We really are:
Specks in the greatness
But still a part of it all.
We grow from the earth
And find
Our own place.

Celebration Of The Seasons

Each year we welcomed summer by erecting a May altar in honour of Our Lady. In this we were motivated less by religious fervour than by a wish to celebrate the long, warm days by bringing the outdoors into the house in bunches of wild flowers which we picked along the ditches and in the open fields. In the bedroom over the kitchen was a large old chest with deep drawers. Over this we draped a white sheet and on top of it we put a box slighly smaller than the chest top and covered this with another cloth. Then another box, slightly smaller again, with another cloth, and so on as high as we could go without causing the whole thing to topple over. On top of this pyramid we perched Our Lady. This was her altar, so she got pride of place, but she was not to have it all to herself. On the steps below her came statues of Our Lord, in case he might feel overlooked, and then Blessed Martin and St Theresa. Also included was St Philomena, but she was actually there under false pretences as the Vatican in later years changed their minds about her credentials. Then came the flowers and greenery arranged in jam pots and trailing down from step to step.

When we were finished we regarded our creation as a masterpiece of sanctity and in front of it we knelt and prayed, feeling that at any moment we might sprout angelic wings and soar heavenwards. Such was our sense of drama that we draped ourselves in trailing bedspreads with pillow covers as haloes on our heads and danced in front of the altar.

One day Connie and I decided that we would bury ourselves in the drawers of the old chest. Maybe we had visions of the popes buried beneath the Vatican. Connie got into the bottom drawer without mishap but as I attempted to settle into my proposed tomb the entire creation of devotion tilted forward and collapsed on top of us. The crash was thunderous, with statues, jam pots, flowers and water flying in all directions. Everybody downstairs in the kitchen came running up the stairs to investigate. We scrambled out of the drawers and under a large old timber bed in the corner of the room where nobody could get at us since the bed almost touched the floor and they were all too big to get under it. My mother was annoyed when she found that Our Lady had lost her head; our sisters were raging over the complete mess, and my father gave out because it took little to start him off and he thought that we were a holy terror anyway. We stayed under the bed for a long time until things calmed down but we finally ventured downstairs when Bill came as he could always be relied upon to pour oil on troubled waters. Our Lady later acquired a concrete neck which was a bit thick, so she lost some of her swan-like elegance but it was the best repair that could be achieved at the time as fixatives had not yet come on the market.

As soon as the sun had taken the cold sting out of the weather we wanted to cast aside our heavy winter clothes and don our summer dresses but my mother put her foot down with her old adage, 'Ne'er cast a clout till May is out'. In winter we wore heavy tweed skirts with hand-knitted jumpers and beneath them grey flannel petticoats. Under the petticoat came a sleeveless jacket called a bodice and then a pure wool long-sleeved vest. We wore long black woollen stockings up as far as possible and secured in place with garters and long-legged knickers with elasticated ends to just above our knees. We spent cold days out in the fields and sat in a damp, draughty, unheated school, so the need to be warmly clad was imperative. But when the weather grew warm we were glad of the freedom that bare limbs afforded.

My mother made all our clothes and for summer wear she bought us a large roll of cotton material and ran up simple, shift-like slip-over-the-head dresses. The primary need was to cover our nudity and elegant cut was not a requirement.

Climbing trees and slushing through muddy gaps was not conducive to model child appearance, so clothes were serviceable rather than flattering.

Each of us girls had a box in which we stored our summer dresses in a big press over the winter. Come summer we brought our boxes out into the garden to lay them out to air in the warm sun. In our garden all the plants and shrubs were called after the people who gave them to my mother, and escalonia was Jer Lucy's bush. On that day Jer Lucy wore a collection of gaily coloured dresses. As the youngest of five girls I was reared on a succession of hand-me-downs but I had a godmother in America who sent me parcels of beautiful frilly muslin and silk dresses which smelt of lavender and foreign places.

When the sun had warmed the heart of the earth it thrust forth white garlands of little button mushrooms. They came up overnight in small clusters where late the night before there had been nothing but green. Now there they were, with their little white faces peeping up from between blades of grass. Some fields were mushroom fields and others were not, and we knew where to look, but so did all the neighbouring children. Where mushrooms were concerned it was a free-for-all with farm boundaries of no consequence. So, if mushrooms were on your mind you rose early because as well as other early pickers there was the fact that cows and horses could trample them into the ground.

Gathering mushrooms in the early summer morning, with the dew washing your toes and the thrill of discovery growing with each white cluster, was a lovely experience. Sometimes, stretching like gossamer across the grass, the dew-glistening cobwebs sheltered the little mushrooms, almost like a mantle protecting them from the world above the earth. Finally, gallon full, we skipped home through the sun-warmed fields to savour our collection. We cooked them for breakfast on red hot sods of turf besides the fire. Each white mushroom was placed on its back, in its pale pink cup a shake of salt which melted and mingled with the juices as it cooked. Picking it up, careful not to spill, first you drank it and then you ate it, a little chalice with the liquid and flavour of the open fields. Sometimes my mother boiled them in milk but somehow that was to reduce to the ordinary this food of the earth that needed no preparation as it was bathed in the morning dew and could be eaten as picked, such was its delicacy and freshness.

As the summer progressed the briars along the ditches burst into blossom with green berries that later matured into large, luscious blackberries which arched and draped themselves around every field, ripe for the picking. Each blackberry was inspected on picking to see that the stem base was free from small tell-tale holes, the tracks of tiny snails that feasted on the blackberries, especially when the rain brought them forth in great numbers; any blackberries with these signs were returned to mother earth. First we ate what we could contain, developing purple-smudged mouths and fingers; then we filled gallons and buckets to the brim. My mother made large two-pound pots of blackberry jam, most of which were consumed at a rapid rate, but some of which were stored to bring the taste of summer to the winter months.

Crab apple trees grew in some of the fields but the crabs were small and bitter; however, they could be made into a sweet-tasting jelly and jam. Picking them was a thorny business as often strong briars and blackthorn branches were entwined in them. Once, having filled a bucket of crabs, I left it in the middle of the field while I drifted away to follow some other diversion. Coming back a few hours afterwards I found that my bucket and its contents had been baptised in amber liquid: of all the places in this wide open field for the cow to stand to do the needful!

My father often came home with his cap full of crabs and once he asked me how valuable I thought a cap full of crabs was; when I answered, 'No value really', he smiled and said, 'Well, a child who does not respect his fellow human beings is as valuable to the human race as a cap full of crabs'. He did not expect much from his fellow human beings but he was very conscious of the rights of other people and always instilled this consciousness in us.

We had a very happy young lad called Christy working with

us. He loved dancing and was often out until the small hours of the morning as he also had an eye for a pretty face. One night, coming out of a dance in the local hall, he found his bike punctured so he helped himself to a tube of another one as he had a girlfriend to take home on the bar of his bike. Incredibly, Christy was later taken to court and sentenced to six months in jail for this offence. My father was stone mad about it, feeling that Christy was a gay-hearted lad and that the punishment was outrageous in relation to the crime. When Christy came out he was quiet and subdued and all his old sparkle had gone. On his first Sunday back my father and mother went away for the day, leaving all of us children and the house and farmyard in Christy's care. A few days later he went to visit his mother.

'Christy,' she asked him, 'will they trust you on the farm after being in prison?'

She afterwards told me that he smiled as he said, 'It made no difference: they went away on Sunday and left me in complete charge.' She said that it did more to restore his self-esteem than any amount of words could have done. And, indeed, Christy soon regained his self-confidence and was his old sunny self again; my father had never studied psychology but he had an innate understanding of human nature.

Wild fuchsia, which we called bell trees, grew along the hedges and, plucking off the bell-like flowers, we sucked their sweet, sticky juices as we had seen the honey-bees do. If thirst overcame us out in the fields fresh spring water ran along by most ditches, flowing down from the hill behind the house. We were expert at leaning into greenery and, using our saucered hands as cups, we scooped up the crystal-clear water and drank from the palms of our hands. The only polluters of the waterways were the ducks and geese and my father often objected to them as the horses and cows often refused to drink the water after them. My mother, however, stood up for their rights and refused to listen to his objections, stating that as they used only one large stream they were entitled to their freedom and the pleasure they got from the water.

As summer turned to autumn we stored the best apples for

Hallowe'en, or Snap Apple Night as we called it. We diligently watched the nut trees, hoping that they would be ripe in time, but ripe or not we always picked them. These trees were tall with high, arching branches far from the ground, so it took all our climbing skills to conquer them. We climbed to the top and then as far out along the swaying branches as we dared, while we swung up and down at precarious angles, grasping bunches of nuts and throwing them down to the collector on the ground. Finally, gallons full, we slithered to the ground and danced home through the gathering dusk, scratched but triumphant. That night we cracked our nuts with a stone on the flagstone before the fire while apples swung from cords tied to the meat hooks on the rafters of the kitchen or floated in the timber tub of water in the middle of the floor.

For Christmas too the land provided what was needed, and the Sunday before we made our annual pilgrimage to the wood for the red-berried holly. It was there in abundance as was the ivy and moss, together with strange, interesting pieces of dried-out timber. We gathered them all and tied them up in bundles with hay twine and we brought them home on our backs, holding firmly to the twine across our shoulders. They would all be used to make different decorations for Christmas. There was no money for shop decorations but we did not need them as all around us the countryside fulfilled our needs.

The Jelly Jug

Sunday in the country was a day of complete rest. Cows were milked, animals and humans fed but, apart from that, we all took time to ourselves. It was a holiday in the kitchen as well so that everyone would be free of the work routine. Unfortunately, we had to rise earlier than usual so that the cows were milked before the early Mass to which my brother went on his way home from the creamery. This left my father free to take the rest of us to the late Mass.

My father was always present for the breakfast on Sunday, and it was a very relaxed occasion as there was no work waiting to be done. It was the only time he ever sang and his favourite was 'The Old Bog Road'. He would tilt back his chair and, rubbing the back of his head with the palm of his hand, he would rumble 'her coffin down the old bog road'. He had a voice like a rusty chain rattling in a bucket but what he lacked in harmony he made up for in enjoyment because he only sang when he was happy. He liked poetry and was much better at reciting that than he was at singing. His favourite poet was Goldsmith and *The Deserted Village* rolled off his tongue with such relish that you knew he approved of all the poet's sentiments. He also had an odd little poem which I never heard from anyone else:

Once upon a time
When pigs were swine
And turkeys chewed tobacco
And little birds built their nests
In old men's beards.

Once the Sunday morning poetry session was over he turned on the Church of England service on the BBC saying,

'Listen to them now; every bit as good as what we will be hearing from our own in an hour's time'.

The pony's job was to take us to Sunday Mass in the trap. This could be a hazardous undertaking in the winter because if the pony slipped on the ice we would all end up out on the road on top of our heads, but in the summer it was a very pleasant way to travel. If we passed anybody walking along the road they were picked up and brought to town. At that time the different premises in the town had backyards where the horses and traps were tied up during Mass. After the ceremony we would call to an aunt's house with a bastable cake from my mother and two large whiskey bottles full of milk and our aunt would offer us tea and apple tart.

Then my mother did her shopping. This was of a very practical nature as money was scarce in those days: there was plenty of everything except money but then the need for money was not great. We produced all our own food and most places we went to we walked, which cost nothing only time, and we had plenty of that. We children stretched our pennies to buy those sweets which cost the least and lasted the longest. The best value was a sixpenny slab of toffee, for which my sister Phil and I pooled our resources, and that lasted us a whole week. It was the lap of luxury to have something to chew on going to school and sometimes it did a two-way journey as we took it out of our mouths half chewed and saved it, wrapped in paper, for the way home.

Sunday in the country was a leisurely day. As well as shopping after Mass, much chatting was done when my mother met her neighbours and often the talking took longer than the shopping. My father went to the pub for a few pints and met up with his friends. We went to change our books in the branch library which had opened in our town, and although it took much browsing and deliberating it opened up new horizons for us. Finally we all drifted back to the pony and trap, with my mother always the last to arrive and my father now nicely relaxed as he lit up his pipe and puffed away contentedly. When we were finally ready to go home the pony trotted off at an easy pace.

Arriving home we had what we called a tea dinner – nobody worked on a Sunday so there was no cooking done, and we usually had a cold meat salad with jelly and cream afterwards. My mother often made jelly the night before for this Sunday treat: I loved making jelly too, and watching it melting under the hot water always fascinated me. One day I put my jelly into an orange jug, not realizing that it was a family heirloom which my mother had got from my grandmother when she married. I poured the boiling water straight from the kettle on to the jelly and the jug split in two halves. I can still see the red jelly flooding out over the table as my mother's gasp of horror conveyed the enormity of my crime. Years afterwards, when I was the same age as my mother was when this happened, we were discussing the orange jug.

'Do you know something,' my mother said, 'I think that the pieces of that jug are behind in the old turf house in a hole between two stones under the back window.'

And back I went into the semi-darkness of the old stone house that was now used for storage and there, exactly where she had said, between the stones under the window, were the pieces of the old jug. It took me back years just to see it. I was delighted and brought it away with me to have it repaired, and it now takes pride of place in my collection of jugs. My mother was a hoarder, a trait that proved a great blessing for us too in later years.

After the dinner on Sundays my father usually went fishing, a solitary pastime from which we were excluded for fear of frightening the fish. But we enjoyed catching the flies that he used. He put a piece of fresh horse dung into a box and this drew the flies; then he closed the box, which had a round opening at the other end, and up against this he put a cow's horn. The flies flew into the horn which he then covered with mesh wire, and the horn full of buzzing flies slipped nicely into his fishing bag. When he came home the bag was usually bulging with brown trout. We washed the fish in the stream at the bottom of the garden and my mother fried them in butter for the supper.

We children usually spent Sunday in the fields. Sometimes

41

we just lay quietly in the long grass watching the rabbits, of which there were dozens along every headland, and if you appeared suddenly they would scamper into the ditches and down their burrows. The ditches were riddled with burrows: very occasionally you came on an extra-large one and this was the fox's lair which was also easy to recognize on account of the strong pungent odour that hung around it. Sometimes, too, you might see the fox running at an easy pace along by a bushy ditch and stopping every now and then with ears cocked for danger. Once ever I saw one out in the open: he ran the entire length of our long fort field where I happened to be sitting at the top of the rise. When he saw me he stood still and stared at me. If he was frightened I was even more so because I had visions of being carried off between his jaws like my mother's hens. We stared at each other for a few seconds and then he sauntered off, dismissing me as of little danger.

Picking wild flowers was another Sunday pastime: the buttercup, the bluebell, the woodbine with its haunting smell, all found their way back to our kitchen where they stood in every corner in empty jam pots. As well as acting as a flower vase the jam pot served many purposes: it kept the goose grease from the Christmas killings, which was used for softening tough shoe leather and easing painful joints; it also served as a fishing net for catching collies, miniature fish that travelled in shoals. We tied a twine around the jam pot's neck and laid it on the river bed where it sparkled between the stones. Standing motionless beside it we watched the collies swim around our toes, tickling them, until one invariably found its way into our pot and then we swung it out of the water. We often caught other types of fish as well but we were scared stiff of eels, convinced that they would bite the toes off us.

Some Sundays we went to the fort which was just behind our house, a very big fort where my father had planted trees years before, so now it was a wood as well. Set on the side of a sloping hill it had huge mounds with hollows in between, and the entire place was carpeted in pine needles so that walking felt like treading on cushioned air. We played hide-and-seek around the mounds and behind the trees and the only sounds beside ours were the birds'. The place was a haven for all kinds of wildlife and here too the foxes often made their head-quarters – much to my mother's annoyance because her geese and turkeys often became their prey.

We had a series of birds' nests which we visited, careful never to disturb anything as we watched the eggs increasing in the nest. We were delighted to see the baby *gearrcaigh* (or nestlings) appear and often hid ourselves to watch the parents fly back and forth feeding their young. Every year the swallows came to our cow stalls and stables where the rafters were a maze of nests, and it was a great feather in your cap to be the one to see the first swallow and to hear the first call of the cuckoo. At night we fell asleep to the sound of the corncrake whom we thought said:

'Corncrake
Out late
Ate mate
Friday morning.'

At that time meat was never eaten on Friday so the corncrake was breaking the fast.

In the grove below the house the pigeons cooed continu-ously. In the orchard beside this grove my teenage brother started beekeeping, but as his hives increased he moved to the grove behind the house. Here a hive was stationed under every tree and it was absorbing to watch the bees at work, especially in the summer when my brother sometimes went away for a week on a beekeeping course and I was left in charge. The first time this happened I prayed that they would not swarm, but of course they did. One afternoon when I came to check them, there, hanging off a branch like a large cluster of grapes, was a fine thick swarm of bees. I knew the procedure and though a trifle nervous I donned the beekeep-ing gear. Approaching quietly, with one hand I held a bucket just below the swarm and with the other I hit the branch a good belt with the back of a hatchet and the swarm fell neatly into the bucket. A share of the bees buzzed angrily at this in-trusion into their peace but I put the bucket under the tree and when they had settled covered it with a sheet. Now at least they could not take off if the notion took them, which was quite possible anytime before sundown.

Late in the evening I returned to finish my job. Having found the old door of light timber which my brother kept for this purpose, I rested one end of it on the landing board in front of the hive and the other end on the ground, and then covered it with a white sheet. Gently lifting up the bucket I prised the covering off and shook the lump of bees out on to my prepared sheet. At first they buzzed angrily but soon they got their bearings. The trick at this point was to spot the queen, who is a good deal larger than the other bees, and make sure that she went into the hive so that the others would follow. I had beginner's luck: there she was heading for the front door, so the rest followed on naturally. There was no need to stay after that as they did the rest themselves, but I came back later in the semi-darkness to check that the sheet was clear of bees. The grove was peaceful at that time of night with all the hives silent after their busy day. If you knelt down beside a hive and put your ear against it you could hear the soft drone within. Our kitchen table was never without a honey supply, whether it was a jar, a section or indeed sometimes a frame of honey straight from the hive.

My mother was the only one of the family to spend her Sunday in the house. She sat inside the open kitchen window reading the Sunday papers, and she always had interesting articles from the weekday papers put aside to be read on her day of rest.

At this time, as well, she had the radio to herself. This was a great luxury in our house as there was usually a power struggle when different channels had interesting programmes on at the same time. My mother was an avid radio listener all her life. At that time *Mrs Dale's Diary* was on BBC at 4.15 every weekday and she never missed it; indeed, we often ran home from school ourselves to be in time to hear Mrs Dale if she was having a family crisis. *Woman's Hour* was another of my mother's favourite programmes.

However, her peaceful Sunday reading and radio listening was usually interrupted as she had many callers; this, especially, was the time when neighbouring farmers' wives came to visit. Apart from these my mother had a varied assortment of visitors. There was one lady gone past her first flush of girlhood, but not realizing it, who came to my mother to get her a husband or a 'little job'. My mother baulked at the first suggestion but set her up in many 'little jobs'. Invariably though, things did not work out and back she would come again looking for another little job. She smoked like a trooper and when we came into the kitchen and sniffed her cigarettes we annoyed my mother intensely by saying: 'Oh, you had 'little job' today'.

Another Sunday evening caller was Andy Connie. He was an uncle of my father so he must have been fairly old, but he had the heart and fitness of a teenager. Leading in to our outside yard was a five-foot-high gate, and into the garden a smaller one, and he never opened either one but jumped over them. He loved singing and dancing and often stood in the middle of the kitchen floor and danced a jig or a reel. He just danced because he was full of the joy of life and we loved to see him coming as he was like a ray of sunshine.

Andy's wife had died at a young age and he was left with a baby daughter, whom he adored. Many of his friends tried to get him to remarry so he composed a little poem to put them off. Mary Barry had been his wife's maiden name and he invoked her support in his dilemma:

> If Mary Barry of old
> Could only behold
> Her own Andy Connie
> Getting married again.
> Her corpse long dead
> In her narrow bed
> In anger and shame
> Would rise again.

Andy stayed with us one stormy night and the following morning at breakfast he told my mother that he hadn't been able to sleep at all as the ash tree at the bottom of the garden was all night calling, 'Andy Connie, Andy Connie'. To this day the tree is known as Andy Connie.

Towards evening, when we all drifted back to the house, the Sunday night jobs had to be tackled as the animals needed to be fed irrespective of what day they had. Two of us went to bring home the cows and two more to feed the calves and someone to feed the hens and other fowl. After milking we all had supper together and there was usually some extra treat because it was Sunday. Then my father went roving and the older ones went dancing but my brother usually had to hive his swarm before he went anywhere. My mother usually went for a walk in the fields, coming back then to finish her reading. Later, when my father returned, she rounded up the members of her household too young or too old for night life and we all knelt to say the rosary.

An Odd Old Codger

Old George was different from the other neighbours. He lived by the letter of the law and if you came into close conflict with him he could run you up the steps of a High Court before you knew how it happened. As far as I know he never studied law but he knew exactly how far he could go without illegally infringing on anybody's rights. He was meticulous in his ways. He drove into town in a pony and trap, the pony fat and well groomed while you could see yourself in the gloss of the shining trap. He wore a dark suit and a black bowler hat and spoke in a slow, measured voice that gave one the impression that he checked every word before it passed his lips. He was not greatly liked but he was part of the place and we accepted him for what he was, an odd old codger. Everybody kept well away from him: rather like our jennet, he was safer at a distance.

A new Guard came to town and decided to flex his muscles with George. We could have told him that he was on a loser but bright young men, then as now, know it all. He called on George to check on his dog licence. At that time the Guards kept a close watch on the canine population and if you were caught without a licence you were summonsed and taken to court. This young Guard asked George if he had the dog licensed and George said no, he hadn't. The Guard cautioned George that he would be back in a week and wanted to see the licence then. A week later he was back and George gave him the same answer.

In due course a summons arrived and George went to court. He loved going to court: maybe at heart he was an actor who loved a dramatic performance. The case was called and

George was summoned to the witness box; the judge, remembering this client from previous experiences, decided to play it cool.

'You appear to have an unlicensed dog,' he said mildly.

'I have not,' George answered.

'But that is the charge,' the judge said.

'The charge is incorrect,' George announced.

'But you do own a dog?' the judge queried in an effort to get things straight.

'I do not own a dog.'

'Well who owns the dog in question then?' the judge asked.

'My son Peter,' George answered, 'owns that dog.'

'And why is he not licensed?' the judge demanded.

'That dog is licensed. My son Peter has got him licensed. I do not own him so I do not license him!'

George enjoyed challenging the establishment. The priests at that time carried mighty clout, or so they thought. Every house in every townland had the Stations in their turn and it was the custom that the house due to have the Stations collected the priest's suitcase from the house in the adjoining townland which had had the Stations the previous day. The suitcase contained the priest's requirements for saying Mass and though this system probably originated when the priests travelled around on horseback it still continued with the arrival of the motor car. It suited the priest and nobody thought to question it: that was, until George came up against it.

On the morning of George's Stations everything was in readiness when the priests arrived. As was customary the parish priest went into another room to hear confessions while the curate, who was a self-opinionated, middle-aged man, started to get his altar ready. He looked around questioningly for the suitcase which was usually in readiness. It was nowhere to be seen. 'Where is my suitcase?' he demanded.

Quite unperturbed, George replied, 'I suppose, Father, it's wherever you left it. That's nobody's business but your own.'

From then on the priests carried their suitcases themselves.

When George died after reaching a fine old age all the neighbours flocked to the house for the wake. His wife had died years before and his son Peter was a pleasant man who had often found his father's approach to life a little perplexing. Wakes could often be sad occasions but George's was almost a celebration: he was different in life so it was fitting that he should be likewise in death. After a night of storytelling and drinking, the neighbours decided to say the rosary in case it might look as if they had forgotten what brought them; Jim, who had worked with George for many years, decided to take charge. George's sense of drama must have rubbed off on him because in order to give out the rosary he decided that he required an exalted position. He climbed up on the kitchen table where he knelt over all the others. 'The man at the helm steers the ship,' he declared, and then proceeded to say the rosary in a loud, measured voice exactly like old George.

Holiday Hens

How do you live to a ripe old age and still believe that this is a wonderful world and everybody in it as good as they can be? My mother never lost her faith in the goodness of human nature. If anybody wronged her she invariably excused them, reasoning that they would not have done it if there was any alternative open to them. Her simple logic often caused frustration. We had one neighbour who enjoyed a good gossip, and the juicier it was the better for telling: he believed that you should never spoil a good story for the sake of the truth. If he was really scratching the bottom of the barrel for a listener he fell back on my mother, and he always lived to regret it. No matter how startling his news, she was totally indifferent, remarking: 'Never heard a word about it', with the implication in her voice that if it had been true she would have heard it.

'Blast it, Lena,' he'd say, 'it could be on the tay bag and you wouldn't hear it.'

One day in desperation he dismissed her totally from his potential audience, telling her in a withering voice: 'You are no company because you won't say a bad word about anyone'.

Despite this implicit belief in her fellow human beings she could still cut you down to size, but so gently that it might be ten minutes before the implications of what she had said would hit you. One of my sisters and I once had a long and complicated argument with her and finally were convinced that we had proved our point and totally outmanoeuvered her. She smiled innocently at us and said: 'For a stupid woman, how did I have two such clever daughters?'

My mother included all old neighbours as part of our household duties and because she was so tolerant she was often imposed on. One of her friends sent us her hens on holiday every year while she and her husband went to the seaside. Not alone did the hens come on holiday but they had to be collected by my father in the pony and crib, and this put him into a rage that lasted for the entire length of the hens' visit. But if my father objected to the whole idea, it was nothing compared to the hens' objection for hens are settled creatures and do not like strange places. Neither do hens make good hosts, and our own hens made the visitors' lives a misery and fought with them in every corner. In fact the only one delighted with the situation was our cock. This extended harem brought new life to his flagging spirits but by the end of the month even he had had enough of this particular pursuit and was in a state of exhaustion from over-indulgence.

Bedtime posed the biggest problem because, whatever about the cock, hens are very selective about whom they let into their beds. So, come dark, the residents retired to their hen-house while the visitors took to the trees. This might have been an ideal situation but for the wily fox, for when dawn came the foolish hens would come down off the trees and then he would strike. A loud squawking would wake the entire farmyard and out of bed we would all tumble, my father swearing vengeance on the hens and the fox and waving his gun. Total chaos reigned in the soft light of the new day. The horses objected to close gunfire at dawn and the complete bedlam woke all the other animals. Pigs who had been sound asleep and cuddled up together comfortably suddenly awoke with the clamour and decided that it must be much later than they thought and that they should be hungry. Hungry pigs set off a high-pitched repetitive peal which penetrates the toughest eardrums and tightens the most relaxed nerves. All hell broke loose and the culprits were, of course, the visiting hens.

The only solution was to get them into bed voluntarily or otherwise every night. This could not be achieved until they had settled for the night. The spot of their choice was usually the tops of the trees in the surrounding grove. The older and more submissive hens we had rounded up and driven into the hen-house at dusk. But a lively pullet determined to get away is not easy to pin down, so on the tree tops we had the lively young ones who had to be grounded and housed.

When dark came and they were all settled we issued forth from the warm kitchen armed with brush handles and long sticks to poke the reluctant hens from the branches. We younger ones enjoyed the climb to the tree tops in the dark. Having grasped an unfortunate hen we sent her flapping to the ground where she was bundled up by an adult and thrust into the hen-house. This operation could take up to an hour, during which time my father cursed and swore at the hens, but not alone at them but also their owners – 'Daft bastards tanning their arses in Ballybunion'.

All this extra night-time activity took place in August at the peak of the haymaking and contributed greatly to frayed tempers on hot days in the meadow. If Dan was with us at this particular time he would announce at breakfast to all and sundry and looking at no one in particular, that 'People usually get what they deserve'. Dan had great respect for my mother and got on with her as well as his cantankerous nature allowed, but her easy-going ways sometimes drove him to distraction and he certainly blamed her for 'these blasted hens' that were upsetting the whole home. After a month everybody had had more than they could take, so when the owners returned bronzed and rested my irate father packed their holiday hens into the crib, tackled the pony to it and brought home their charges. I often wondered how he resisted telling them what to do with their hens. But even though her calm acceptance of other people's problems drove him to the outer regions of a nervous breakdown, he loved my mother greatly and would do nothing to hurt her family or friends. 'Don't upset the wife's people,' was one of his favourite bits of advice.

Open Spaces

 P aul's farm stood on the hill across the river from our house. He had spent many years out in the Australian bush and was accustomed to the solitary life, having no desire for human companionship. His male neighbours he tolerated but women seemed to be outside the realms of his comprehension and he kept as far as possible away from them, viewing them as members of a dangerous species that threatened his safety.

His neighbours respected his privacy and kept their distance, and if he needed help at any time he would stand on the hill outside his house and shout across the river. If trained in operatic circles his remarkable vocal cords might have brought him fortune, their volume and vocal range were so extraordinary. A neighbour almost as well endowed was Jack, who lived to the west of us, and it was not unusual for a long-range conversation to take place across the valley, and we used to listen happily to the shouted communications of what we called the Lisnasheoga telephone.

Paul had long white hair with a matching beard and wore a loose white, flannel waistcoat to his knees. In summer he peeled off his pants and went around in his white long johns. He presented a strange biblical appearance out in his meadow on a summer day. Once ever he was unfortunate enough to be taken ill and had to go into hospital. It was the small local cottage hospital where a domineering matron ruled with a rod of iron: that is, until she met Paul. For a man who had spent most of his life out under the stars a rigid hospital bed was a new and unwelcome experience. The matron insisted, however, that the bedclothes be tucked in firmly, but as soon as her nurses had achieved this Paul whipped them out again. A battle of wits and words raged daily between Paul and this iron lady who confirmed all his worst fears about women. Finally, one day the matron herself tucked in the bedclothes so rigidly that Paul was almost strapped to the bed. In a glorious fit of pure rage he gave such a violent tug at the bedclothes that he turned the whole bed upside down. From underneath the bed poured a tirade of abusive language describing the matron in terms hitherto unheard. Paul won the battle and his bedclothes hung freely from then on: a free republican bed of defiance in a ward where absolute dictatorship was otherwise the rule of the day.

Paul attended no Sunday services. His God was out in the fields with him and as he did not think too much of his fellow human beings he could not see how they could be of any assistance in getting him into heaven. Our saintly old parish priest accepted Paul's thinking but he moved to another parish and a new priest arrived who believed that conformity was the road to salvation. He rode a saddle horse and one day called on Paul. Without even showing him the courtesy of dismounting, this priest lectured him from his superior position in the saddle. Paul listened wordlessly, but when the priest hesitated in order to gauge the impact of his words Paul raised the stout crop that he always carried and brought it down sharply on the horse's rump. The startled horse bolted out the gate and was halfway back to town before the priest succeeded in bringing him to a halt. He had discovered that Paul might send him to heaven a lot faster than he could get Paul there.

Paul lived to a ripe old age and despite his innate distrust of women it was one of that dreaded species, in the person of a kind cousin, who cared for him lovingly at the end of his days. One hopes that heaven has open spaces for someone like Paul, who never liked to be fenced in, or maybe his spirit is free to ramble along by the banks of the Darigle river where he herded his cattle and saved his hay.

Back To Simplicity

Oh, clergyman all dressed in black,
What a mighty church is at your back.
We are taught that by your hand
We must be led to our promised land.
Jesus is locked in your institutions
Of ancient laws and resolutions,
Buried so deep and out of sight
That sometimes we cannot see the light,
Behind huge walls that cost so much
Where simple things are out of touch.
But could it be He is not within
These walls so thick, with love so thin?
Does He walk on distant hills
Where long ago He cured all ills?
Is He gone out to open places
To simple people, all creeds, all races.
Is Jesus gone from off the altar
Catching fish down by the water?
Is He with the birds and trees,
Gathering honey from the bees?
Could it be in this simple way
That God meant man to kneel and pray?

Mrs Casey

 rs Casey lived two fields away from our house. She had never heard of Women's Liberation but she was herself a liberated woman. She was an integral part of our lives and attended our coming and going as she laid out the dead with dignity and love, and welcomed new-born babies with open arms. Babies at that time had the luxury of being born at home where they were welcomed not alone by parents but by grandparents, aunts, uncles and caring neighbours.

Eight generations of our family have lived in our house and Mrs Casey was present to welcome the first of the seventh generation when my parents' first-born arrived. Waiting with my father on the night in question were my maternal grandmother and my uncles, but when the nurse finally brought the new-born son into the kitchen it was Mrs Casey who, with her great feeling for place and tradition, stretched out her arms and said, 'Welcome to Lisnasheoga, James Nicholas!' This was no wrist-tag baby whose name was as yet open to question: this was a child whose grandfather's name was waiting for him and whose roots in this very house stretched back through many years.

After that first son my parents had five daughters, which Mrs Casey regarded as rather unfortunate; baby girls she accepted but did not rejoice in. Then, on a cold January night, my younger brother Connie was born. Mrs Casey had a healthy respect for the spirits of the dead and the 'little people' as she called them, so, when my father called to her on his way into town for the nurse and the doctor, she lit a blessed candle and holding it high above her head she walked from her cottage to my mother's bedside with the candle still lighting.

'They came with me when I had the blessed candle,' she told my mother.

She had a strong, implicit faith. Once, she was very ill just before Christmas, and the doctor told her to stay in bed; however, on Christmas morning, as she afterwards told my mother, 'I felt that I'd get up and go to Mass, so we tackled the black pony. When I went into the church I went to the holy water and washed my face and hands in it and the strength flowed back into me.'

She was her own faith healer. She held nothing in awe, only the spirits of the dead and the 'little people'. She was convinced that the 'little people' of the fort helped our family. But it was not within the power of man or animal to frighten her. Most women find rats a frightening sight but when one made an unwelcome intrusion into her bedroom she bundled him into a towel and choked him.

She regarded being childless as one of the worst afflictions that could befall a couple, and when this was the case with a neighbouring couple she ascribed it to the fact that when the husband went to bed he went to sleep. As a little girl I remember her making this pronouncement to my father, who was highly amused, while I was intrigued and felt that it had implications beyond my grasp. She was very tolerant of the weakness of human nature and if the first baby arrived ahead of schedule to a newly married couple she always smiled kindly and said:

'Wasn't it great to have so much done before they got married.'

She loved children and could see no wrong in them. If any one of us was in a sulk and my mother was trying to straighten us out, Mrs Casey would say, 'Don't cross them'. That was her full philosophy where small children were concerned and we still quote it. Mrs Casey was a great believer in the natural order of things and breast-fed all her children whenever and wherever the necessity arose.

She had great faith in marriage as a builder of character. If any selfish young woman who always had to have her own way was getting married, Mrs Casey would smile wisely and say, 'The baba will straighten her out.'

Or if the head of the family was very troublesome and aggressive, she would remark, sagely, 'His own will level him; it always takes your own to level you. The same bad blood is in the veins, you know.'

The dead she attended with loving reverence and a thoughtfulness all her own. When Mike, an old neighbour, died suddenly Mrs Casey did the needful. This old friend had always worn a hat and when he was laid in the coffin Mrs Casey told my mother, 'He looked so cold and not himself without his hat on. So I looked around and there was none of his own to be seen, but on the sideboard beside me was a small black hat. I put it on him and pulled it down over his ears and he did look better and more like himself, so we closed the coffin on Mike with the hat on.'

As the hearse was moving out of the yard his sister came looking for her hat. Mrs Casey recalled afterwards: 'I knew then that he'd be back. He had the hat and he'd come back for her.' Strangely, the sister died within the week.

Mrs Casey worked hard all her life both indoors and outdoors and knew few luxuries. Every year she fattened two pigs in a Baby Ford car parked in the garden of her cottage. They announced their hunger pangs by putting their heads out of the windows and squealing to be fed. When they were the right weight she had them killed and salted and put into two timber barrels at the bottom of the kitchen. She loved her food and could eat large amounts of fat meat but never suffer indigestion. Early in their married life her husband made the mistake of praising his mother's cooking. As she told my father, 'I took it from him for a while, but then one day I stood back and gave him a swipe of the *ciotóg*.'

She was left handed, and always referred to her left hand as 'the *ciotóg*', almost as if it belonged to someone else. Any problem which she failed to settle amicably brought the *ciotóg* into action.

Her husband was a dapper little man with a neat black moustache and she always referred to him as 'My Jack', or 'My little man'. He loved his porter but was drunk after two pints.

At a time when women seldom frequented pubs, Mrs Casey always stood at the counter with the men to have her pint. Similarly, at the Stations the men usually had breakfast with the priests while the women ate elsewhere, but Mrs Casey never failed to seat herself at the priests' table and often brought them to task about any matter in the parish which she felt was not in order.

Every year she planted fourteen drills of potatoes in one of our fields and she dug them out with a spade, while Jack followed on, picking them into a bucket. It was a very long field, with a rise at the top, and sometimes she would be gone over the rise and out of Jack's sight. If my father came on them, she would look back and say, 'He's failing, my little man is failing'.

Then, further back, Jack would say to my father: 'I have to let her forge ahead, you know. She'd think that she was failing if she couldn't keep ahead of me.'

They had each other's measure and were very happy together.

Mrs Casey picked potatoes, cut turf, thinned turnips and bound the corn. Cutting the corn took place in early autumn when my father, with two horses tackled to the mowing machine, usually started the work on a mellow September day. One of us children, sitting on one seat, guided the horse while my father, on a lower seat, would create the swarths suitable for the sheaves. All around the field the workers would bind up the corn into sheaves. Mrs Casey worked across the bottom of the field and always had the way cleared before the horses. The cutting started at the outside, working all around the field and gradually, as the day wore on, the swaying corn turned into golden sheaves which were then stood in stooks before night fell. Mrs Casey worked hard all day, her small sturdy figure dressed in flowing black moving back and forth. Sometimes her hearty laugh pealed across the field as she enjoyed a good-humoured exchange with a neighbour. She understood her neighbours and if she did not like them she never pretended otherwise, but with those she loved her great heart knew no boundaries and she brought colour and richness into their lives. She had a wealth of character and though the winds of change blew around her they never carried her with them. She was a strong woman and her philosophy of life was all her own.

Earth Woman

She was as real
As the dark brown
Bank of tiered turf
With the promise
Of warmer days.
She was as solid
As a great oak,
Unbending with
The winds that blow.
She was as strong
As the hard rocks
That weather the
Crushing waves.
Her core had
The luxuriant glow
Of the black, rich,
Sensuous soil.

Tea In The Meadow

When the summer had proved its intention of staying with us, cutting the hay began. With his meadows ripened to a honey coloured hue by the sun, my father went to the haggard and, taking his old mowing machine firmly by its long shaft, he eased it slowly from under the overhanging trees where it had sheltered throughout the long winter.

A simple, solid machine with two small wheels and drawn by a pair of horses, it had a raised seat for the driver at the back. On one side was a cutting knife which lay flat on the ground when in use and ̃was raised up for the journey back and forth from the meadow. Inside this knife was a long blade with diamond-shaped edges called sections. At first my father oiled and greased the entire machine, which had seized up during the winter; then he sat astride the shaft of the mower and laid the long blade across his knee. There was a skill in edging the blades in which he took a particular pride. He had a long edging stone with a timber handle, which he kept on top of a high press in the kitchen. This was taken down and inspected and when found to be in perfect condition was the cause of great satisfaction. What could possibly have gone wrong with it is difficult to imagine, but I suppose he had discovered over the years that very few of his tools were safe from his energetic brood. Now, sitting in the warm, sheltered haggard, beginning at one end of the blade and taking it section by section, he edged along with a balanced rhythm, occasionally dipping his stone in a rusty gallon of water which stood on the ground beside him. Gradually the rusty, archaic blade assumed a new life, its teeth gleaming with a razor sharpness, and along its base lay a ridge of brown and grey froth like the moustache of a monster man. I sometimes sat on the ground and watched this deadly weapon come to life, in awe of its power for my father gave us strict instructions regarding the dangers of farm machinery and the use of his gun, and his commands were obeyed unquestioningly.

The following day cutting the hay did not commence until the sun was high in the sky and the gently swaying hay was well dry of the morning dew. Paddy and James were rounded up, eager for work as they were after a long rest since the spring ploughing. That had been heavy, cold work and they had come home at night with their hooves covered in mud, but the hayfield promised to be soft and pleasant underfoot, with ample juicy mouthfulls available to satisfy any pangs of hunger.

The two horses were tackled to the mowing machine and, arriving in the meadow, they cut the first swarth along by the ditches and continued all day around the field, their rounds becoming gradually shorter. My father always watched out for birds' nests hidden in the hay, and the one most likely to be found was the pheasant family. If the birds rose from the hay he would halt the horses and walking into the high grass he would gently lift up the nest and carry it to the mossy ditch. Some nests, however, did not transport very well and once he brought home a few pheasant eggs to be put under a hatching hen. They hatched out along with her chickens but they were much smaller and far more active. When they grew bigger they were carried to the fort where several families of pheasants lived, and there they returned to their own lifestyle.

The blade of the mowing machine gave off a plaintive whine which carried across the valley and told of busy times. And so, hour after hour, my father and his horses worked in companionable silence while all around them lay the moist swarths of newly mown hay. Coming into the meadow in the late afternoon, bearing a jug of tea and home-made brown bread, I was enfolded in a wild, sweet essence that was moist and sensuous, stimulating some deep-rooted feelings in my inner being.

Now my father sat in a shady corner under a tree and drank his tea straight from the jug, while the horses also relaxed and sampled some freshly cut hay, flicking their long tails to keep the flies at bay. I explored the newly exposed ditches around by the headland, as we called the outer edge of the field after the first swarth was cut. In some of the meadows a stream ran along by the ditch and here floated all kinds of interesting insects sheltering under the overgrown grass and ferns. Here too, earlier in the year, frogs' croak was to be found, a jelly-like substance encasing an abundance of black dots trailing little floating legs, the baby frogs in neo-natal condition. Those tiny tadpoles who had squirmed out of that quivering quagmire were now grown into frogs of all shapes and colours: there were yellow, green and sometimes black frogs to be found jumping along the moist ditches of the meadows.

The rabbit families lived on the other side of the meadow where conditions were drier. The whine of the mowing machine and all the unexpected activity in their quiet corner had sent them scurrying underground, but now, while there was a temporary lull, they ventured out to see what was going on. They stood transfixed in amazement to find their familiar scene totally changed; gone was the high sheltering grass, and now the entire meadow lay exposed before them. But then, seeing the horses and humans, they turned tail and disappeared, to return no doubt when all was finally quiet and their domain was no longer disturbed by human intruders.

One of the meadows had a complete hedge of wild honeysuckle or woodbine, as we knew it, and this sent out a soft, wild, heady perfume that mingled with the smell of new mown hay. You had to stand still and close your eyes to fully absorb this feast of fragrances.

When my father resumed cutting I usually stayed on, wandering around, exploring mossy ditches and picking wild flowers, until finally the last swarth fell and the day's work was over. The long knife raised, the horses felt the sudden easing of their straining chains and set off briskly towards the gap that led to home. Here was a stream of spring water where they drank, spattering spray with their quivering nostrils.

Back in the haggard they were relieved of the burden of the mowing machine and tackling; then they trotted off to the freedom of the green fields with only the dark patches where they had sweated beneath their tackling to show that they had spent a hot day working in the meadow. Often times they lay down on the cool grass and rolled over on their backs, with legs cycling in the air. Then, righting themselves, they jumped up and galloped around the field, exulting in their freedom from restraining ropes and chains.

The next step in the cycle of haymaking depended on the weather and if it was less than perfect a process known as turning the hay had to be endured. This was sometimes done by hand with a hay pike: the swarth of hay which was now dry on the top side had to be turned over and its damp underside exposed to the sun. It was a slow, monotonous process which could raise blisters on little hands unaccustomed to gripping pike handles for long, but the monotony was relieved by the companionship of many people working together. Oftentimes this job was done by a machine, aptly named the swarth turner, and why it could not always be used I found hard to understand, but maybe on some occasions manpower was more plentiful than horsepower. The swarth turner was a strange looking machine on two extremely large iron wheels with two timber shafts to the front, and to the rear two giant iron spiders that sped around tossing the hay in all directions, exposing it to the sun and air. It was drawn by one horse and the driver sat on an iron seat perched high over the twirling spiders.

When the hay was sufficiently dry it was raked into rows with the wheel raker, a machine similar in design to the swarth turner which pulled a giant iron rake behind it. This gathered up the hay and then the driver pulled a lever which raised the rake, leaving the hay in a tidy row; down banged the rake again and the next row was collected. The aim was to have each row of hay parallel to the previous one and this required split-second timing and good horse control. That was the ideal, and when it was not achieved the driver of the wheel raker would be subjected to much derogatory comment from his or her fellow workers.

And so at last we arrived at the actual point of haymaking. The interval between cutting and haymaking could vary from two days to two weeks, depending on the weather, but the shorter the interval the better the hay. Hay, fast-dried in the hot sun, with all traces of green and moisture evaporated, was far superior to a dark brown version that had soaked up rain and had to be shaken out to be re-dried. Haymaking and wet weather made bad working companions and turned a pleasant experience into a long-drawn-out hardship. However, when the sun shone all these difficulties were quickly forgotten. When the swarths were ready for saving the meadow was full of blond, crinkling hay. The smell of the hay had changed, becoming more aromatic and varied as it matured, and on the day of the cutting the meadow was perfumed with a wild, sweet fragrance that filled your nostrils with the essence of summer.

A day in the meadow was sunshine and sweat, hard work and happiness. Hayseeds and innumerable forms of insect life found their way into your hair and clung to your damp back. We were usually barefoot so we picked up numerous thorns, but this annoyance was relieved by the soft feel of mossy patches beneath our feet and we developed a second sense about where it was safe to tread. Luckily, some of our meadows lay by the river, and oh! the joy on a hot day to plunge into the icy water and rid yourself of all this sticky irritation.

A contraption called a tumbling paddy was used to collect the rows of hay into big heaps. Made entirely of timber it was like a giant comb with two handles at the back; when it was full to overflowing with hay the handle was thrown forward so that the comb tumbled over and all the hay fell out. This was then used as the base for the cocks of hay, or wyndes as we called them. When the butt had been made somebody stood on it and packed the hay down while the tumbling paddy collected more hay which was piked on to the wynde until gradually it grew tall and pointed.

Standing on the wyndes was a job for somebody light and

agile. Pikes of hay were thrown up at you and had to be pulled in under your feet and danced on to firm this wavering creation. Sometimes the hay would hide an odd scratching briar or a soft yellow frog to stimulate an unplanned high jump. Things going to plan, however, you slid down the side of the wynde when it had reached its peak, then it was pared of loose hay at the base and finally tied down. A piece of hay with its ends firmly embedded in the base of the wynde was wound around the hay twine and knotted with it. The ball of twine was then thrown across the wynde and tied at the other side in the same way, and this process was repeated cross-ways.

And so it continued all day, wynde after wynde, while we got hotter and thirstier as the heat beat down on us. Then somebody would call in a voice full of elation: 'The tea is coming!'

My mother usually brought the tea in a white enamel bucket and maybe a tin sweet-gallon full as well. We made ourselves comfortable on various heaps of hay and passed around cups of tea with slices of homemade brown bread. We watched my mother's basket eagerly and usually she came up trumps with a big juicy apple cake. It is said that hunger is a good sauce but hunger and thirst certainly made the tea in the meadow a feast with a special flavour, like manna in the desert. The aroma of the sweet-smelling hay blended with the tea, funny stories and riddles made for great laughter and fun, and the whole occasion took on the atmosphere of a gay picnic.

Tea over we got back to work but there was new pep in our step and gradually the wyndes rose like mini pyramids around us. Towards evening, as the shadows lengthened across the field, we gathered up our rakes and pikes, and together with the horses made our weary way homewards. Sometimes, though, one of the more energetic members of the family would shout: 'Race you home!' and we would all take off, weariness forgotten in the challenge to be the first one home.

My father remained on to rake down the wyndes and tie them firmly with binder twine. I often saw him in the dusk of the evening standing by the gap of a field counting the cocks of hay, the satisfaction of a job well done all around him.

After the work in the meadow was finished the hay was drawn into the barn. We all enjoyed drawing in the hay; there was about it an air of achievement, a fulfilment of the basic need of man to fill the barns and prepare for winter. Next to his family's needs the welfare of his stock was closest to the heart of the farmer and it was every farmer's dread not to have enough to feed his animals in the harsh days of winter. My father had taken on the farm when he was sixteen years old, after the death of my grandfather, and his first winter had come long and harsh and left him with too little hay for the animals. It was a cruel experience for one so young and he never forgot it: at the end of every winter now our barn had a spare block of hay, a monument to my father's hard-earned lesson.

The hay was drawn home in the horse and float – a big sheet of solid timber with two iron wheels and two shafts in front. In the meadow it was tilted up in front so that the back edge lay along the base of the wynde of hay. Then the thick float ropes that were wound around an iron roller at the front of the float were unwound and tied behind the wyndes. The roller was turned, winding up the rope and bringing the cock of hay up along the float. The horse then drew home his load with the driver sitting on the setlock or on top of the wynde, while the children sat along the back of the float, their feet trailing along the fields. Drives in the float were part of their summer entertainment on the farm.

When they arrived in the barn the load was tilted out and, while the man with the horse set off for the next lot, the workers in the barn cleared the way for his return. My father usually piked the hay up and one of us took it from him and passed it back to another who packed it farther back. While the hay in the barn was low the work was very easy, but as the hay rose it became more difficult, and we had to work fast if we wanted to have a rest before the float came back. If the draw was long – coming up from the fields down by the river – we had a nice leisurely time when we could take down the books we had stored on the rafters of the barn. But when the hay was coming from a field near the house, on a hot day and the barn almost full, perspiration ran down your back clogged with dust, hayseeds got into your hair and down your throat, and the break between loads was all too short.

The day the last wynde was drawn home marked the end of the haymaking season. Now the barn was full of soft golden hay, and our animals were safe against the ravages of winter no matter how harsh it might come.

Free To Be Children

Give our children
Time to be children,
To savour the wonder
That is theirs.
To blossom in the world
Of their simplicity,
Not darkened
By the shadows
That are ours.

Let them bask
In the warmth
Of their sunshine,
Cleanse in the
Softness of their tears,
Be kissed by the
Beauties of nature,
Let them be free
In the kingdom
That is theirs.

Their beauty
Is the purity
Of heaven,
Not tainted
By the ugliness
Of man.
Oh, let's not destroy
Their simplicty.
We never can
Improve
On what they have.

Going To Ballybunion

The hay in and the barn full, it was Ballybunion time before the horror of going back to school befell us. The whole family did not go together: my father went by himself after the threshing when Listowel races were on while my mother took the two youngest in August. When we arrived in Ballybunion we checked around in a couple of the guesthouses we usually stayed in, and there were sure to be vacancies in one of them. Some were ordinary guest-houses but others worked an arrangement whereby you bought your own food and they cooked it for you. As they usually had a couple of families staying at the same time, I'm not sure how they sorted it all out.

In the guest-houses we met up with various families, some of whom we knew from previous years. One family I remember was like the steps of stairs, one after the other, and they had a mother who never stopped shouting. At that time there were no wash-hand basins with running water in the bedrooms: instead we had large jugs of water with basins underneath for washing and enamel buckets to hold the used water. One morning this particular family were about to bring their bucket of dirty water down the stairs when they started a fight on the top step. The bucket was turned upside down and rolled down spilling water in all directions: that gave their mother something to shout about!

But the most important job on arriving in Ballybunion was to make our way to the 'Tricky Tracky' shop for buckets and spades. Tricky Tracky was a marvellous shop full of seaside paraphernalia and it always had a small, brightly coloured merry-go-round twirling in the breeze on the low wall in front of the shop. Then, the first smell of the sea was heaven to our nostrils and we saw the donkey carts with their loads of sea-weed trotting along the strand. Sunbathing bored us: we climbed rocks and investigated damp eerie caves and packed the long warm day with endless activities. We headed straight for the strand after breakfast and with the exception of meal-times we never left again till dark.

The headland cliffs of Ballybunion are wild and beautiful but also very dangerous for the unwary. My mother was forever cautioning us about the dangers but her warnings went in one ear and out the other; to us the sea was great fun, where we splashed and dived under waves and got mouths full of salt water. There was a huge cluster of rocks called the Black Rocks which were covered by the full tide but when it was out it left warm pools which sheltered many little sea creatures. We loved investigating all of these and gathering shells and sea grasses. The 'Nine Daughters' Hole' was our chamber of horrors: there was a legend attached to it that a man drowned his nine daughters there because they would not each marry a man of his choice, but I secretly believed that nine daughters were too much for any man and he had gone berserk. We were under severe threat not to go to Nine Daughters' Hole, but of course we did. It was a huge, gaping hole set well back from the edge of the cliffs, but the sea had burrowed its way through the rock at the bottom and thun-dered in and out with a menacing roar. I always felt the hair rising on the back of my neck as we lay on our stomachs to peer down over the edge. The possibility of slipping brought me out in a cold sweat as I looked down along the sheer black face of the rock at the grey sea belting in and out below.

Sometimes at night – if we promised to behave ourselves – we were taken to the bumpers. Each car took two people but even so they were expensive by our standards and we did not get to go very often. They were inside in a large hall that had other games and kiddy rides, and it was here that I had my first experience of dishonesty. I had a shining silver half-crown which I was keeping in case something special re-quiring big spending turned up. My father had given it to me before leaving home, and now I took it out of my pocket every so often to savour the thrill of having so much money at my disposal. A big girl began to chat me up with a sad story of having no money because her mother was away and wouldn't be back until the following day: if I gave her my half-crown, she said, she would give it back tomorrow night. My half-crown and I parted company. The next night there was no trace of my new friend and the following night she ran in the other direction as soon as she saw me. It had never dawned on me that she would not give it back, but then the penny dropped. I had lost my half-crown, which was painful, but I also felt let down in a way that was quite new to me.

The old travelling theatre companies were based in Ballybunion for the summer and they brought a new dimension to my thinking: every night a whole new world opened up before my eyes. I soaked in every performance, absorbing the different emotions flowing across the footlights, but the play that made the biggest impression on me was *My Cousin Rachel*. How I suffered with the young wife and resented the black-garbed, threatening housekeeper! However, the one who really got to me was the leading man, who stole my heart away. It was the first yelp of puppy love and I wallowed in its agony and ecstacy.

My mother spent her days sitting on a rug in a sunny cove where she met up with many old friends. Ballybunion at that time was the holdiay centre for Cork, Kerry and Limerick, so she met far-flung relations and 'connections'. She was the only person whom I ever heard use that word: it meant somebody whose family was connected to yours by marriage. There was no blood relationship but they were still in her calculation on the outer fringes of the family circle. She loved talking to people and she would listen to the most boring old crones for hours on end and sympathize with all their sad stories. But she met some great characters as well. I remember one happy fat lady who never had a swimming suit and used to go into the sea in an overflowing bra and big pink knickers. She swam like a giant fish and would carry you so far out to sea that you had to sink or swim. Another great source of entertainment was the sight of pot-bellied men and large-bottomed women; bare flesh got rare exposure in Ireland at that time. Listening to these strangers, we found the Kerry accent soft and caressing but the Limerick people had a way of saying 'Are you here for a forthnight?' that we would mimic endlessly.

For the entire two weeks in Ballybunion we never wore shoes except when going to church, to which my mother dragged us protesting every morning for Mass. She thought it was marvellous to be able to get daily Mass but we did not think that it was so great; however, the strand and the sea at that time of morning looked calm and peaceful and it felt good to run down and be the first to leave your footprints along the wide expanse of golden sand. My mother visited the church at night as well to say her rosary, but when I got bored I would leave her at it and ramble off outside. Religion, I discovered, could be very time-consuming. Across from the church was a wide area of waste ground overgrown with weeds and briars, and strangely enough right in the middle of it was a bright red flower. I sat on the wall and imagined all sorts of fantasies about that flower: in one I was an orphan on a desert island who turned into a red flower. My mother praying gave me plenty of time to dream.

At the end of the holidays we came home bronzed and my fair hair was always white from the sun. We were ready but reluctant to face back to school.

A Memory

The waste ground was choked with weeds
They grew above her head
But in the middle of this waste
One flower of golden red.

The little child came every day
To gaze upon this scene
The flower it was the loveliest sight
That she had ever seen.

This flower took root and blossomed
It grew inside her head
And led her on to lovely things
Long after it was dead.

To School Through
The Fields

Going to school and coming back was so enjoyable that it made school itself bearable. My main objection to school was that I had to stay there: it was the first experience to interfere with my freedom and it took me a long time to accept that there was no way out of its trap. I could look out through a window in the back wall of the schoolhouse and see my home away in the distance, with the fields stretching out invitingly and with the Darigle river glinting in the valley. I made many an imaginary journey home through that window: it was not that I wished to be at home so much, but that I wanted to be free to ramble out through the fields. I envied the freedom of the crows on the trees outside the window, coming and going as they pleased.

But school became an accepted pattern and even though it had its black days it had its good ones as well. The black days were mainly in winter when we arrived through the fields with sodden boots and had to sit in the freezing cold with a harsh wind whipping in under the door and up through the floorboards. The school was an old stone building with tall rattling windows and black cobweb-draped rafters, and when the wind howled the whole school groaned and creaked. The floor had large gaping holes through which an occasional rat peeped up to join the educational circle.

The educational process of the day was based on repetition: we repeated everything so often that it *had* to penetrate into our uninterested minds. A booster, by way of a sharp slap across the fingers with a hazel rod, sharpened our powers of perception. Learning was not optional and the sooner you learnt that fact, the freer from conflict life became. All the same, most of the teachers were as kind as the system allowed them to be, but inspectors breathed down their necks and after them came the priests to check our religious knowledge. One stern-faced priest peered down at me from his six-foot height when I was in third class and demanded to know: 'What is transubstantiation?'

Education was certainly not child orientated but our way of life compensated for its shortcomings. Sometimes, though unaware of it, we tried to educate our teachers, especially the ones that came from nearby towns to do part-time duty. One of these asked us to write a composition on 'Life on the Farm'. I loved writing compositions and my problem was not how to start but how to finish. I included in my account a description of the sex life of a cow and when I got my copy back from the teacher this section was ringed with a red pencil. A red mark meant an error so I checked every word for spelling in my dictionary but found nothing wrong. I returned to school the following day to ask the teacher what was wrong.

'That sentence should be left out,' she said.

'But why?' I asked.

'It's not suitable,' she answered, giving me a strange look.

On returning home in a very confused state I explained my problem to my mother. She read my composition, smiled and said: 'People from a different background do not always understand'. It took me another couple of years to understand why the teacher did not understand.

Ours was a mixed school and this suited everybody because families and neighbours were not split up but could all go to school together. The boys played football at one side of the yard and the girls played hunt and cat and mouse at the other side. At the back of the school the boys' and girls' toilets, which consisted of a timber bench with a circle cut in it to facilitate bottoms of all sizes, were separated by a stone wall. The little toilet building was partly roofed with galvanised but this had grown to a complete roof by years of free-growing ivy.

The school had just two rooms. The master had a room to himself and the second room was shared by the two other teachers: one taught infants and first class at one side of the room, while second and third classes were taught by the second teacher at the other side. It was open plan education and if you got bored at your end you could tune in to the other side, at the risk of a slap across the ear if you were caught out.

We ate our lunch, which consisted of a bottle of milk and two slices of home-made brown bread, sitting on a grassy ditch around the school, and we fed the crumbs to the birds. In winter the milk bottles were heated around the fire during classes, often resulting in corks popping from the heat and, if the cork could not pop because it was screwed on we had a mini-explosion and a milk lake.

There was a cottage near the school from which we collected a pot of tea each day for the teachers, and this provided a welcome diversion, especially in summer. We went down a narrow lane which led into a long garden abounding with rows of vegetables, fruit trees and flowers. These flowers overflowed on to the paths and climbed up over the windows and on to the thatched roof of the cottage: it was almost buried in flowers, and when you went down the steps and through the doorway you stepped into another world. Inside the cottage was shadowed and had an air of mystery because every available space seemed to be filled with the treasures of the old couple who lived there. All around was the smell of flowers and on the table were bowls of fresh fruit from the garden. When you arrived into the kitchen you were seated on a soft *súgán* chair and given a cup of scalding tea coloured with goat's milk and a cut of bread with a thick layer of homemade jam, and afterwards you got a fistful of strawberries or raspberries that were soft and luscious. The little window on the back wall of the cottage was frilled with a lace curtain tied back with a ribbon and through the sparkling glass you could see the back garden as profuse and colourful as the front. It was a dream cottage and John O' and Mrs O' were ideal occupants. They were gentle people; she wore a long skirt with her hair coiled in a soft roll on top of her head, he was a neat little man with a black moustache, and always wore a navy suit. The trip to John O's cottage brightened up many a school day tinged with monotony.

Going to school in the winter mornings through the grey frosty fields had its own beauty. The bushes and briars took on unearthly shapes of frozen rigidity and the trees glittered with outstretched arms like graceful ballerinas; underfoot the grass crunched beneath our strong leather boots. The muddy gaps through which the cows waded up to their knees in gutter were now strangely transformed into frozen masses of intriguing shapes. In their frozen state you could dance from one strange pattern formation to another or try to crack the black ice with the tipped heel of your boot and create your own strange designs. This grey frozen land was much more interesting and comfortable than its rain-soaked winter companion. In the rain you could slip on the wet grass and have a wet bottom to sit on for the day or, going through the gaps between the fields, an unwary step could land you with two boots full of mud and water. We had two glaises to contend with; these were waterways larger and rougher than streams but smaller than rivers. Now swollen with floods they provided an additional hazard and we crossed them on stepping stones while the brown foaming water swirled around our boots. I had mental images of slipping off the stones and being carried by the rushing water down to the river that was roaring through the valley below, but somehow we survived all these winter threats and they added a sense of adventure to making it through the fields every day.

Summer came at last. We welcomed it and the freedom it brought from the shackles of winter. When the warm days were firmly established we kicked off our heavy boots and long black stockings and danced through the warm grass in delight, the morning fields moist with dew that ran down our bare legs and trickled between our toes. Cobwebs sparkled on the bushes and cascaded on to the grass, joining the fields and ditches in a shimmering web. The sun warmed us and set our journey aglow. The day in school was just an unwelcome interlude then between the morning trek and the return home, and if the journey to school took about thirty minutes, the coming home could take anything up to two hours.

On leaving school we ran down the lane and over a wooden

fence into a large hilly field. We ran around in circles flinging our sacks ahead of us and running after them, like young calves kicking up their heels at the first taste of freedom in an open field. Half way down that field was a small well in the side of a mossy ditch with a grey timber gate covering it. This was John O's well and the gate was to keep his goat away from it, so the goat had to content himself with the stream outside. This was our first stop. Here we collapsed on the warm grass and stretched out in the sun. We swapped stories, one more far-fetched than the last, and one of the boys sometimes made pools in the well stream for the birds to bathe in. He loved the birds and they reciprocated his feeling because they showed no fear of him.

Then we washed our lunch bottles and filled them with cold spring water and, having drunk enough, we refilled them for the safari home. We ran to the bottom of the hill and in under the overhanging trees where our first glaise tumbled over green mossy stones. Here, if the humour was on us, we might block up a large pool and paddle in and out of it, hitching up our skirts by tucking them up the legs of our knickers. The boys had short pants, but they rolled them up further, re-vealing patches of white above their mahogany brown knees. Tiring of this we rambled along the next field which led to the only stretch of road on the journey home, a short bit of road made up mainly of a long stone bridge. Under this bridge the Darigle river hid itself between deep grassy banks, and some-times we went over the low wall of the bridge to catch collies. Other evenings we hung over the bridge watching the water-hens darting in and out beneath the bank. The hens' hatching time was eagerly observed and the evening the chicks appeared was as exciting as the arrival of a new baby at home.

It was difficult to drag ourselves away from there, but leav-ing the road we parted with some of our friends and took to the fields again. Rambling on through two more glens we came to another glaise, which was covered with briars and bushes. We burrowed underneath them and splashed into the cool green water before climbing up a stone ditch at the other side. Now came our greatest test of strength: a steep hill which we zigzagged up very slowly, stopping half way to replenish our strength with our water bottles. Finally we reached the top where we sat down for a long time to finish our bottles. From this hilltop perch we looked back over the valley we had just come through and the school looked small in the distance, which felt most satisfactory. We watched the different herds of cows grazing and picked out the bulls. These were something to be reckoned with constantly on our journey to and from school: some were killers and had to be kept at a safe distance, which often necessitated putting extra fields between us and them. We recognized their different roars and checked every field to make sure of their whereabouts.

Having recovered from our hill climb we often picked buttercups and made daisy chains. Then, as we sauntered on through the remaining fields, we checked our birds' nests to see how things were progressing. An odd time we met one of the neighbours and if we were lucky got invited in for a cup of milk and currant cake. The last few fields were flat and mossy and we picked blackberries or sometimes, when they were in season, we filled our bottles with black sloes and buried them to make sloe wine – only we could never remember afterwards where we had hidden them. Finally we arrived home sunsoaked and relaxed, with school almost forgotten because it was, after all, only one part of a much larger cycle of education.

A School Friend

We walked to school
Through the dew drenched fields
Meeting where our paths crossed
At the foot of a grassy hill.
If one ran late, the other
Left a stone message
On the mossy bridge.
He had muddy boots,
A jumper torn by briars
And hair that went its own way.
Trivial details to a mind
That raced amongst the clouds
And followed rabbits down brown burrows.
Gentle hands, twisted by a bad burning,
Reached out towards the birds,
And they perched on his fingers
At ease with one of their own.
Blessed with a mind that ran free
From the frailties of his body
He walked during his quiet life
Close to the gates of heaven.

Our Daily Bread

The day on the farm started at about 7.00 a.m. with a quick cup of tea. Then, when the cows had been milked and my father had gone to the creamery, the rest of us sat down to a long, leisurely breakfast. Preparations for dinner meant going to the field where the potatoes and vegetables grew and digging a bucket of potatoes and cutting some heads of cabbage; a big black pot of potatoes was boiled every day and whatever was left went with the other scraps to feed the farm dogs and the pigs. Dinner itself was at one o'clock, and a shrill iron whistle that hung beside the kitchen door summoned us: we could hear it fields away. At four o'clock we had afternoon tea, and whatever time the cows were milked in the evening was supper time.

The evening milking was a restful moment in the day. Men and women, tired after their work, slapped their little milking stools on the ground beside the cows. We called the stool 'the block', maybe because it consisted of a two-inch block of solid timber with three legs broadening out at the base to give balance. Having made sure that your block was secure, you sat down with a bucket between your knees and rested your forehead against the soft, silken flank of the cow. Then, wrapping your fingers around the cow's warm teats, you milked to a steady, soothing rhythm. At first the milk hit the tin bucket with a sharp metallic sound but as it filled it mellowed to a drowsy hum and the cold bucket grew warm between your legs.

Milking time was singing time; it was debating time if your fellow milkers felt so inclined; or it could be just dreaming time. If, however, the cow felt that her presence was being ignored she could draw a sharp kick and send you sprawling into the centre channel of the stalls, baptizing you with the bucket of warm milk. Most were tranquil animals but we had a few of what my father called 'kickers'. Each cow had a name and the kicking strain could follow from mother to daughter, and often we had a mother and daughter in the one herd.

The cows were of many different strains and colours; specialization had not yet come in. We had a family called 'Legs': these were long-legged white cows; and the white cows were termed 'baney'. There was a strain of small brown ones we called 'Mouse', and we had both a mother Mouse and a young Mouse; I liked the mother Mouse particularly because she was so quiet and easy-going and never kicked.

We carried the buckets full of milk to the churns, which we called 'tanks', on the stand outside the stalls, and around the top of each tank was a muslin cloth through which we strained the milk. When Dan was staying he rather than my father might sometimes take the milk to the creamery; however, this occasionally led to problems. These were the early days of hygiene inspectors and Dan resented inspectors in any form: he absolutely refused to allow any inspection of our tanks, demanding to know of them,

'What did you ever do for your country that entitled you to go around smelling our milk?'

After such an altercation a hurried SOS would come from the creamery to channel Dan in another direction.

In early spring or late autumn when milk production was at its lowest we separated our own milk and made butter. We poured the milk, still warm from the cow, into the separator – a large iron dish with two pipes, which was attached to a motor with a handle. It gave off a soft whine when the handle was turned, and out of one pipe came cream, out of the other skim-milk. It was a simple but ingenious device and while my father manned it we young ones lined up with cups for drinks of cream.

On the following day the cream was put into the churn to make butter. We had two churns: a hand one which sat on a table and could be worked by one person and a barrel churn which stood on a stand and required two churners, though if woman power was scarce, which seldom happened, one could manage it. After a certain amount of churning the thick cream formed into lumps of butter. The faster one could achieve this the better the butter, and this was the source of the country saying that 'Long churning makes bad butter', a saying which was considered applicable to many situations in life. The butter made, it was washed and salted; what remained in the churn was buttermilk, a grand drink on a hot summer day and a great favourite of the men coming in from the fields.

The crops we had planted in spring grew through the summer months and as they ripened the differences between them became evident: the wheat was a golden brown, the oats a butter yellow, and the barley with its bearded head the old man of the three. Cutting the corn in the autumn meant the winding down of the year's work, and it was a task in which the neighbours came together and helped each other out. When the corn had been cut and bound into sheaves, stooks were made and finally handstacks; then the handstacks were drawn home with the horse and float and the different ricks (or 'reeks' as we called them) were made.

The threshing was one of the biggest events of the farming year; the sowing of the seeds in the spring, followed by the cutting of the corn, were all a build-up to this point. Now the wheat would be threshed into grain, which would in turn be ground into flour to give us our daily bread.

Coming home from school through the fields we heard the hum of the thresher in the different farmyards and counted the days until it would pull into our haggard. Finally, on coming home one evening, we would be told that the threshing machine was coming to our farm that night. We waited in the haggard and kept our ears strained for the sound of the old engine, our eyes peeled for the sight of the smoke above the trees. Living still in the age of the horse, anything motorised that moved on wheels on the farm was to us a kind of miracle.

At last we heard the engine grumbling its way along and saw the high, pink-timbered threshing machine between the hedges; as I watched it coming down the laneway I felt thrills of anticipation shooting out through my toes. Getting the long, unwieldy paraphernalia into the haggard was a slow and complicated ordeal and it was a great place to be if you wanted to learn any new curses. The greasy overalled engine men twisted and manoeuvred this iron monster which all the time belched smoke and spluttered in protest. Finally, after much discussion and pacing of distances, the most suitable position was achieved: she was set and ready for action the following morning.

After breakfast the engine was coaxed into life and as it coughed and finally roared it sent out smoke signals that brought the men from miles around. They came from across the river, down from the hill, across the fields and down the laneway. They were weather-beaten, work-hardened men and each one carried a pike; they came at a lively pace with a hunger for work in their stride.

The threshing was a test of working skills in which men showed their mettle and, even though they often worked hard days at home, they did not always have such an audience. It was also one of the most sociable days of the year, for some of these men met only at threshings and so had a year's events to discuss. Some of them opened the reek and threw the sheaves to those on top of the thresher. At the back of the thresher where the straw poured out was one of the toughest jobs in piking away the straw. Here a reek of straw was made, and as the reek of corn reduced in size this rose higher; there was skill in making a well balanced reek.

The story of the harvest was told at the front of the thresher. Here the golden grain poured out of little trap doors into jute bags. This was where my father took control: he scooped up the first grains anxiously into his fist and examined them on the palm of his hand; then he put a few into his mouth and chewed them thoughtfully with his eyes closed. He was like a connoisseur sampling wine as he tested his year's work. Finally, he opened his eyes and, rubbing his hands together, declared: 'Great stuff, that'.

It was lovely to watch the gold grain pour into the nut-brown bags. When it was about four inches from the top we quickly changed bags; then the full bags were carried on the backs of the men across the haggard to the loft, a long, low stone building with a timber floor. The grain was poured from the open bags on to the floor, starting at the back wall. As the bags were open-mouthed on their backs the men just bent forward without removing them and the grain poured out over their shoulders. I helped my father switching the bags at the mouth of the thresher and a sense of togetherness and harmony with the satisfaction of a job well done built up between us during the day.

All that day the thresher droned and the men worked steadily, breaking only for dinner and tea. It took large supplies to feed the hungry *meitheal* (the group of neighbours who had come to work with us) and if Napoleon believed that an army marched on its stomach my mother believed that the threshing men worked on theirs. There was an air of good fellowships and fun both in the haggard and around the kitchen table. At the side of the thresher a large pile of chaff – featherlight bits of straw and empty ears of corn – built up and here, after school, the neighbouring children played, burrowing into it and throwing it at each other while the men shouted at them to get out of the way. The haggard was the realm of the men and children to which the women, busy in the kitchen, rarely came.

Gradually, as the reeks of corn disappeared and the reeks of straw towered high, the threshing wound down; we children were sorry to hear it shuddering to a halt. Then the men helped to get the thresher and engine out, a complicated business because the wheels were so heavy that sometimes they sank into the soft ground. After much pushing and shunting she finally got going and it was with a sense of sadness that I watched the whole gangling procession steam its way up the passage. The top-heavy thresher frequently swayed at precarious angles but always recovered in time to right itself.

The threshing was over for another year and the men went home to their various farms to milk the cows, their children with them. The haggard, a hue of different shades of yellow and brown, was silent at last. The bright yellow straw, the soft yellow chaff and the rich dark earth where the wheels of the thresher had cut. My father stood with one hand on his hip and the other rubbing the base of his neck: it was his stance when everything was right in his world. He walked to the open door of the loft where the rich-coloured grain spread out in waves to the four corners. I stood beside him, silent lest I break the magic of his moment of inner peace. He was a man who was often aggravated by some of the aspects of farming, but at times like this he reached a high plateau of fulfilment, and later he and my mother would go together to view the loft.

When the geese and ducks arrived back for the night from the fields there were shrieks of joy, for the haggard after threshing was a haven of rare delight for them. They screeched and they quacked and they tore into the chaff with all the sounds of ecstasy. They ate it, they burrowed into it, and they rolled over in it: such was their harvest thanksgiving.

Later some of the grain was taken to the mill for crushing. A large quantity of the oats was left as it was to be fed to the hens and horses. The crushed oats and barley were used to feed the pigs and some of the cows, and the wheat was milled for flour. Some of the wheat was sold and more returned for our own use. My mother baked every day: big circles of brown and white bread baked in the bastables over the fire. Shop bread rarely appeared on our table. She made big currant cakes and apple cakes with the apples from our own orchard. We had huge old apple trees that produced an abundance of fruit which my mother stored in boxes in the loft; they seldom had time to dry out as our consumption was heavy and demand always exceeded supply. After a stormy night the pigs had a feast in the orchard eating the windfalls, but when my brother started beekeeping the hives were under the apple trees and the pigs were forced out. They resented this infringement of their rights but when they made any attempt to force an entrance the bees went on the attack. I often saw the herd, with tails curled high, screeching in protest and running as fast as their short legs would carry them.

A Rusty Love Affair

In a sun-baked shed
With black grained hands
These iron men of steam
Sweat oil pursuing an ideal.
There she sits in state,
This queen of the past,
Waiting for her archaic
Limbs to be greased
Into motion, her joints
Soothed gently by her
Black lovers, unquestioning
In their complete adoration.
In this brown station yard
Carriages grey with old age,
Retired queens, proudly wear
The grandeur of another day.
Here, a dream in creation,
An old train being reborn
When men became gods
Breathing life into dead iron.

My Father's Butter Box

In our local creamery butter was stored in solid boxes, about two and a half feet wide, made of fine timber with a yellow waxen sheen. Many found their ways into local farmers' houses where they were put to good use; one such was the butter box that came into our house and became my father's tool box.

It had lost its former waxen elegance and had turned a muddy brown, with a bit missing off the top at one side. Into this my father had collected a miscellaneous assortment of hammers, wrenches and screwdrivers, together with nails, washers and screws of varying degrees of antiquity. On top came bits of timber and rubber and all kinds of odds and ends left over from previous jobs. He never threw anything away in case it might come in handy in the future, but this practice was self-defeating as he could never find anything he wanted. His box was packed full to the very top and had to be dragged rather than lifted due to its immense weight.

When he had a job to do out came the butter box. The jobs could vary from putting a handle on a brush to replacing a window or fixing the leg of a chair that was unable to withstand our daily assaults. The butter box was an essential part of these undertakings. At first my father dug and poked into its depths looking for a nail of the required length. Many were discarded in a rising tide of frustration and annoyance at their unsuitability until eventually, in a final crescendo of pure anger, the whole box was turned upside down on the kitchen floor. Ours was a large kitchen but when my father's box was upended its contents scattered to the four walls with screws and nails rolling under all the presses and chairs. As most of the contents of the box had rusted to various shades of brown over the years, our kitchen now took on the appearance of a ploughed field. At this stage the whole house came to a standstill while my father poured a tirade of colourful language on the head of any nail that had the audacity to bend before reaching its prescribed destination. His favourite expression when he had reached the limits of his endurance was 'hoor's bastard!' and when I was young I thought that a 'hoor's bastard' was a crooked nail and that a 'hoor' was a cow who would refuse to go through a gateway when my father intended that she should.

The job, depending on the size of the undertaking, could go on for many hours during which time we children ran back and forth answering his every demand and sometimes anticipating them like a team of nurses tending a surgeon during a major operation. I will say one thing for this exercise: it certainly sharpened our reflexes and if the hammer slipped and he hit his thumb instead of the nail we heard adjectives hitherto unknown to us. Finally the mission was accomplished and our carpenter downed tools. He then found other more important things to attend to and walked away leaving chaos behind. It was our job to pick up every single item and throw it in the butter box, and this we did with a vengeance so that the final state of the box was worse than the first, thus guaranteeing another performance at a later date. The cleaning up was a slow, laborious, monotonous job and we hated every minute of it, though it was surely a great training in the development of patience. When the kitchen floor was finally brushed and the last bit of rubbish shovelled into the butter box, the floor which was normally a stone grey was now a symphony of browns and greens of sufficient variety to thrill the heart of any landscape artist.

My mother, a wise woman, was seldom in the kitchen for these performances. This was not by chance but part of her marital strategy. She was very happily married for over forty years to a man who was an excellent husband but whose threshold of tolerance was very low. She thus avoided direct confrontation and quietly out-manoeuvred him, believing that in marriage, as in battle, strategy was of all importance.

In after years my father's butter box became a joke in our family and we often wondered how he would have fitted into a modern semi-detached in suburbia with an equal-rights wife and modern teenagers. He was never designed for 'little boxes' living.

The Last Litany

Despite the fact that my mother was tolerant and flexible in most situations, she did have streaks of uncompromising rigidity. The family rosary was one of these: sick, maimed or crippled, we were all on our knees for the rosary, and helpers, visitors, or anyone who happened to call at the wrong time were apt to be included.

During the summer months I knelt inside the kitchen window looking down over the fields where the cows were grazing after milking. When my turn came to give out the decade I used the cows in the field to count my ten Hail Marys. I mentally sectioned off ten in a corner, but as my mind floated back and forth across the valley the cows naturally moved around so my ten could decrease to five or six. If I said the Glory before schedule my mother gently intervened in the background – 'Two more'. Or if my herd increased and my Hail Marys swelled beyond the ten she interrupted with 'Glory, now, Glory'. She also fought gallantly to keep us all supplied with rosary beads but they were continually getting lost or broken. She never tried to convert my father to beads, so he cracked his knuckles as he went along to keep count.

Her rosary was one thing, but her additions to it were something else. First came the litany starting 'Holy Mary', and we would all chant, 'Pray for us' in response. After Holy Mary came a long list and somewhere down along the list came 'Ark of the Covenant' and 'Gate of Heaven'. After 'Gate of Heaven' one night my mother lost her concentration and she floundered and repeated it a few times, failing to remember what came next. Finally a little voice in the background piped up helpfully: 'Try Nelson's Pillar!' Everybody fell around the floor laughing, and my father took advantage of the opportunity to call a halt to the litany for the night.

But the litany was only one of the many additions. There were three Hail Marys for this neighbour and a second lot for another one, until my father would start complaining, 'For God's sake, we'll be here till morning'. We prayed diligently for years for one neighbour who was studying to be a teacher and of whom my father voiced the opinion that 'if a bumble bee had his brains he'd fly backwards', but despite this pronouncement on the neighbour's grey matter he still qualified. It was my mother's conviction that prayer could move mountains and indeed hers often did; at least they moved mountains of ignorance. During exam time she always lit a candle in the centre of the parlour table. I would come home during exams and peep into the parlour to check if she had remembered. It was always lighting. It was a symbol of caring and in later years her children wrote as adults to her from many corners of the world asking her to light her candle and pray for their special problems.

She had an implicit faith in the goodness and power of God but despite this she was always late for Mass. If left to her own devices she would never have made it at all, but my father was a punctuality addict. He was ready half an hour before time and paced up and down the kitchen floor ranting and swearing; then he would go to the kitchen door and, scratching his head and raising his eyes towards heaven, would declare: 'If ever a man suffered!' I think that he was imploring God to witness that this was his agony in the garden. Finally he would stand at the foot of the stairs and shout: 'Missus, is it today or next Sunday we're going to Mass?' Normally he called my mother Len, but if she was pushing him to the limits of his endurance it changed to 'missus': this was his signal to her that thus far and no further could she go. Finally she arrived, pulling on her hat and calling instructions back over her shoulder to those staying at home. She was only going to be missing for a few hours, but a stranger could be forgiven for thinking that a world voyage was on the agenda.

Organized planning and good housekeeping were not on

the top of her list of priorities and it was to people she gave her number one commitment. She always had time to listen and chat. If you ever had to leave the house very early in the morning she was there. She was with you having the breakfast to listen to any worries troubling you; late at night she was in the kitchen waiting to have a cup of tea. She never told us that she loved us but she wrapped us in blankets of love and did not need to use words. Her love and serenity filled the house and she herself was one of the most contented people I ever knew. In an era when corporal punishment was the rule of the day she did not believe in smacking children; she maintained that slapping them made children bold and aggressive. One day I came home from school to find a stream of water pouring out the door against me. She was baby-sitting a neighbour's little girl, an only child who was always beautifully dressed, and in the middle of the kitchen she had a wheelbarrow full of sand and water; not a little wheelbarrow mind you, but a large rusty, iron model. When I asked her the reason for the wheelbarrow I was informed that it was good for children to make a mess and that sand and water was of great benefit to them.

She absolutely forbade bad language from any of us children, and though my father indulged in all sorts of colourful phrases it was accepted that it was his prerogative and did not extend to the rest of us. She amazed me in later years by quite blandly informing me that my father used only the words necessary to describe any given situation, and she was quite right.

Togetherness

Forced apart
By busy days
We who belong
Together
As the interlaced
Fingers
Of praying
Hands
Join again
In quite times
At peace
In our
Togetherness

The Cut-Throat Nuns

We lived about three miles from the nearest town but the passage, as we called it, from the road to our home was another half a mile. On each side of the passage from the gateway were high mossy ditches where birds and rabbits nestled, and further down were seven gates marking the divisions between the fields as this was also the access lane for the cattle and machinery going along the farm. Lorry drivers dreaded our farm and one cranky individual once poked his head out of his cab at my father and demanded: 'Does the Almighty God know that people live down here?'

I loved walking down that laneway and I knew every twig and branch along the way. The first time that the joy of returning home along it hit me was after my first enforced absence from home, when I had to go into hospital in Cork for a week to have my tonsils removed. The prospect had not worried me greatly to begin with; however, when I had seen my mother's hat disappearing out the hospital gate I had begun to feel abandoned, and the week that had followed was to put me off hospitals and nuns for the rest of my life. The nuns in their virginal white habits sailed around the wards like billowing swans and, when the operation left my throat feeling as if the French guillotine had done a job on it, I discovered that their snowy white exterior penetrated to their inner regions as well, for the nuns treated us with cool efficiency but with very little of the milk of human kindness. I do not think that they believed in the approach expressed in 'suffer little children to come unto Me'.

At home whenever one of us had a sore throat my mother soaked bread in warm milk and this remedy slid down a raw throat like soft butter. Now in hospital my throat screamed in agony with every swallow and my stomach groaned because its food supply was cut off. I thought with longing of my mother's solution: we called it 'goody', a childish word and, like most children's expressions, an apt description. But when I asked one of the nuns if she had ever heard of 'goody' she threw back her head, gave a braying laugh like our jennet when he had been tied up for too long and, looking around the ward, she asked in a high, nasal voice: 'Did any of you ever hear of "goody"?' She pronounced it as if it were a dirty word, and I wished that I could have used some of my father's favourite phrases to tell her what I thought of her.

The week in that hospital was a bewildering experience. The babies in the ward cried all the time they were awake; it was the era of restricted visiting and the children cried from loneliness. At home on the farm we cuddled our baby animals when they were sick: here in hospital these children fared far worse and it was heart-breaking to see the little tear-stained faces peering through the iron bars of the cots.

After a few days, when I had begun to recover and to get my bearings, I began to plan my escape. Nobody, I decided, could survive in this set-up for very long. Across the road from the hospital was a hotel. I sat on the verandah outside the children's ward and watched the comings and goings at the hotel hoping to see a familiar face, and finally I spotted an old friend of my father's. The next day I watched my chance to make my way out the front door of the hospital and I shouted across at Jack when he appeared. I poured out my troubles to him, and discovered that he was going home by bus that evening. I asked him to call for me on his way to the bus; then I went back to the nuns and told them that my father was collecting me that evening. Eventually they relented and agreed to let me go. I felt like somebody released from jail after serving a sentence of hard labour. As we travelled to Lisnasheoga the engine of the bus was happily singing 'Going Home'.

As I opened the gate of the road to our farm I felt such a surge of joy pour over me that I could have flown over the fields. I sat on a stone and my eyes roved over every familiar detail of that view; in the haze of the late summer evening it looked serene and welcoming. I was so glad to be home.

That was my first experience of a deep-rooted love of the very fields of home. Every evening my father would walk these fields, checking the animals and seeing that everything was as it should be. It was not actually necessary to do this every day but he enjoyed walking the fields – you were never alone in them, with the farm animals and the wildlife all around you. At that time there was a lovely practice known as blessing the crops: these were days of supplication when God was asked to bless the harvest. The farmer went to every field with a bottle of holy water, and he sprinkled the holy water and said whatever prayers he thought suitable, giving special attention to those fields in which crops were planted. I accompanied both my father and my mother as they did this, and I felt a great sense of harmony, a blending of man, nature and God in complete unity.

Yalla Bacon

We killed two pigs every year for our household needs. On the day of the killing my father acted as butcher and the neighbours as fellow executioners. A big timber table was scrubbed white and beside it a timber barrel of boiling water was placed in readiness, and these were positioned outside the old, disused turf house. The pig was then led to the slaughter, but you could not say that he came like a lamb: he fought every step of the way. It took four strong men to hold him down on the table until my father, with the expertise born of years of practice, brought the whole drama to a speedy conclusion with his long, deadly, butcher's knife, while my mother held the white enamel bucket into which the warm red blood gushed forth. When the killing was taking place I stayed upstairs with my head under a pillow; I could not bear to see my friends meet their deaths.

Once dead the pigs were scalded in the barrel of boiling water, washed and shaved clean of hair. Then they were hung by the back legs from the rafters of the turf house, slit down the lengths of their bellies and their insides removed. Then my mother set to work, sorting every bit of the pig into her white enamel bath and buckets. Very little was discarded. The insides of the pig were then washed down with buckets of water that ran out the door and into the stream outside. When the cleaning was complete three ash rods, peeled and pointed, were used to keep the sides apart: one at the shoulder, one at the ham and the third in the middle. The turf house door was then shut and bolted. I used to peep in through the slits in the timber door to see the two white carcasses hanging in the semi-darkness and I felt very much in awe of these ghost-like figures.

They hung there for two days, during which time my mother was preparing for filling the puddings. First the puddings were washed and re-washed so many times that our fingers would be numb from cold water. The final washings were done in spring water from the fairy well and this water, because it came straight from the bowels of the earth, was ice cold on even the hottest day. When the puddings were snow white they were left soaking in a bath of spring water, and looked like a nest of slithering eels. The lard was removed from the pig and rendered down in the bastable until it was clear liquid; then it was poured into an enamel bucket where it formed a solid block which was used for cooking and frying. When the fat was run off left in the oven were the graves – bits of gristle and meat that were embedded in the fat and would not melt – that were later minced for the puddings. My mother cooked the pig's blood and liver and many other bits and pieces that only she could identify.

When everything was cooked and in readiness, filling the puddings would commence. All the meats were put in the mincer, herbs and spices were added, and once the mincing was completed a filler was attached to the mincer. We filled white and black puddings; the basis of the black ones was the pig's blood and the white ones minced belly meat and breadcrumbs. A huge black pot of boiling water bubbled over the fire and as soon as each ring of pudding was complete and tied firmly it was plunged into the boiling water. As the pudding cooked an aromatic smell filled the kitchen; it was then lifted out of the pot using a clean handle of a brush and rested across the backs of two chairs where the steaming puddings gave off a mouth-watering fragrance. Row after row of puddings replaced each other on the brush handle, enough to feed an army and, in fact, because all the neighbours got a supply, there was almost a small army to be fed.

The salting of the pig took place the second night after the killing. As soon as darkness fell that night all the neighbours came to help with the work. The backbones were removed from the pigs and they were brought into the kitchen in four sides of pork. First they were cut into sections large enough for our daily needs and then the salting began. A big jute bag of salt sat in the middle of the kitchen floor between the two tables on which the pigs were being salted and we children distributed it in basins to the men who rubbed it into the meat and under the bones. Then the meat was packed between layers of salt in a big wooden barrel which was later filled with fresh spring water. The pork steak, backbone, and some choice pieces were left free of salt.

When the work was finished the tables were scrubbed and the kitchen tidied, the bastable put over the fire and filled with pork steak. The two tables were set for a late supper and when the steak was golden brown we had platefuls of it with tea and brown bread. The following day we went around to all the neighbours with pork steak, fresh pork and puddings – and they did likewise when they killed their pigs. We had the homemade puddings for breakfast, dinner and supper while they lasted; the backbone roasted was a tasty dish, and the pig's ear was grilled over the open fire. Even the pig's bladder was used; seasoned up the chimney and then pumped up to become next season's football. Every last scrap of the animal was put to use.

If my mother could get away with it she hid some of the puddings, which she hung up the chimney to be smoked. Gradually we ate our way down that barrel of bacon: we had bacon and cabbage, bacon and turnips, and once or twice a year – when my mother decided that the iron in nettles was very good for us – we had bacon and nettles, which we ate under loud protest. The remaining bacon was taken out of the barrel and hung off the hooks in the rafters of the kitchen, where it turned a golden yellow from the smoke of the open fire. If real smoked ham was required the bacon was hung up the chimney, which had ample accommodation in its cavernous interior.

Practically all the meat we ate was produced on our own farm. My mother reared and fattened chickens which she boiled and roasted; we also had roast duck and, on festive occasions, roast goose or turkey. Trout was a regular Sunday dish and, as my father also liked to shoot, pheasant sometimes came our way.

In the autumn the potatoes were picked and drawn home from the field. They were then stored in the potato pit, a six foot-long trench that was about two feet deep and three feet wide. Butt loads of potatoes were poured into it and stacked high, and then thatched with straw to ward off the rain and frost. The turnips and mangles were treated in like manner. The turnips were for kitchen use while the mangles, chopped up in a machine called a pulper, were fed to the horses and the pigs. The pig was the waste disposal unit of the farmyard and ate anything that came his way. Any heads of cabbage still remaining in the field were cut and brought home to be fed to the cows because cabbage, unlike the other vegetables, could not be stored over the winter. And so the fields were cleared of crops and when the weather got cold the cattle were also brought off the land, back to the farmyard, where they slept in their comfortable straw-filled houses at night and went out during the day for water and exercise in a field near the house.

The turf was drawn home from the bog and built into a rick behind the house. The turf house was also filled to the door and here what we called brus, the broken up sods of turf, formed on the floor over the following weeks. The brus were used for lighting the fire, with little bits of kindling which we collected from under the trees in the groves and the fort.

At the beginning of winter a mountain of logs was stacked high beside the house. We were surrounded by trees and when some were brought down by storms they were cut up with a large saw called the cross-cut which was worked by two men. Then they were split with the sledge and wedges, and finally chopped smaller with the hatchet. I loved sitting on the pile of freshly cut logs, running my hands over the different shapes and smelling their woody fragrance. To this day I think that there is nothing as interesting to look at as a heap of newly cut logs, the delicate colouring of their veined insides telling their life story, while they wait to bring warmth and comfort.

And so, a bit like the squirrel, we gathered in our stores for the winter, and if the snow came heavy and we were cut off from the outside world, we were safe and self-sufficient. Our wheat, which had been ground into flour at the mill, was now stored in bins to make white or brown bread. The timber barrel was full of meat and eggs came from the hens daily. When God's light faded we had the candles in the sconces and the lamp casting a soft glow around the kitchen. Facing into winter the entire work of the farm wound down, and we looked forward to the long, leisurely nights around the fire.

One of the last jobs to be done on the land was the winter ploughing. Our work was carried out in groups but my father spent long days alone with his horses when ploughing. One winter's evening I went up in the early dusk to the field where my father was ploughing; I walked in the gap and there across the furrows of brown earth the man, the plough and his horses were silhouetted against the darkening sky. The last rays of the winter sun haloed these three in a fusion of soft light: I held my breath, afraid to intrude because I felt that I had come on a holy communion of nature, God and man. My father, who worked with the earth, had a closeness to nature and a full acceptance of its laws and the laws of God. Years afterwards, when he was a very old man, visiting him I would ask, 'How are you?' and he would smile serenely and say, 'Waiting'. Death was as natural to him as the seasons and he had come to terms with his God out in the fields. He was not a praying man but he was a thinking man and he had thought it all out right to the end. In old age he found an inner peace; it was as if, coming near the end of the road, he looked back and saw that all the turnings had led him in the one direction.

Give Me My Shirt

H e was not blessed with a sunny disposition but possessed a razor-sharp brain and a biting wit. His role in life could best be described as a part-time travelling farmworker. How much he travelled and for how long he worked was entirely of Dan's own choosing; he was a free spirit and marched to the sound of his own drum. Trade unions would have been completely unnecessary to Dan because if conditions did not suit him he just moved on. He was master of his own destiny, but he never wronged anybody and he was completely honest.

Dan came to our house a couple of times a year and the length of his stay depended on many factors. His wardrobe consisted of a brown paper bag containing his spare shirt which he entrusted to my mother on arrival and demanded back when he made his sometimes hasty exit. Some people believe in making an entrance, but Dan was one for making an exit and his parting shot was always: 'Give me my shirt – I'm going'.

He usually arrived at Christmas time, because then he had the farmyard more or less to himself. At that time farmworkers went home on Christmas Eve and did not return until the 1st of February, which was the beginning of the working year, and Dan would survive longer if he had only my father to contend with, though even he was too much at times. At the end of our house was a large room where my brother slept, with a bay window opening on to the garden. There was always a spare bed in the room and some mornings Dan would be in the bed, having arrived during the night without disturbing anyone. More mornings the bed would have been slept in but Dan missing as he would have gone to bring in the cows for the early milking. He was a light sleeper and an early riser, and when he had the cows brought in he'd rattle around the kitchen and make such an infernal racket that he would wake the whole household. If anyone complained the only satisfaction Dan gave them was to remark: 'Don't be sleeping your life away'.

Among the other farm houses that he favoured with his presence was a widow woman who lived across the river from us. She was very mean where food was concerned and Dan enjoyed dragging the last bite from her. One day for dinner she gave him a huge plate of cabbage, which was plentiful on the farm, and a tiny bit of beef. Dan demanded more beef and got a little, with still more cabbage, and when he demanded more beef again she said:

'Dan, that heifer will be bellowing inside in you if you eat more beef.'

'Jakus me, ma'am,' Dan snorted, 'If she will it won't be because she's looking for cabbage.'

Eventually he got fed up with the widow woman and one morning, bright and early, demanded his shirt and was gone. She met him a couple of months later in town, and complained bitterly about how wrong it had been of him to desert her when she had needed him so badly.

Dan drew himself up to his full five foot two and, glaring at her from under his bushy eyebrows, he snapped: 'Madam, I deserted the King of England, so where does that leave you?'

Dan usually got on well with my father, but they could have their differences too. One winter's day Dan left the cows a bit short on hay so my father asked him to give them a little more. (The cows were kept in for the winter and tied up in their stalls in a comfortable cowhouse where they were fed with hay daily.) The next day my father went to the cowhouse to find the cows up to their ears in hay: Dan had decided to go overboard on it. My father pointed out that this was too much, whereupon Dan said:

'Jakus me, Boss, hot or cold won't please you. Give me my shirt and I'm going'.

We never knew where he went to and we were never surprised when he reappeared. Once when he returned after an
absence of about twelve months my father remarked that we
had not seen him for a long time.

Dan looked up at him and said, 'I was a guest of His Majesty
the King'.

We children often came under fire from Dan's erratic temper. One day during one of these forays I called him 'Daneen'
in a fit of annoyance. My mother intervened, reprimanding
me for being so cheeky, but Dan soon put things in perspective. 'Missus,' he said, 'children have only what they hear.'
We heard a rare deal of things from Dan. Across the valley
from us was a large fat man with an enormous pot-belly. Dan
described him one day: 'Jakus me, Boss, if he was cleaned out
he'd make a fine duck house'. Ever after when I saw a pot-
bellied man I had visions of rows of ducks sitting comfortably
behind the straining waistcoat.

Dan was a little man and he carried a large walking stick
with a big knob on top. He would put his two hands on top of
the kob and rest his chin on them. Then with a faraway look in
his eyes he would say,

> 'For man to man
> Is so unjust,
> We do not know
> What man to trust.
> We trusted many
> To my sorrow,
> So pay today
> And we'll trust tomorrow.'

He was a man of little sentiment and held few illusions
about his fellow human beings. One day he stood watching
Mick trying to put a handle on a hammer and failing to make it
firm. Finally Dan could take it no longer and grabbed hammer
and handle saying in a withering tone of voice: 'No wonder
Oisin came off the horse'. When Mick's father died later in the
year, leaving a lot of money after him, Dan's only comment
was, 'Jakus me, but he killed awful well'. Death, to Dan, was
nothing to mourn about, and the practicalities of life had

always to be faced.

He had spent many years in the British Army and had served in the Boer War where his job had been burying the dead. He claimed that no man was ever killed whom he could not lift by himself: he was able to shift bags of coal and meal effortlessly as a result of the muscles he developed lifting dead Englishmen. A bag of coal, Dan declared, was a tidy bundle compared to a gangling corpse. After the excitement of the war Dan, with his appetite for the unusual, found the army boring so he deserted. On the night of his return to his home village he met up with his old buddies and got uproariously drunk. After closing time he staggered up the centre of the village singing at the top of his voice. At the end of the street was the barracks where a six-foot sergeant stood at the door and viewed this miniature troublemaker but Dan, oblivious to all but his own happy state, never saw the sergeant until he got a crack of the baton on top of the head. Dan's head, however, was immune to all kinds of bangs so he just stepped back and beheld his long-legged opponent. Perhaps Dan thought he was back in battle and that this was an upright corpse to shift; anyway, he put his head down and charged. He rammed the sergeant with his cast-iron skull, keeled him over his head and, grasping a long leg over each shoulder, gave the big man an upside-down piggy-back down through the village before throwing him, stunned, over the graveyard wall. He then beat a hasty retreat across the fields.

Needless to mention this encounter did not endear him to the law, who were also after him for desertion from the army. Dan enjoyed the chase and if he passed a barracks late at night he loved to leave a note on the door to annoy the occupants: 'The great Dan passed this way'. But finally he was caught, court-martialled and sent to jail.

The policeman who had been taken for the piggy-back informed the army sergeant who took Dan into custody that Dan had broken his mother's heart. This piece of information confirmed the sergeant's already low opinion of Dan, and when he marched the reluctant soldier around the barrack square he shouted: 'Man, you broke your mother's heart: but you won't break mine!'

But neither could be break Dan because Dan thrived on controversy and *cleampar*. Finally, the army gave up on him and, after putting him on bread and water for a month, discharged him. But as Dan loved a good fight, especially with someone in uniform, he was often a guest of the prison service and of His Majesty.

When Dan ended up in court it was usually on a charge of disturbing the peace. On one occasion an attorney by the name of Burke prosecuted for the state and took great pleasure in listing out Dan's long litany of misdemeanours. Burke had a dark scar on his cheek as a result of a brawl in his student days. He completed Dan's history of wrong-doings saying, 'Your Honour, this man has spent his life going from fight to fight'.

'But,' Dan shouted across the court, 'at least I brought a clean face out of all of them!'

The entire court was highly amused, including the judge who had often suffered the long-winded, pompous Burke. The case was dismissed.

Dan had one special fighting partner whom he called 'The Boar'. This man was the local undertaker and as soon as Dan and himself sighted each other the coats were taken off, sleeves rolled up and a fight ensued until one or the other was knocked senseless. Dan always insisted that 'The Boar' was the only man he knew worth fighting with: he provided a real challenge. Why he called him 'The Boar' was known to Dan alone. One day, when they were both old men, Dan called on his opponent and just as 'The Boar' stood back ready for action Dan held out his hand in friendship, saying: 'We had many great fights and you gave me much enjoyment, but now I'm giving you the last round. I am going to die soon and nobody else would enjoy burying me as much as you would.' Before the surprised undertaker could open his mouth Dan slapped an envelope of notes on the table and, going out the door, he looked over his shoulder and said: 'I will call you Boar no more'.

When Dan died he left a will bequeathing thousands of pounds to all the people he disliked most, and they were many. The fact that he did not have a penny to his name proved that Dan marched to his grave to the sound of his own drum.

A One-Way Ticket

Children who die very young leave a warm memory in the hearts of those who loved them. It is as if their candle of life, because it glows for such a short time, shines especially bright. Connie was the youngest of our family, born in the autumn of my parents' childbearing years. He was a long-legged, fine-boned little boy with silken blond hair that touched his shoulders. His birth brought great joy – if nothing else, after five daughters, he was a welcome change. An imaginative, sensitive child, he blossomed in the adoring love of this predominantly female household. My older brother at this time had left the free world of childhood behind and was finding his feet in the quicksands of adolescence.

There was just a year between Connie and me, so we grew together in early childhood like a pair of twin lambs. In my earliest memory I am sitting on a warm flagstone outside our house while Connie sits in his pram under a huge palm tree. The palm tree dominated our garden and its branches brushed against the window panes, filling the rooms at the end of the house with moving shadows.

Connie and I spent our days in the grove behind the house. The others were gone to school so we were left to our own devices. We played imaginary games beneath the trees where the ground was soft with the fallen leaves and pine needles of many years. One old tree had a huge hole in its trunk and into this we sat and pretended that we were travelling to many strange places. Because we could not see the top of this tree, as it seemed to go up and up and up, we believed that it grew into heaven. Heaven in those days was very real. The sky was our roof and the ground floor of heaven; up there were God and the angels and our cat that had died the year before. Everything that left our world finished up in heaven and we never questioned that it was a one-way ticket; after all, if heaven was where we all hoped to end up who would think of coming back?

We fed the ducks and the chickens every day and the baby calves were our favourites, though all the young animals around the yard were very much loved by us. We often visited Bill at the top of the hill, where he told us stories and gave us rides on the donkey. We could ramble through the fields and be missing for hours and nobody had to worry because the countryside was free and safe. The only disappearance that ever created panic happened one wet winter's morning when Connie went missing. The stream at the bottom of the garden had turned into an angry torrent of flood water that backed up the garden and overflowed into the grove behind the house. Connie was nowhere to be found, and the terror was that he had fallen into the flood water. A thorough search proved that this was unlikely but the possibility could not yet be overruled. Every corner of the house and farmyard was searched to no avail. Most of this consternation sailed over my head, and I decided that I would visit our sheepdog in the haybarn who the previous week had had a litter of cuddly puppies. And there, curled up with the new mother, was Connie, sound asleep, almost indistinguishable from the pups who were draped all over him.

At night we slept together in a big bed that had a high old-fashioned timber base and headboard. The fluffy tick filled with soft duck and goose down collected over the years from the Christmas pluckings provided warmth, and fun too as we stood on the timber headboard and dived into its comforting fullness. It had sunken pathways and fairy tunnels and countless hidden possibilities. Going to bed early, when sleep was the least of our interests, we turned the bed into a playground peopled by who- and whatever took our fancy; we scratched pictures on the headboard and Lowry men and women pranced around our pillows. Nobody cautioned about damaging the paintwork. There were no dolls and teddies to cuddle in bed as these were the war years and such luxuries were non-existent – but never missed. Instead, our resourceful mother provided us with two little statues, one of Saint Theresa and the other Baby Jesus. There was no shortage of statues in Irish homes at that time so every night we took our battered and chipped and much-loved statues to bed.

Once a week my mother left home to visit my grandmother who lived a few miles down the road. She was never missing for very long but home lost some of its warmth when she was gone, and if she was not back by bedtime my oldest sister Frances did the needful. This was the case one winter's night, so my sister changed us into our night-clothes and, lighting a candle, led us upstairs to bed. The older children were trusted with candles in their bedrooms but the younger ones settled for moonlight once they were tucked up in bed.

On that particular night, however, the moon did not oblige so we were in complete darkness. Tucked up snugly in our comfortable feather tick we did not mind, but just as we were dozing off to sleep I realised that we had no statues to keep us company. We knocked on the wooden floor to summon help from the lower regions and when Frances came in answer to our call we explained about our statues. She went in search of them. After a long time she came back and tucked the statues under the bedclothes beside us.

I ran my finger over Baby Jesus and thought that he was a strange shape. Then Connie's sleepy voice whispered to me in the darkness, 'Saint Theresa has a very long neck tonight'. However, we were too tired to investigate any further and drifted off to sleep. We awoke the next morning to discover that instead of our two statues, which had gone missing, we were holding on to two bottles of porter.

I got my first doll the following Christmas, and Connie got a little cloth man he called Patsy. That morning I awoke and when I moved my legs something clanked off the bottom of the bed: it was a doll with a ware face, and we named her Katie Maria. We had many hours of fun with our new friends Katie Maria and Patsy, but we did not abandon our two old pals who stood guard on our bedside table.

When summer came round again we returned to the grove and our tree house. We lived in a child's wonderland and the harsh face of reality had never frowned on us. But then, suddenly, an icy draught blew around us when Connie got very sick. He had been part of my day and night, sharing every childish secret, and now suddenly he could laugh no more. He lay still and quite like a little bird in the middle of the feather bed. I sat on the floor and played with Patsy and Katie Maria. I talked endlessly to Connie, feeling that even though he couldn't answer he would know somehow that I was there. The doctor came every day and I shrank back into the corner while he examined Connie. My mother and the doctor had long discussions and I could see the pain in my mother's face.

Then one day after the doctor had been my mother told me that Connie would have to go into hospital and that he might get better, but she was not sure. Looking into my mother's stricken face I feared that Connie would never come back. Since he had got sick I had felt that something terrible was going to happen and now the certainty formed a hard lump of terror in my heart. I went up into the grove and sat into our old tree. A black car came into the yard and through the trees I watched my mother come out with Connie in her arms. He was wrapped up in a white blanket but my mother's face was whiter still.

I stayed in the tree house all day, feeling close to Connie there. Tears never came to my eyes – crying was something you did when you cut your finger. This was beyond all tears. Finally, as dusk came, I heard the pine needles crunching as someone approached. It was Bill. He sat outside the tree as he could not fit inside; just sat saying nothing while the tears ran down his face. I crept out of the tree and on to his lap, putting my arms around his neck. And so we sat, Bill and I, locked together in our terrible grief, I silently while my dear friend shuddered with great heart-broken sobs.

The next day Connie died. I did not feel any worse because it was as if it had already happened. I actually felt better because I decided that now he had left the hospital and gone to heaven he would come back. Every day I checked the tree house a couple of times in case he would be there. When this did not work out I decided it was back to the bedroom he would come. Our little room had been stripped bare and the curtains drawn, and a sulphur candle stood guttering and spluttering on our bedside table. The nuns in the hospital had given my mother a relic of Saint Theresa and a waxen pink rose which were also on the table. I hated that pink rose. In some way I had come to the conclusion that God had taken Connie and sent back this stupid rose. One day when I peeped in to see if Connie was there I could stand it no longer so I caught the rose and tore it up, petal by petal.

My refusal to accept the fact that Connie was gone must have added greatly to my mother's anguish at that time. One day in order to try to solve the problem she asked me if I would like to visit his grave. I was delighted and tore upstairs for Patsy and a bag of Connie's favourite sweets that I kept hidden under our bed: it took a long time to realize that heaven was, indeed, a one-way ticket.

Years afterwards I opened the door of a room in a strange house and the smell of a sulphur candle hit me with such an impact that a memory box in my subconscious snapped open and I was once again back in that little room. I stood rooted to the floor as tears streamed down my face while some of the anguish of those days washed over me.

Healing Place

The frosty, feathery grass
Crunched beneath my feet
As my warm valley
Caressed me in welcome;
Bejewelled with frost
The trees and grass
Sparkled in the morning sun
And across the river
The mothering mountains
Shrouded in a misty light
Stood ground. Not a sound
But the gurgling of the river
And the companions of the solitary
My feathered friends
Echoing my thoughts
Pour forth their ecstasy
In unrestrained delight.

Oh, to hold these thoughts
And this place forever
In my mind
This beloved place
So much part of me.

I stood
And let the essence
Of this balm of my growing
Soak into the inmost regions
Of my soul,
To be printed
On the back pages
Of my mind,
To be re-read
In some far distant hour
When my need

Would be great
And I could no longer
Come to this
My healing place

A Touch of Oliver

My grandmother was a formidable old lady. She was six feet tall and, dressed in flowing black with a crochet shawl around her shoulders, she carried herself with grace and dignity. In later years she used a walking stick, but she walked with regal bearing until the day she died at ninety-eight years of age. It could be that she needed the stick to maintain law and order when she was unable to move as fast as she wanted, for while grandmothers are supposed to be loving and soft-bosomed, mine certainly did not fit into that picture: she was strong willed and domineering and ruled the house with a rod of iron. Her husband was dead with years so she ran the large farm herself and thrived on it. She was a fore-runner of the struggle for equality and she was confident that most women could run a business as well if not better than men. She did just that, but in her time she was no ordinary woman. She killed her own pig and seldom sent for a vet as she could dose cattle and repair fractures like an expert. Some of her mother's people were doctors so she maintained that medicine was in her blood and, indeed, when one of her workmen was gored by a bull her fast, skilful action saved his life.

Though in some ways she was ahead of her time, in others she belonged to the era of the French Revolution. When our revolution came and the Black and Tans rampaged around the country my grandmother, a staunch Republican, was in the thick of it. Anyone on the run knew that they could get safe harbouring in her house. The Black and Tans knew this as well and many nights when the family were fast asleep the lorries drove into the yard, loud banging started on the door and the house was searched.

One night a young man called Larry, who was on the run, was asleep upstairs in the same room as her young son. Her two daughters were in another room. Suddenly the loud knocking started and she woke up. Realizing that they had not heard the warning noise of the lorries, she got out of bed slowly, hoping to give Larry time to get away, but she did not know that the house was surrounded. She still delayed in answering and the knocking turned to banging, demanding that she: 'Open in the name of the King!' Eventually she opened the door and the soldiers trooped in past her. They searched the house thoroughly, even turning the bedclothes out on the floor, but finding nothing they became very annoyed because they seemed certain that there should have been somebody there.

My grandmother was a tough woman who did not know the meaning of fear: she asked them to leave now that they had searched her house. She refused to get drawn into an argument with them but stayed tight-lipped – which could not have been easy for her as silence was not one of her virtues.

The officer in charge, who had called many times, looked at my grandmother and remarked, 'You remind me of my mother'.

'Well, indeed,' she snapped back, 'your mother must not be up to much to raise a blackguard like you.'

At last they left, warning her that they'd be calling again and that she'd be caught eventually. She went to the door and listened to hear the lorries starting up down the lane; then she put her children back to bed and sat by the fire for a long time. Opening the front door she checked in the half light of the dawn to make sure there was nobody about. It had happened before that the Tans had doubled back, hoping to catch them unprepared. Eventually, when she was convinced that they were safe, she stood in the middle of the kitchen and called aloud: 'In the name of God where are you?'

Beside the fire in the kitchen was an old settle bed which appeared to be a timber seat when it was closed up. The Tans had checked it but when the cover did not rise they had assumed that it was just a seat. Out of this, with his face white as a sheet, rolled Larry. It had been a narrow escape. She was convinced that the Tans had known that somebody was there that night so they must have been tipped off; she suspected a family further back the valley and she never forgave them. If ever their name came up in conversation her face would darken and she would say, 'Bad blood there'.

When I was young I never stayed at her house as I was half afraid of her though, gradually, as she got older, she grew a little bit more mellow, or else I got braver with the years. Working for her in the house was a saintly girl called Mary who often stood between me and my grandmother's wrath. Once my grandmother had boiled a chicken and she loved the chicken broth which she had cooling in a jug on a table at the bottom of the kitchen. I decided to do a big clean up and finding this jug full of water – as I thought – I threw it out the door. When she discovered what I had done I had to spend the rest of the day out on the farm with my uncle.

As my grandmother grew older she spent more time sitting on a chair beside the fire, from where she talked non-stop. Later I regretted that I had not paid more attention to her as she had a tremendous memory and a great mind with crystal clear thinking to the very end. She was a constant reader of the *Irish Press* which my uncle brought to her every day when he went to the creamery. When he came in the door she would say: 'Give me that paper until I see what old Brookeborough is saying today'. All her life she took a keen interest in politics and was a fanatical supporter of de Valera. As my father was on the other side of the coin she was always slightly suspicious of him; however, politics apart, they had great respect for one another.

My grandmother had one strange chink in her armour: every couple of years she took to her bed and decided she was going to die. Admittedly this idiosyncrasy did not begin until she was over seventy so on the law of averages she could have been right. But she was no average woman and when the local doctor came he always annoyed her intensely by telling her that she was fine and had years to live. She got over this problem by contacting one of her own relations who was a doctor in the next parish. He understood what was expected of him and prescribed tablets and told her that, yes, she was quite ill and should stay in bed. My uncle regarded all this with great amusement and referred to these outbreaks as 'a touch of Oliver'. Why he called it this I do not know, but when he came to our house and said that 'herself has a touch of Oliver' we all knew what he meant. But perhaps the doctor understood more than he got credit for. This strong woman who never showed any softness needed to go to bed and be comforted occasionally, and after a few days she would be back on her feet again.

When she had come to live on the home farm after getting married her mother-in-law, father-in-law and a brother of her husband's were already in the house before her. The brother-in-law later got married and had two children before leaving to set up in business. Despite this extended family living together under one roof complete harmony prevailed, and all attributed this fact to my grandmother. She was a woman of many parts. She had a constant flow of visitors, including one old friend who always brought her a present of a bottle of whiskey which he drank before he went home.

She was very lucky in the fact that when my uncle married she got a splendid daughter-in-law. I was there the first morning she took over the kitchen and I was open-mouthed in astonishment at her efficiency. Grandmother had great admiration for capable people, so if the daughter-in-law had been lacking in ability it could have caused a problem. My uncle was a happy, big-hearted man who lived very comfortably between his two remarkable women. He was a sociable person who visited us regularly and always loved to have us call when we were home on holidays. In later years when television came and he had acquired a set, he put it in a cupboard. When the television was on naturally the cupboard was opened, but as soon as anybody came in visiting he turned it off and shut the cupboard. He maintained that television should be kept in its place and never take precedence over people.

When grandmother died it might have been expected that some of her old pictures might be taken down off the walls. However, when I called some years afterwards I was surprised and delighted to see the same old great-grandaunts and uncles still smiling down at me. Her daughter-in-law remembered the old lady with love and affection.

As my grandmother was such an overwhelming personality there was a danger that she might have over-shadowed her only son but this, however, was not the case because, while she was forthright and domineering, he sailed through life on a sunshine cloud. They were two very different types of people. My uncle believed that life was for playing hard and working hard, and he never did anything by half measure. Sitting at the top of the kitchen table he would bang it with his fist and sing 'I'm sailing along in a trolley. I feel like a big millionaire'. And indeed he was very generous; when we stayed with my grandmother he never came from town without something in his pockets for us.

He put me on a pony for my first time, gave the pony a slap on the rump and set her galloping across the field with me clinging on for dear life. Finally, all the tackling which was on the pony – she had just come from the creamery – slid off and I came with it. I kicked him hard on the shins in retaliation, but he only laughed and said 'Get back up now again'. In a temper I did just that, but became so thrilled by this new experience that I rode the pony bare-backed all day and could not sit down for a week afterwards.

One winter we had very heavy snow which stayed on the ground for almost two months. There were drifts over six feet high along the fields and, as if this was not bad enough, a very severe flu came at the same time. When some of our family caught it we found it difficult to try to keep the cattle fed, but my uncle arrived on horse-back every day and stayed until all the work was done, even though he had to go home then and see to his own animals as well. He had a great sense of family loyalty and togetherness. 'That's all that counts at the end of the day,' he told me once.

On the morning of his wedding we were walking down the

passage from the house on the way to the church. Suddenly, he shot in a gap and fled across the field. When I caught up with him I asked what all that was about.

'Very unlucky, Alice, to meet a foxy woman the morning you're getting married and Kate was coming around the next corner.'

Kate was a red-haired women of the roads whom we met every day, but my uncle was taking no chances this morning.

The only time I ever saw him sad was the day that Connie was buried. He sat in our kitchen, pale faced and silent, one of the images that impressed on my child's mind that this was a terrible day. I supposed that small children, to whom death is incomprehensible, can only judge its seriousness by the reaction of familiar adults. I decided that anything that could wipe the smile off my uncle's face must be disastrous.

In his autumn years my uncle developed terminal cancer. I visited him in hospital after his operation and was shattered by what illness can do to a great-hearted man. His wife nursed him in the last months and it was awe-inspiring to see the dedication and care which true love can create.

Walk The Fields

When I go home
I walk the fields,
The quiet fields
Where the warm dew
Had squelched between
My childish toes.
To sit beneath
The cool oak and ash
That sheltered
My adolescent dreams.
These trees stand
With leafy arms
Outstretched
Like lovers',
Not in passion
But with gentle
Sighs of contentment.
I watch the cows
Graze peaceful
Beside the river
Curving its way
Through furzed inches
Into the woods beyond.

This is a holy place
Where men have worked
Close to God's earth
Under the quiet heavens.

A Country Child's Christmas

Christmas in our house was always magical and for weeks beforehand my toes would tingle at the thought of it. The first inkling of its reality was Santa's picture in the *Cork Examiner*: we pored over him, loving every wrinkle in his benevolent face. At first he was a small face peeping from an obscure corner, but as Christmas drew nearer his presence became more reassuringly felt as he filled a larger space on the page.

The first step in the preparations in our home was the plucking of the geese, not only for our own family but also for all our relations. A night in early December was set aside for killing and plucking; homework had to be completed quickly after school that day and when the cows had been milked and supper finished the kitchen was cleared for the undertaking. I never witnessed the actual killing because my mother performed this ritual away from the eyes of us children, but when she brought the geese still slightly flapping and warm into the kitchen I always felt that she, who was gentle by nature, had been through some sacrificial fire which but for necessity she would have avoided.

Each member of the family with arms strong enough sat on a *súgán* chair with a warm goose across their knee. My father, however, washed his hands of all this crazy carry-on and, after imparting a lecture about relations providing their own Christmas dinner, he set out across the fields roving to a neighbour's house where 'sanity' prevailed. Strong feathers were eased off first and put into a big box and then the pure down was stowed in a smaller one. As the night wore on our arms ached and our noses itched with downy fluff, but my

mother coaxed and cajoled until half a dozen geese lay stark-
ers on the floor. With our mission accomplished we viewed
each other with great merriment, our white downy heads and
eyebrows lending us the appearance of white-haired gnomes.
We tidied everything up then and gathered with cups of cocoa
around the open fire, where my father would join us with perfect timing, bringing with him the tang of night air and frost
glittering on his high boots.

During the weeks that followed the outside walls of the
farmyard were whitewashed or cement washed and all the
yards and passageways were brushed. Inside the house itself
was washed and polished, but first the wide chimney was
brushed. Standing close to our fire and peering up the chimney you could see the sky: it was a perfect Santa chimney. The
kitchen floor was scrubbed, as were two tables and the chairs
used to seat the lot of us. Our household seldom numbered
less than ten: my parents, six of us children, a man who
helped my father, a girl who helped my mother, and invariably one or two others, either miscellaneous relations or extra
helpers.

The next step was 'the bringing of the Christmas', as we
called it. My father and mother would set out early one morning for the nearest town to buy everything that was needed for
Christmas. At this stage we usually had our holidays from
school and we waited expectantly all day for the homecoming;
usually night had fallen by the time we heard the pony's
hooves in the yard. Bubbling with excitement we watched the
succession of interesting boxes being carried in and stored
away in the parlour and glimpsed bottles of lemonade sparkling amidst red and white Christmas candles which foretold
their own story. Other goodies were skilfully obscured from
our prying fingers and inquisitive eyes.

At last, Christmas Eve dawned. We brought in the holly
which we had collected from the wood the previous Sunday
and in a short time holly branches were growing from behind
every picture – everywhere but around the clock, which was
my father's sanctum and could not be touched. Then the
Christmas tree. Our house was surrounded by trees: my

father planted them all his life and he loved every one of them. At Christmas he suffered deciding which of his little ones had to be sacrificed. We usually ended up with a lop-sided branch instead of a full tree, but when it was dancing with Christmas cards and balloons it always seemed a beauty. We ran streamers across the kitchen and did everything our way while my mother made the stuffing and ignored the bedlam.

A big turnip was cleaned and a hole bored in it for the candle; this was decorated with red berried holly and placed in the window. That night no blinds would be drawn so that the light would shine out to light the way for Joseph and Mary. Before supper the Christmas log was brought in and placed behind the fire in the open hearth. Banked around with sods of turf it soon sent out a glow of warmth to make the toast that was part of our Christmas supper tradition. But before anything could be eaten the Christmas candle had to be lit. We all gathered round and my father lit the candle and my mother sprinkled us with holy water. Then we sat around the kitchen table, my father at the top with my mother on his right and each of us in our own place. I feasted my eyes on the white iced cake, the seed loaf and barm brack, but most of all I gazed at the mountain of golden toast streaming with yellow butter. After supper we had lemonade and biscuits and the ecstasy of the gassy lemonade bubbling down my nose remains a memory that is Christmas for me.

Our gramophone was normally kept safe in the parlour but at Christmas it took its chance in the kitchen. Every Christmas my father bought new records and we played them non-stop. Silence was restored for the news on the radio but we young ones had no interest in the news; to us there was no world outside our own. After the news we all got on our knees for the rosary, something I never enjoyed usually, but on Christmas night it became real: this was the actual birthday of the baby. Looking out of the window into the dark night, thinking that the same stars had shone on him so many years before, in my imagination I saw the cave and the animals in the warm straw and heard the angels singing. On that far-off Christmas night I was there in my child's mind.

Off our knees my father performed the usual ritual of winding the clock. Then, standing at the foot of the stairs, his last words to my mother were: 'Len, come to bed before morning'. My mother, a night person who always got a second wind facing midnight, had jelly to make, stockings to darn, underwear to air around the fire. We hung our stockings on the old-fashioned crane convenient for Santa as he came down the chimney, and then mother ushered us all off to bed, the more responsible ones with a sconce and candle.

Ours was a large room with two beds and an iron cot with shiny brass railings and knobs. If the night was very cold we had a fire which cast mystic shadows along the low timber ceiling while the moon shone fingers of light across the floor. Anything seemed possible. Try as I might to keep my eyes open to see Santa appear out of the shadows, I was soon carried into the world of nod and awoke to the excruciating pleasure of sensing that Santa had been. No sensation in later life could compare with the boundless joy of those early Christmas mornings when Santa was an unquestioned reality. The gifts in the stockings were always simple and indeed often of a very practical nature but the mystique of the whole occasion gave them an added glow.

Having woken mother and father to display for them Santa's benevolence, those of us going to first Mass set out in the early dawn to walk the three miles to the church. Candles glowed from the farmhouses in the surrounding valley, making this morning very different. The lighted church welcomed us, but it was the crib rather than the Mass that was special to me, to whom these were no plaster dummies; they were the real thing. Afterwards we either walked home or got a lift from a neighbouring horse and trap. Breakfast was always of baked ham, after which the remainder of the family went into the second Mass of the day. Before leaving for Mass my mother placed the stuffed goose in a bastable over the fire with layers of hot coals on the cover. There it slowly roasted, filling the kitchen with a mouth-watering aroma.

The clattering of the pony's hooves heralded the family's arrival home and finally after much ado we were all seated around the table for the Christmas dinner. Was anything ever again to taste as good? My mother's potato stuffing was in a class of its own. We finished our dinner as the King's speech began on the radio. My father had Protestant roots and always instilled in us an appreciation of things British as well as Irish. My mother listened to the Pope, my father to the King of England, and to us they were both as much a part of Christmas as Santa. Our new records were played again and again, and toys were savoured to the full until after supper exhaustion finally won the day and we dragged our small, weary feet upstairs to bed.

It was all over for another year, but each year was another page in the book of childhood.

Children of A Changing Time

Thing is the story of country living that revolved around the hearth, the family, the farm animals, and the neighbours. The people we lived amongst provided us with companionship, whether out in the fields or around the fire, and the farmyard and household chores gave a pattern to our days. But as we left childhood behind and put tentative toes into the adult world, that pattern changed, rural living moved forward into a bright new world and we became the last children of the old ways.

So this is also the story of a changing time, a time when rural Ireland quenched the oil lamp, removed the po from under the bed and threw the black pots and iron kettles under the hedge. We who were the children of the forties came in the fifties into the challenging, exciting world of adolescence.

Rural electrification flooded our homes with light, clearing away old ghosts and beliefs and sending fairies scurrying underground. Modern plumbing replaced the bucket of spring water from the well and the timber rain-barrel at the gable end.

Corners hitherto shrouded in dust and tranquility suddenly found themselves scrubbed clinically clean with the new and plentiful supply of hot water and disinfectant. The flush toilet replaced the chamber-pot, bringing an instant solution to a basic problem. The wide, warm comforting arms of the open fire were folded up and into its corner came tight-lipped ranges and shining enamel-faced cookers.

Out in the farm the clip-clop of horses' hooves gave way to the roar of engines; cows, accustomed to the soft glow of the storm-lantern as we checked them at night, now blinked in the glare of the harsh electric light.

The older generation stood and hesitated on the brink of this bright new world, but we of a younger generation opened wide our arms and swam happily with the tide. We became the young parents of the sixties and seventies and brought children into a world totally different from the one of our own childhoods. Economic prosperity boomed and our teenagers grew up far from the shadows cast by the oil lamp and the plaintive call of the corncrake.

Look back with me to when we changed from the old ways to the new and left behind a world now almost forgotten.

Going For The Messages

I always stopped for a few seconds outside Ned's door to sniff the air appreciatively as we walked up the winding street past his little shop on our way to Mass. The whiff of tea, loose in a plywood chest; a wheel of cheese wrapped in muslin cloth; candles piles on top of each other in a timber box: all mixed with the strong smell of snuff, which he kept in a tall tin can under the counter. He cut plugs of tobacco off a large block, filling the little shop with rich aromas which blended with the other fragrances that made up the unique mixture that was Ned's shop.

Ned was a little man clad in a brown overall and because he seldom came out from behind his high timber counter he created a head and shoulders image in our minds. His hair had receded well back from his forehead but had decided then to go no further. His hair-line was a blend of grey and brown, matching his brown overall which was streaked with white as a result of his constant weighing of flour. He viewed the world with kind, brown eyes from behind steel-rimmed spectacles.

Although his working hours often extended far into the night he was always, it seemed, in a pleasant frame of mind and when he was not serving customers he was busy weighing out supplies into stiff, brown paper bags. Goods were delivered in large jute sacks and heavy timber boxes and had to be measured out into weights suitable for purchase by his customers. Tea, sugar and flour were all poured into these strong brown bags with different sized scoops. They were then thumped gently on the counter to settle down the contents before being put back on the old iron scales for the final test of precise weight. The balancing weights ranged from small round brass ounces to heavy oblong iron pounds which had holding bars for convenience. Ned had a white enamel scales as well, but this was for the weighing of lighter items which called for greater precision, like cheese, tobacco and sweets. The long needle waved back and forth like the hand of a clock gone crazy until finally it settled and pointed out the exact weight.

On the floor inside the counter Ned stood surrounded by a circle of bags of varying heights. He usually began Monday morning with flour weighing and as the day progressed the shelf behind him filled up with paper bags of different sizes while the white cotton bag of flour declined in stature. The jute sack of sugar was next on the agenda and Ned weighed away, in between patiently serving and chatting to customers as they came and went, and after that he started on the tea. His appearace always told the tale of exactly what he had been weighing because evidence of it clung to his overall.

High on the shelves behind him, flash lamps, bicycle repair kits, Sacred Heart lamps, alarm clocks and all sorts of things stood. Below them were tins of biscuits that had to be weighed out when customers made their choices. Some containers had glass tops so that you could peer in without Ned having to remove the covers, and below the biscuits came the tin gallons and high glass jars of sweets whose colourful contents provided temptation beyond resistance. There were black-and-white bull's-eyes which were hard enough to damage the most perfect teeth and 'brown cushions' with their strange, minty taste; but the conversation lozenges made for the brightest jar of all, with their gay pinks, reds and yellows. They were exactly as their name implied, but the conversation was not one to be had with a casual acquaintance, as the messages had a decidedly intimate flavour. 'Kiss me quick' or 'Love me' or 'Hug me' were not invitations to be extended to all and sundry. As if to counteract these amorous sweets came the acid drops that made you catch your breath with their sharp tang. Gallon sweets were the poor relations; the grander ones came in the glass jars. Top of the market came the sweets that had their own coats on, the wrapped variety. We seldom rose to those heady heights but the plain-wrapped toffees at six for a penny came within our reach. For long-lasting sucking the slab of hard toffee was the best value and came with the titles 'Captain Mac' and 'Half-Time Jimmy'; the full slab was usually beyond our means, so Ned cracked off the required amount on the edge of the counter.

Everything that Ned had to handle was inside the counter, while outside was anything that did not require weighing or wrapping. A stack of enamel and tin buckets stood guard on each side of a pile of enamel pots and pans. Spades, shovels, two-prong and four-prong pikes and pickaxes all stood shoulder to shoulder, while milking stools could be tested for balance and comfort by waiting customers or anyone stopping in for a chat. Hanging off the ceiling was a miscellaneous assortment of goods, including kettles and teapots, balls of binder twine, strong nailed boots, and occasionally a pig's head. You had to keep your eye on the pig's head as sometimes if you stood underneeth it you could get a cold drip of salty brine on top of your head. If you looked up, the pig's eye would peer contemptuously down at you. On Friday the pig's head gave way to strips of salted ling that hung off the ceiling like items of forgotten underwear.

Window-dressing was not Ned's speciality; out there stood sun-faded advertising placards of teas being sampled by rosy-cheeked ladies and foggy mirrors etched with happy, pot-bellied, bearded gentlemen advocating the bliss of St Bruno tobacco. Ned's cat used these mirrors to admire her tawney good looks and to improve on them. The window was the cat's department and from here she watched life pass by with the disdainful air that only a well-bred cat can impart, her unblinking stare occasionally punctuated by the flick of an aristocratic feline whisker. A sliding timber shutter, which no longer slid but reluctantly shunted, gave access to this view of the outside world.

Ned's burning passions in life were horses and greyhounds and his 'mother bitch', as he called his oldest greyhound, was usually to be seen stretched out on the shop floor between the buckets and shovels. She knew all Ned's customers and if a stranger called, which was rare enough, she slowly drew herself off her haunches and sniffed him out, much to the customer's surprise, because a sniffer dog was something one did not expect to find in this little corner of the world. But the greyhound, like Ned himself, was not aggressive, merely curious.

Ned used the evenings to do his accounts, which meant adding up the totals in a stack of little notebooks. Each of his customers had a notebook into which they wrote their messages, and these they handed in to Ned together with their shopping bags. Many farmers called to him for their messages on the way home from the creamery and scarcely needed to write down their orders since he knew better than they did what they needed. He filled each bag and wrote the prices into each notebook, and once a week or twice a month, whichever the arrangement was, he added up the list and was paid.

When he had his accounts finished he folded his arms on the counter-top and became the ideal chairman who skilfully directed heated arguments into calm waters and often supervised the sale of greyhound pups and promising yearlings. The shop, as well as being a place for trading, was also a select men's club where male views were aired and membership was based on a man's knowledge of horses and dogs. Not that anyone was refused entry, but as the main topic of conversation were racing odds and filly fitness, unless you were that way inclined you could not take part in the discussions that went on late into the night. Men sat around on milking stools, upturned buckets, tea-chests and indeed sometimes on an upturned po and, as the talk flowed, the smoke from their pipes and cigarettes curled upwards, blending with the pigs' heads and balls of binder twine, giving them a smoky, well-seasoned look. Speedy greyhounds such as Spanish Battleship and Prince of Bermuda were discussed, their finer points closely analysed, and the chances of local horses Sheila's Cottage and Cottage Rake winning the big races were argued back and forth at length.

The only night that Ned had early closing was when the track was on, but that did not upset his regulars as they were all at the greyhound track as well. He closed down completely

for Listowel and Galway races, and sometimes for other meet-
ings if a horse of special interest happened to be running. No
one else could follow the geography of Ned's shop, so the
simple solution was to shut down altogether. Everybody
understood that when Ned's door was closed he had gone
racing. Perishable goods he sold off to his pals the night before
and it was not unusual to see a man walking home from Ned's
with a pig's head under his arm.

My mother brought the messages from town every Sunday
after Mass but sometimes during the week one of us might be
sent in to bring home extra requirements. We loved to be sent
to town so there was great competition to be the one chosen to
go. Walking along the road I enjoyed looking in through the
iron gates on my way and watching the animals in the different fields, or climbing to the top of the ditch and looking
down over the valley. Arriving in town I went straight to
Ned's shop, where I was always sure of a fistful of sweets; he
made no profit out of me and I had it eaten before I left the
shop. Children and men were Ned's best customers because
some of the less understanding women felt that in the interests of hygiene his cat should be evicted from her viewing
perch in the window.

Across the road from Ned lived two old ladies, the Miss
Bowlers, who had a big stone-floored shop that was scrubbed
out daily. It was a contrast to Ned's, where the timber floorboards, ingrained with knots and seams, sank and squeaked
as you clattered across them. Whereas Ned's little shop was
packed to overflowing, the Miss Bowles' large shop had all the
activity packed into one corner where they dished out squares
of home-made toffee, sold brown lemonade and cut up blocks
of ice-cream and sandwiched it between two wafers. A penny
ice-cream only served to stimulate the taste-buds, a twopenny
one was more satisfying and a fourpenny one bordered on
extravagance, while a six-penny one was sheer, gorgeous
gluttony. They also sold puffy buns with dollops of cream and
jam inside; when you sank you teeth into them the cream
oozed around the corners of your mouth and along your
fingers and, like Ned's cat, you had to whip your tongue

around vigorously lest you lose any luscious lick.

One of the sisters was like the cream-buns she sold and had folds of soft double chins, beneath which rows of white pearls continued the cascading descent into her enormous cleavage. Her hair was snow-white, and even though it was caught up at the back it still curled down over her forehead and ears, from which long pearl earrings swung, while her large, soft bosom encased in a white, satin blouse rested on the counter-top. She always reminded me of a downy feather pillow, soft, white and comfortable. The other sister paled by comparison. She was tall, thin and spare and was like the tall bottles of lemonade whose tops she whipped off with the iron bottle opener.

What Ned lacked in fastidiousness the Miss Bowlers made up for: their shop and they themselves were spotless. The hands of the small, cuddly Miss Bowler were white and soft, with pale pink fingernails which curved to slight points, and she always smelt like a rose garden, waves of light, flowery perfume wafting from beneath beneath flowing folds. The tall sister seemed clinically clean and wore a white, lace collar and cuffs over her long black dress; her auburn hair streaked with grey stayed in a tight knot at the base of her poll where it was secured firmly with a few barbaric-looking hairpins.

As well as serving us ice-cream, buns and lemonade, they taught us manners in a very gentle fashion. So restraining was their influence that once you stepped inside their shop-door you slowed down to a ladylike pace and approached their counter with a sense of decorum, stating your requirements in a clear, precise voice and never omitting 'please' and 'thank you'. The Miss Bowlers dealt only in the luxuries of life and graced each transaction with such a sense of occasion that you felt they lived in a special world and you were their welcome guest rather than a child with a few pence in your fist.

Around the corner from the Miss Bowlers was Con the baker who every day turned out rows of high-backed crusty loaves on his low timber counter while the smell from his little bakery behind the shop spilled out into the street and sig-nalled that another batch was fresh out of the oven. Big currant-buns with sticky white icing pouring down their sides clung together at the base, and if you wanted one Con eased them apart, but if you were lucky enough to be buying more they came in a row with the currants protruding through the icing like stones on a snow-covered hill. He made huge bracks and seed loaves that were only bought if you were expecting visitors or having the Stations, or if Christmas was around the corner. But his hot, golden doughnuts, oozing warm, syrupy sugar, that melted in your mouth and slid down your throat like butter in a warm dish were the best of all. Tuesday and Thursday were doughnut days and their smell transcended all others, enfolding us in delightful waves of anticipation before we ever sank our yearning teeth into their steamy sweetness.

All our clothes, or the material for making them, were bought in the one shop. Here my mother could buy elastic for our knickers or material to make an overcoat for my father. Here, indeed, she could buy cover of all kinds for bodies of all shapes and sizes, from inside out and from top to toe. Long rolls of material stretched out on the high shelves and when Jack unrolled it in great thumps it fell into billowing folds on top of the long timber counter. Catching up fistfuls of it and shaking it like a dog might shake a rabbit, he would say, 'Look at that for quality'.

He had a fascinating practice, which he shared with my mother, of catching a little bit of the material between thumb and index finger of both hands and giving it a few hard, fast pulls which caused the cloth, if it was heavy, to give a dull thud or, if lighter, a hard, sharper sound. This was known as testing the bias. A lot of discussion went into assessing the quality of the weave and testing the bias. Buying material was not something to be treated lightly and often the decision would be stretched over a few Sundays before all were satisfied that a particular cloth was the right one to see father through the next ten winters or to provide a daughter with a Sunday coat which would have the handing down potential to serve a couple of younger ones in succeeding years. Purchasing the material was only the first step in this process. The next necessitated a visit to the tailor or dressmaker, and would inevitably be followed by several further visits for fitting at later stages. And because the full creation of an outfit was a long-drawn-out process, it was of the greatest importance to make sure that the first step was the right one. All in all, such purchases could not be concluded in a hurry and Jack, fortunately, had all the time and patience in the world to devote to discussing the pros and cons of pure wool versus velour or tweed. When the material had finally been decided upon he measured it along the brass rule on the counter.

Jack had big boxes of shirts and stockings and endless varieties of underwear. Heating everywhere was of a limited nature and layers of underwear provided vital protection against the cold. My mother fought valiantly to force us into a scaled-down version of long johns called combinations, and their name was very apt because they combined total cover from wrist to knee with a built-in back door providing the necessary outlet. They were hideous and uncomfortable and we refused, point blank, to be fettered by them. My mother believed that if you were warm, all other considerations were secondary and such thinking led to many protestations from her five daughters; sometimes she got the better of us, but not where the combinations were concerned.

Our footwear, too, was bought at Jack's. He lifted us easily on to the counter and marched us up and down to ensure a good fit. A fine, tall man of ample proportions, he was always well turned out, as befitted his business, in a grey or navy suit with matching waistcoat and a gold watch-chain draped across his broad chest. Completely bald, his face and head knew no boundaries and his skin had a pale, polished look, in contrast to the brown, weatherbeaten appearance of his customers. His spectacles, when not in use, he wore perched on top of his head, a feat that I greatly admired.

Paying Jack was a seasonal event, depending on many things: a good milk cheque, the sale of fattened pigs, or a good harvest. When the farmers did well, Jack did well. He recorded all transactions in a big leather-bound ledger which he kept on a little rostrum inside the window.

Only rarely did we visit the harness-maker as my father repaired most of the tackling himself. A tall, rangy man, he doled out good advice as well as leather work. Once, when my father and he were discussing the women in their lives and the reasons why sometimes they were a bit touchy, Billy's prescription was: 'Let the women out to take the edge off them'. Housebound women, he figured, were cranky women. Billy himself was not endowed with a great amount of patience. Big-hearted, colourful and generous he certainly was, but he was not easily amused. Many years after I had left childhood behind me I went home to the funeral of an old man who was also noted for being particularly serious by nature.

'Taylor,' he said (he called us all Taylor because he never knew which of us girls he was talking to), 'how well you came down for old Bob's funeral.'

'Well, Billy,' I said, 'he served us faithfully all his life.'

'Yes,' said Billy solemnly, 'without a smile on his face.'

What made me relish the remark was the fact that Billy himself rarely smiled.

The same families had been in most of the shops for several generations and had built up and passed on a deep understanding and knowledge of their customers. It was a relationship that worked both ways, and when money was scarce we gave each other mutual support. While all the shopkeepers were our neighbours, my mother always bore in mind that we were related to some of them, for she was a great believer in looking after the needs of the extended family. Allegiances of all kinds were important to her, and if somebody's grandmother had been good to my mother's grandmother then my mother was not going to forget that, and so all the shopkeepers – Jack, Ned, Con, Billy and the Miss Bowlers – were not just shopkeepers to us: they were our friends, and shopping was as much of a social outing as the acquiring of goods.

Mrs Tom's Tan

At the age of ten I received my first lesson in male treachery. I was naive and trusting at that point of my development and thought that life was a fairy-tale full of happy endings. He was twelve; tall, thin, blond and devastating, the only boy in a family of four girls, the family treasure. Our mothers were cousins and he came from the city to spend one long, hot summer on our farm – his first visit to the country. On his arrival I viewed him with a certain amount of suspicion. Dressed in immaculate white shorts and pullover; he possessed long, brown, unscratched legs. It was the unscratched legs I distrusted most because they must have been acquired by sunbathing on a manicured lawn, an activity that was almost inconceivable as far as I was concerned.

Another possible explanation seemed even more unthinkable. The only time I had seen legs like those was when Tom's wife decided for herself that summer had arrived. Tom was a neighbouring farmer who had emigrated and had then returned home bringing a glamorous English wife with him. We children referred to her only as Tom's wife, which was strange really because she was a colourful person in her own right, but I never learned her own name so we called her Tom's wife or Mrs Tom.

One year, after a long, cold spring, the first sunny day of summer came and on the way home from school that evening we met Mrs Tom walking along on a pair of positively golden, tanned legs. How was it possible? Legs that had been clad in lyle stockings and which I had assumed to be pale and milky underneath, now were suddenly golden brown. Surrounded as I had always been by all the natural voices of the countryside telling me of seasonal change, I knew that in nature nothing was instant, and so the extraordinary spectacle of Mrs Tom's legs turning brown overnight captured my imagination. It puzzled me for days and then, in order to solve my problem, I eventually went straight to the heart of the matter and asked her to explain the transformation. She looked at me in surprise for a few moments, causing me to think that I had pushed my luck too far, but then she smiled.

'Come with me,' she said, 'and I'll show you.'

Taking me into her bedroom, she picked up a bottle from a bewildering array of pots and jars on her dressing-table and clarified the mystery of her instant tan. And from that day onwards I marked the arrival of summer by the change in the colour of Mrs Tom's legs. The first daffodils heralded the arrival of spring and Mrs Tom's legs announced when summer was here.

My cousin with legs like Mrs Tom's was the cause of great curiosity and my first impulse was to run this paragon of perfection through a *glaise* to discover if the tan would wash off. I also felt that a struggle with a blackthorn hedge would do him no harm and might even make him look more like one of us. However, his mother and sisters stayed for the first few days of his visit and decorum had to be observed while they remained on the scene. During those few days, as if to emphasize the wild state of my own legs, I scratched myself on barbed wire and gained a scar which, though not deep, ran from my knee to my ankle. In ordinary circumstances it would have been left to heal of its own accord but my mother's cousin was a nurse and she insisted on washing the wound with disinfectant and putting a big long strip of sticking plaster on my leg. This made the whole thing look a lot more serious than it really was and I went around explaining to the less well-informed that I could actually have died from blood poisoning.

Robert – for that was my brown-legged cousin's name – was left to fare for himself when his mother and sisters had departed, and he and I teamed up together. I took him catching 'collies' and discovered that his tan did not wash off, walked him in his snow-white canvas sandals into his first cow dung, and took him picking blackberries. He worked in the meadow making hay, blistering his hands on the pike handle, and went for spins in the float, tearing a hole in the backside of his pants. People who came to the house gradually stopped asking who was the visitor because he no longer stood out from the crowd.

Sometimes late in the evening we went to the well for water and, sitting down on the side of the mossy hill with high ferns forming an umbrella over our heads, we told each other stories in a cool green fairyland where the evening sun slanted through the serrated fronds of ferns. Walking through the dry gap, we cooled our dusty toes in the ice-cold stream that overflowed from the deep well into the adjacent *glaise*. The stones in that stream were black, flat and smooth and, stacked on top of one another, made a rocker which tested our ability to balance as far forwards and backwards as possible without toppling over. Frogs, too, liked this little corner because it was moist and cool, sheltered by overhanging trees. We rested hands and knees on the large grey stone that fronted the well which arched back into the hill and, leaning forward, we watched our wavering reflections in its depth. At that time I had a story in my schoolbook about Narcissus who, looking into a well, fell in love with his own reflection. I pondered on the improbability of this as I watched my long blonde hair blend with Robert's in the water of the well.

Getting up early in the morning, we went out picking mushrooms in the clinging, misty dew of the new dawn. We watched the sauntering cows scattering moisture along the high grass as they went in for milking, and on reaching home we grilled our salt-sprinkled mushrooms on a hot sod of turf by the open fire.

Catching collies was our favourite occupation. Late in the evening we came with our swinging jam-crocks to the river which curled between high banks over dark brown stones, sometimes shallow and sandy and then curving into deep, still pools where trout jumped with a splash, sending ripples circling to the bank and diffusing the midges which hung suspended over the water. My dream was to catch a trout in a

jam-crock and the practical impossibility of such an achievement never dampened my enthusiasm. We splashed around
in the river until daylight moved towards dusk and then we
rambled home in semi-darkness through the fields, where the
cows now rested chewing the cud.

I loved the cows and introduced Robert to them individually
by name. Back in the stalls I showed him where each one
belonged and told him how they all knew their own places.
When he suggested that they should have place names over
their heads I was fascinated by the idea. That each cow would
have her own name over her head was a new and wonderful
thought. Ours were going to be the first cows in the country to
have their names mounted in their executive offices. But how
to achieve such a dream was the question, and Robert had the
answer. Back in the city the railway station had a machine that
could print on tin and he would do all the cow's names and
send them on to me. It seemed a dream come true and I was
sure that the cows would be delighted as well. With a stubby
pencil and a notebook I laboriously wrote out each cow's name
and, for good measure, added the horses as well, in case they
might feel neglected.

I was sorry when the time came for Robert to go home, but
the thought of the cows' name-plates arriving compensated
for any pangs of regret that I might have felt at his departure. I
got a jamjar and filled it with short, shiny tacks which I dug
out of my father's butterbox, doing untold damage to my
fingertips and nails. I also helped myself to a small, stubby
hammer, which I knew he would go rooting for, but as he
could never find anything anyway I felt that one more missing
item would not make that much difference.

With everything in readiness for action, I waited for the
name-plates to arrive. Every day I watched for the postman
and every day I drew a blank but decided, each time, that
tomorrow my parcel would surely come. Eventually, after
many weeks, I finally gave up hope. I felt betrayed on behalf of
my cows, who were to remain apparently nameless, and I told
myself that I should not have expected much from a boy who
had legs as smooth and perfect as Mrs Tom's tan.

Old Bags

The art of making do was a virtue passed down from my great-aunt Susan through the female line of our family – mere males were not considered to be safe custodians of such gems of wisdom – and practised in our constant saving and re-using of almost everything. Containers of many kinds were used and used again and the only waste-disposal unit we knew was the pigs' trough.

Jamjars were washed and stored carefully for future use for home-made jams and preserves, and any we couldn't use ourselves we returned to the shop for a penny for a two-pound pot and a halfpenny for a one-pound one. As potential sources of pocket-money, few jampots were left lying around for long. Another container with multiple uses was the tin sweet gallon. Having booked a gallon with Ned, we got it after a while with little bits of sweets clinging to the bottom, but we soon cleaned it out and had it ready for its new life. Tea was taken to the meadow in a gallon if the *meitheal* was small or to supplement the white enamel bucket if the workforce was strong, and sometimes a lone man would drink straight from the gallon. It also served to take milk between the houses when supplies were low in the winter time, and for bringing water from the well, especially if you were too small to carry a bucket.

Some farmers kept a goat with their herd of cows, and people without grazing for cows usually had goats which fed off ditches and were satisfied with limited supplies of grass. The versatile gallon was used for milking the goat, though the milker had to take care not to get more than milk in the gallon – the odd angle from which goats were milked made this a tricky exercise. And the gallon was also one of the many different kinds of containers used for collecting eggs.

The soft brown tissue-paper around the Sunday loaf of bread was folded carefully to be used later for wrapping up our school lunches. Empty bottles of many kinds were rinsed with water and sand and re-employed as lunch bottles. The milk of magnesia bottle gave its contents a blue look; small Paddy whiskey bottles also made the trip to school, but old sauce bottles accompanied us more often because we used more sauce than either milk of magnesia or whiskey. Corks were carefully kept but nevertheless on many a morning there was none for the school bottle and the art of making do saw an old newspaper torn into strips and rolled up to form a makeshift stopper.

Our newspaper, the *Cork Examiner*, was a multi-purpose item. It cleaned and polished windows and it covered bare timber floors before the first lino or tarpaulin went down, thus providing underlay and insulation. Placed in layers on top of wire bed-springs, it eased the wear on the horsehair mattress; cut into the right shape, it became insoles in heavy leather boots and shoes and, later, in wellingtons when they became part of our lives. Even though it could never be described as baby soft, it was the forerunner of the multi-million pound industry that subsequently provided soft solutions in the toilet-paper business. Rolled into balls it was a firelighter, its effectiveness improved by a sprinkling of paraffin oil. Ned shaped it into funnels and filled it with sweets to make a *tóimhsín*, as he called it. At home it lined drawers and was considered moth-proof and, when nothing else was available, it was used as a dustpan. One of our more industrious neighbours regularly covered her potato stalks with newspaper at night and this protected them from frost.

An item used to great effect by good housekeepers was the goose wing. It was particularly useful for high-flung cobwebs, and where the wing could not reach the eye would not see. It was just as well, however, that some cobwebs remained after the goose-wing's flight because they were nature's flykillers, ready and waiting to trap the flies which had not been discouraged by the nicandra or shoo-fly we hung around the windows.

Necessity was the mother of resourcefulness and everything available was put to good use. Horse manure fortified our roses without any assistance from shop-bought preparations and garden sprays were unheard of. The suds from the washtub were used to keep slugs off the cabbage. If the tub itself leaked it could always be sealed with a mixture of curds and lime brushed into the base and allowed to harden. Leaking buckets were repaired with a 'mend-it' which consisted of two little circular bits of tin with a sandwich of cork in between. One piece of the mend-it was put at each side of the leak and the two pieces were then screwed into each other, the cork acting as a sealer. Care had to be taken when hand-mixing animal foodstuffs in a bucket that had been mended in this way because the tin could pierce deeply beneath your fingernails. Travelling knights of the road repaired items that needed more skill than we possessed; they also made tin gallons which were bigger than the normal ones, though quality rather than quantity was the hallmark of their trade. Every house had a last on which shoes and boots were repaired, and on Saturday nights the children's boots were lined up for repair with iron tips and protectors, and sometimes for patching, which was done with an awl, wax and a ball of hemp.

Mending was a basic skill in our household arts, and was much relied on. Old sheets, worn down the centre where the most pressure was brought to bear, got a new lease of life from a centre-to-sides piece of surgery. When the collars of men's shirts became frayed they were still a long way from becoming dusters, because the collar was turned and the shirt salvaged though admittedly not as Sunday best anymore. Some shirts were collarless and an attachable collar was clasped into position with studs; collarless during the working week, these were what are now called grandfather shirts. My First Communion dress was a hand-me-down belonging to my sister, with a band added on around the tail because my legs were longer than hers.

We had no need of proprietary cleaning agents because our

own remedies were always close at hand. If the cat did what he must where he shouldn't, turf dust was the removal agent which deodorized and eradicated all in one go. If the hens committed the same offence on the kitchen floor, a shovel of ashes from behind the open fire came into action, and ashes were also used for cleaning the silver and aluminium teapots. The bag of lime was essential for keeping things clean around the farm. During the summer months, when the animals had gone to the fields leaving their houses empty behind them, these were whitewashed and disinfected with lime.

Almost everything had more than one use. Warm covers of pots and bastables wrapped in old sheets became bed warmers, and our hot-water bottles were earthenware jars; sometimes, too, the clothes-iron was heated and wrapped up well to warm the bed on a very cold night. Cord which arrived on parcels from town was never thrown away: it was rolled up in a ball to be available for emergency service as garters, to keep up knickers if the necessity arose, or to act as a belt. Hay twine kept buttonless coats closed on cold days or secured the bottoms of wide-legged trousers against the perils of both winds and rodents.

All boxes were made of timber, and these were prized acquisitions. When Christmas supplies came in them you treated them with respect because, whether you got timber boxes, and how many you got, depended on your standing with the shopkeeper. The long double-department orange box served as two semi-detached nests in the hen-house, as did the smaller apple and orange boxes. The long orange box, stood upright, became a bedside locker and, when it was fronted with a frilly curtain, could look quite decorative. The butter box was the most solid and the most prized of all the boxes and had many uses, including those of tool box and lady's work box. It became fashionable to cover the butter box with leatherette and put a padded cushion on top, and in this way it served the dual purpose of work box and fireside seat. The five-pound cheese box held nails or other odds and ends in many houses. My mother bought our tea by the chest, and this was a large, plywood box, lined with silver paper. We stored our summer clothes in it during the winter and our winter blankets during the summer.

But the flour bag was undoubtedly the queen of all the objects that entered our house with the potential for alternative use. A soft, white cloth sack, across which was written the weight and source of the flour, it was apt, if dropped suddenly, to engulf you in white, billowing clouds, and if you travelled with it on the creamery cart you might very well come away from it with a piebald look. But once the sack was empty its reincarnation began.

The first step was to render it anonymous by removing the marks of its previous existence, the blue or red stencil which told its story. It was soaked in a tub of very hot water laced with washing soda, which soon bleached out its identity and the details of its weight – of 112 or 140 pounds. Some people ignored this eradication process and once our old friend Dan came across such a case when he was out looking for one of our horses which had strayed. He had travelled through many fields and over distant hills, searching and enquiring if anyone had seen the horse when, as he told my father later, 'Jakus me, boss, I came to a little house up on the side of a hilland knocked on the door. It was opened by a fine ball of a woman in a long white nightdress with 140 pounds written across her chest.' These nightdresses made from sacks were long-wearing and comfortable, but most people removed the printed statistics lest they end up on sensitive areas, either front or back.

The flour bag often became a tea-towel, in which capacity it had great absorbency. It might also become a table-cloth, pillow-case, bed-sheet (known as the 'bageen' sheet) or apron, or answer other female needs when nothing else was available. It lined children's winter clothes or became the top half of a grey flannel petticoat. It lined a patchwork quilt or, when well worn, was tied around the top of the milk churn as a strainer. The Christmas pudding was boiled in it and then wrapped in another, dry one for storage, and it was wrapped around the hot bastable cake to soften the crust.

Some of the flour bags were made of better material than

others, and the flake meal came in a very good quality bag which was used for making tea-cosies which were lined inside with sheep's wool. Often they were embroidered with bright colours or the threads were drawn to create interesting designs for colourful, durable tray-cloths, dressing-table mats and runners for the tops of chests of drawers. Some artistic souls painted pictures on this fine, closely woven material.

Its uses, like its life-span, were endless. It had a soft, pleasant feel, and when put out to dry it soaked in sunshine and every country smell; the older it was the more pliable it became, making it the ideal absorber in which to wrap babies' free-flowing regions. In its old age it served as a softly caressing facecloth, or a soothing bandage to wrap up bloody cuts and support damaged limbs. During its existence it went through many transformations, until finally it was as fine as tissue-paper. So delicate and transparent was it then that I sometimes thought it could come again into another life as the gossamer wings of white butterflies.

Of course, those who perfected the art of making do ran the risk of being regarded as thrifty to a fault. A mild enough saying was that 'she could live under a hen', but if Dan was describing someone he considered to be very tight-fisted and conniving he would remark: 'That one could live in your ear and rent out the other one without you knowing it'.

In our house we made do, practising the art with the best of them, but somehow my father was never satisfied and we were reared to a background chant about waste and extravagance, as he constantly complained that there was enough food thrown out of our house to keep another family well fed. One day he was going on yet again about how thrifty they had all been in his young days when my sister Lucy, who could always be depended on to take the wind out of his sails, came out with the comment, 'God, the dead were lucky they were buried or else ye'd have made soup out of them!'

Nell's Christmas Spirit

Old Nell, our nearest and most eccentric neighbour, did not believe in Christmas. Despite all my efforts to convert her and re-introduce her to a child's view of Christmas, she stubbornly remained a non-believer. It was the one point in our relationship on which we could not reach a compromise. To me Christmas was wonderful, thrilling, magnificent, an absolute high point of the year, but Nell dismissed all my excitement and all the general fuss as a load of old rubbish. In this she was, in a way, simply being consistent: after all, she did not observe any of the rituals most of the neighbours considered to be important elements of normal life. Funerals, for example, she dismissed scathingly as 'queues of crazy men following dead men'.

Her main objection to Christmas centred around the question of goodwill to all men. If Nell did not feel goodwill towards you for the rest of the year she saw no reason why Christmas should change anything. What she hated above all else was the expectation that money should be spent; she had no intention of allowing Christmas to force open the brass clasp of her scruffy black purse. If other people wanted to spend money, and if Nell should happen to be at the receiving end of their generosity that suited her fine, but she never felt the need to acknowledge gifts, still less to reciprocate; she believed in one-way traffic and that all roads should lead to Nell. Not afflicted with a sensitive nature, she accepted everything that came her way, without any sense of obligation to express or even to feel gratitude.

Shopkeepers at that time gave out Christmas presents to their best customers and Nell expected to be numbered amongst the recipients, though so meagre was her spending that she could scarcely be described as a customer at all. If she had any doubts about a shopkeeper's generosity, she presented herself at his counter a few days before Christmas. Having purchased as little as possible, she gave him a big smile. In Nell's case this could be a rather intimidating experience because her false teeth, which she wore only on special occasions, often came adrift, and when this happened she promptly whipped them out in front of the surprised shopkeeper. At this stage he felt so put out that he handed Nell the first thing available to cover her – as he imagined – embarrassment. What he failed to realize was that he was the only one feeling embarrassed, and in his ignorance he finished up giving her far more than he had intended. By the use of such tactics she succeeded in scoring very well in the Christmas stakes and it always amused her particularly when she managed to drag something out of someone who was like herself, tight-fisted.

One Christmas Jim the hackney-man, who owned the local pub where Nell sometimes bought a bottle of whiskey to warm her at night, decided that he was not going to be bullied by her into parting with a free bottle. Having pulled every stunt, including her false teeth trick, there was still nothing doing, so finally she asked straight out: 'Jim, what about my Christmas box?'

'What about it, Nell?' he answered.

'Are you forgetting it?' she asked.

'No,' he replied.

'I'll take it now so,' she told him, 'because I might not be in again before Christmas.'

'Nell,' he said looking her straight in the eye, 'you don't deserve a free bottle and you're not getting it.'

'Well, Jim,' she said heavily, 'you're a bad boyo in these festive times.'

That was a bit rich coming from her, but she held no ill-feelings towards him; if he had parted with a bottle she would have enjoyed it, but when he did not she admired his astuteness in getting the better of her.

Nell allowed me to decorate her house at Christmas time, and I enjoyed doing so. At home I had to share the decorating with four sisters, and much arguing and disagreement went on, but at Nell's I had it all my own way. There was no question of her spending any money on decorations, but then we did not buy any at home either, making use of our Christmas cards and balloons which were already in the house. Nell's one Christmas expenditure was on a big red candle, so that was the centre around which I accomplished my transformation of her long, thatched house.

On the days leading up to Christmas I prepared her for the festive occasion in which she had not the slightest interest. It was a measure of her tolerance that she never objected, or else it was the fact that, having spent so much time with her and come to know her so well, I sensed instinctively just how much she would endure. The big clean-up that went on at home was definitely not possible in Nell's house. At the very mention of washing the floor and cleaning the windows she would roll her eyes to heaven.

'Child! Don't be disturbing clean dirt. My mother used to get the spade to the floor every Christmas.'

And that brought that discussion to a quick stand-still.

She had great respect for cobwebs, maintaining that they possessed both practical and beautiful qualities; the evidence of her admiration was draped in every corner of the house. She regarded them as the original and best flykillers, and if the spiders had put so much creative energy into weaving them, Nell was not going to destroy the products of their artistry. When we studied the delicate threads of a new creation I had to agree with her, but I found that I did not share her enthusiasm for the furry and soot-laden specimens which hung from her rafters like so many black rags.

Christmas cards were not plentiful at home but some were quite beautiful and ours were not thrown away after Christmas but were carried forward from year to year as decorations. In a box at the bottom of a press in the parlour my mother kept these cards and I would always appropriate a few. So, on Nell's window during the festive season cards could be found which wished her and all the children a very happy Christmas. Indeed, anyone who was inquisitive enough to read the cards in Nell's house would end up completely confused, for there were loving greetings from brothers, sisters and cousins who she simply did not have. Uninterested in communicating with anyone, she lived in an isolation which was almost complete apart from my intrusions. She would pick up some of the cards with which I had decorated her house, read their inscriptions, and snort in disgust at the stupidity of their senders.

Every year my mother invited Nell to spend Christmas with us and every year she refused. She did not believe in togetherness, preferring the quietness of her own place, as she bluntly told my mother, she could do without the aggravation of a crowd of children making noise around her. However, she usually called on Christmas Eve on her way home from confession, where she went to impress on the priest how lonely Christmas was for someone like herself – though she never tried this stunt on our veteran parish priest who knew her too well and saw through her manoeuvres. But if we had a new curate she would put on an act worthy of Siobhan McKenna and have him almost crying into his soutane. If he called to her later with something to brighten her Christmas she would say, 'God bless him, wasn't he very soft? For all the learning they have, they must come to the country to be educated'.

All of her strange pronouncements she made in a high-pitched, piercing wail which made it practically impossible to carry on normal conversation with her. If she was imparting to you anything that she considered to be of a confidential nature, she would warn you in a voice that everyone within half a mile could hear. 'Keep that in your belly,' she would say. If this conversation was taking place, as many of them did, inside at Mass, Nell's whisper would be heard all around the church, rendering the priest mere background noise.

One Christmas Eve she sat at the end of our kitchen table having tea while my mother stuffed the goose at the other end and we children sorted out decorations in between. Finally the clamour reached such a level that Nell could stand it no longer; just before heading for home she told my mother how glad she was that she had not inflicted on herself the persecutions that my mother had to bear – namely her children. Nell's particular way of expressing how she had come to be so lucky was, 'Thanks be to God that I never felt the need of a man in my bed'. Men were in general, as far as Nell was concerned, the begetters of a wide variety of undesirable after-effects.

On the following day, just as we sat down to our Christmas dinner, Nell tore in the door, demanding in her piercing wail, 'Did ye find my teeth?'

'Your false teeth?' my mother enquired in some amazement.

'Yes!' she shrieked at full volume. 'When I looked at the jam pot on the dresser this morning it was empty, and you know my teeth are always inside there except when I'm going out.'

'But Nell,' asked my mother in a soothing voice, 'what makes you think that they're here?'

'Because when I was having the tea yesterday evening I took them out. They were getting stuck in that cake and could have choked me,' Nell shouted, determined not to be soothed.

'Holy Christ,' my father prayed at this stage, but before he could launch into his 'if ever a man suffered' routine my mother interrupted.

'Nell, when I was tidying up last night your teeth were not on the table; so you must have taken them with you,' she said.

'No,' Nell insisted, and then her eye fell on the still-sizzling and golden goose which was lying in state at the centre of the table, and she pointed her black finger at it. 'That's where they are!' she shouted in excitement as if she had been struck by divine inspiration. 'They must have got mixed up with the sliced onions because I remember seeing a dish of them near me and they are gone into the goose with the stuffing.'

'Mother of God!' my father started again, and this time there was no way my mother was going to stop him. 'That's all I need now for my Christmas dinner – Nell's gnashers grinning out at me through the arse of the goose!'

'Nell,' said my mother firmly, 'if we find them we'll bring them back to you, or would you like to stay for dinner?'

'Stay for dinner,' cried Nell, 'and eat my own false teeth!' And with that she departed, banging the door after her.

'Dear God,' my father breathed, 'but she is one galvanized hoor!' He seldom used what my mother termed 'farmyard language' in the house, but where Nell was concerned his patience quickly reached breaking point.

After Nell's departure we all sat horror-stricken, gazing at our golden goose which a few minutes earlier had had our mouths watering but which now apparently held an appalling secret. It seemed a tragedy had intervened to cast a shadow over our young lives. Normally the goose filled with our mother's beautiful potato stuffing was one of the highlights of Christmas, but Nell had certainly snuffed out that light with the prospect of what might lie within.

My mother had a simple approach to the sticky situation. 'I will dish out all the stuffing and then we will know one way or the other,' she said. So she carved the goose and dished out the stuffing from both ends. Because there were many mouths to be fed our goose had no unfilled cavities and was stuffed to capacity in all departments. As my mother spooned out the stuffing we all watched intently and it was one of the few occasions on which silence had ever prevailed at our table. Even my father, apart from an occasional appeal to the Lord to witness his suffering, saw it all through in silent apprehension. Finally the last spoonful proved that we were in the clear and we all cheered, relieved that the horror of Nell's teeth had been lifted from our minds. And because we had come so close to losing it, the dinner tasted all the more luscious. Our dogs would never know how close they had come to enjoying a full Christmas dinner.

Later that evening I went across the fields to Nell with a plate of dinner wrapped in a tea-towel. The countryside had a special stillness and I watched my breath fuse into the cold, crisp air. The water in the *glaise* looked black against the grey, frosty grass and the cow tracks, frozen hard, bore a multiplicity of designs. As I jumped between them Nell's dinner cooled in the freezing early night air. Feeling no need to hurry, however, I ambled along and finally arrived at Nell's house at my ease, to find her sitting by a big fire surrounded by her dogs and cats. From her chair by the fire she had viewed through her kitchen window my progress across the fields.

'Child,' she said, 'you took your time. My dinner will be frozen.'

She put the wrapped plate on a black pot by the fire and the dogs and cats jostled for position to sniff at it. I lay down on Nell's old timber settle, dislodging some of her cats who had made it their bed. I admired the red-berry holly I had placed above it where it contrasted vividly with the black rafters. I decided that all in all Nell's kitchen wore a festive air, despite her reluctance to be part of the season that was with us. The red candle flickering on the window and the yellow flames of the turf fire filled the room with a warm glow. The colourful Christmas cards stood on the deep window-sill and between the brown lustre jugs and bowls on the dark dresser. The stillness of the room was disturbed only by the tick-tock of the old seven-day wall clock and the hissing of resin from the logs as the flames of the burning sods licked around them. It was then that I saw, out of the corner, grinning whitely in the shadows, the false teeth resting in the jampot which held them more often than Nell's mouth. How long had they been there? For some reason I did not ask her.

Goody, Goody

Goody was a balm to bruised minds and bodies and held a special place in all our hearts. Mothers made it when we were feeling sick, but not sick enough for medicine and definitely not needing the doctor – maybe feeling just a little out of step with our fellow human beings and in need of loving or the knowledge that somebody loved us. It was a simple but effective antidote to all ills and was within the scope of all budgets.

Tufts of white bread were plucked from a thick cut or a well-padded heel of a loaf to line the bottom of a cup or a basin, depending on the size of the consumer. Some dressers boasted a colourful, flowery basin which was reserved especially for making goody. On top of the foundation layer of bread came a generous shake of sugar, and sweet-toothed people turned the sugar bowl sideways and poured freely. Then another covering of bread was added, and more sugar, and so on, layer upon layer until it rose, dome-like, over the rim.

While this tiered miracle was being created a wary eye was kept on a saucepan of milk heating on a rake-out of hot coals by the fire. You forgot it at your peril; if you took your eye off it for one second it could erupt in billowing bubbles and overflow on to the fire, scattering ashes and filling the kitchen with an acrid smell. Experienced goody makers managed to get the two jobs to reach completion simultaneously. Then the boiling milk was poured gently in a circular motion over the soft, spongy bread and sugar, which sank with a subdued sigh beneath the scalding waterfall. Some discerning people liked to hold back the skim at the top of the milk, which might be flecked with turf dust and ashes, while other, less fastidious souls let it all pour in. Then, with a big spoon, the entire concoction was squelched up and down, the spoon making a slurping passage through the goody to meet the bottom of the bowl with a dull thud. As the mixing progressed the goody cooled and the connoisseur knew when the precise point for satisfying expectant taste-buds had been reached. Thus was created a soft, sweet, creamy bowl of delicious, slushy sedation.

With this soothing seductive mush babies were weaned off the breast and introduced to solid food. In later years the goody was there when no other comfort was available. Many a hardened bachelor, long in the tooth, coming home on a cold day from the fair and having no welcoming arms to erase the memory of a bad bargain, found his solace in a basin of hot goody. His blood chilled by a long trudge up a mountainy road with a cold wind whipping around his ears, he was rejuvenated and reheated by this bowl of warm comfort. Often an overly discerning lady, unwilling to wrinkle her linen sheets with what she considered the unsuitable manhood available, took a china cup of consoling goody to see her through the night. Happy couples, too, having bedded down their young after a hectic day, shared a bowl of warm goody before going on to share greater comforts. Then, in old age, when sensitive molars could send searing pain through brittle jaws, goody gently weaned them off solid fare with its delicate touch.

Chewing, which rocked unsteady teeth in their shrunken rooting ground, was no longer necessary as goody slid effortlessly over flawed masticators.

Goody was a source of consolation for all seasons. It was an infantile soother, a male menopause stress-reliever, a female oestrogen replacer and, in old age, the last comfort against the ravages of time.

Cow Time

Come the first glimmer of light and the slight twitter that introduced the dawn chorus, the cock crew loud and clear. I imagined that he must sleep with one eye half open in case he might miss that little splinter of light in the dark sky. He was our alarm clock and his cock-crow was a call to arms and a salutation to the new day. There was nothing half-hearted or hesitant about it: his 'cock-a-doodle-do' rang out bright and clear. The vibrant call cut through waves of muzzy sleepiness and was repeated every five minutes until the cock was assured that the coming of the dawn was not going to be ignored by those who lacked the sense of occasion he possessed.

He was a fine-looking fellow, with a bright red cock's-comb which contrasted dramatically with his snow-white feathers. His long, strong, yellow legs spread into gripping claws and he had a vicious beak; he used both beak and claws to keep his huge harem in submission. He strolled arrogantly around the farmyard and occasionally during the day he perched himself on top of a dunghill or on a shed and crowed out his superiority over his flock which was now scattered around the haggard and farmyard.

Our first job after answering the cock's morning call was to bring in the cows. They had no built-in mechanism like the cock's to tell them that the time had come to head home for milking. Usually they were spread out around the field, some grazing, some lying down contentedly chewing the cud. They rose at their own pace when they saw you coming and meandered towards the gap. Rounding up cows in the early morning was a soothing experience. They looked at you out of large, moist, trusting eyes and obediently complied with whatever it was you wanted them to do. As you walked along behind their swinging tails they exuded a warm contentment with their lot that was contagious. The rhythm of their gait compelled you to slow to the relaxed pace of their bovine world. Arriving in the stall yard, each went to her own stall and put her head into her own place. While the sleepy-headed milkers arrived, some of whom were perpetually bad-tempered in the morning, the cows stood impassively chewing the cud, with faraway looks in their big eyes as if dreaming of green fields and mossy streams. With their long tails they flicked away annoying flies.

We had three cowhouses or stalls, and they were known as the new stalls, the middle stalls and the old stalls. The new and middle stalls had grain lofts over them and these my father had built. The old stalls, however, had been there for many generations in a lovely old stone building which was partly covered with ivy and had deep, narrow windows and a cobbled floor. Here in the crevices between the stones the swallows nested and swished in and out above the cows' heads and in the straw loft overhead at the peak of each rafter were rows of nests.

The milkers went to their own stalls and milked their own cows. There was never a worked-out arrangement about who was to milk any particular cow: the system just evolved whereby certain people liked to milk certain cows and that was it. The full buckets of warm milk were carried out of the stalls and across the yard to the stand where twenty-gallon churns stood on a concrete base, and into these the milk was poured and strained through a white muslin cloth tied around the top of each churn. My father left the stalls early to catch the pony and have his breakfast. Pony tackled to the creamery cart, it was backed in beside the stand and the covered churns were rolled into it.

When the cows had been milked and let out again the only other job that was usually done before breakfast was feeding the calves. They were by now bellowing their heads off: having heard the rattle of the milk buckets, they knew that breakfast time had come. All the small calves were individually fed and each one would be at a different milk strength; there were calves on pure fresh milk, calves on a mixture of fresh and sour, and calves on sour milk only, and bearing in mind each calf's requirements was a bit like preparing the feeding bottles in a hospital nursery.

Before opening the door of the house to feed them you had to be thoroughly organized as their bucket manners were not well cultivated and each had just one aim in life: to get its head into a bucket, any bucket. Sometimes you might finish up with two heads in one bucket and a spare bucket with no head in it. But to get a calf's head out once it was in was almost impossible, as the only lever you had to pull them by was their ears and, pull as you might, this had no effect. When the calves were finally matched with their correct feed, the bucket had to be held firmly while the calf was drinking because calves had a strange habit of butting with their heads, almost as an expression of appreciation. They could turn the bucket upside down or, worse still, give you a pair of black and blue shin-bones as a result of a belt of a bucket.

After wrestling with the calves we took a break and fed ourselves. When breakfast was over the rest of the morning jobs were done, but somehow they never seemed to take as long as the evening ones, which was strange because the routine was almost exactly the same.

In the summer, as soon as the first evening shadows stretched their slanting fingers across the fields, all the animals converged on the farmyard. Hungry animals are noisy animals and the only ones who were not hungry were the cows but they bellowed too because they wanted to be milked. The demanding clamour could be deafening. Permanently stationed in the yard was a house of pigs in for fattening and they now gave off a shrill, demented scream as they jumped against their door and rattled their empty iron trough around the house. In the next few houses baby bonhams might be squealing for their mothers who had been out eating grass and rolling in mud. Two large gates led from the fields into the yard and these were closed at this point to bring a bit of law and order to the situation. Outside one gate the big calves, who had spent their day out in the fields, were now bellowing for their supper with long, plaintive maa-maa-maa sounds that went on non-stop. Outside the other gate the returning sows screeched with continuous determination. Already in the yard were hens, turkeys, ducks and chickens, all adding to the chaotic chorus of wailing animals and birds. It was pure and absolute bedlam.

First to be dealt with were the hens, because they were everywhere, jumping into the other animals' feed and scurrying around between your feet, so you had to get rid of them first. A bucket of oats was taken to the front of their house and a call of 'tioc, tioc' brought them clustering after you. The oats were scattered on the ground and they pecked it up. Next came the ducks, who would actually eat anything, which my father maintained was the reason why their eggs were not up to the same standard as the hens' eggs. The turkeys, however, were a finicky lot and the baby turkeys were actually fed on scrambled eggs and nettles. Sometimes they got a strange complaint called the gapes and then they were put under a cardboard box where a pink powder was blown around them. Turkeys were delicate and demanding, but the turkey-cock was a colourful old boy who would fan out his bright feathers and huge wings and dance sideways like an excited matador going into attack. And attack he would, because he was an aggressive devil and would fly at you with wings spread out in full flight.

The fowl quietened, the background wailing still continued and the pigs were the next to be tackled and reduced to comparative silence. In the yard was the 'mess house', as it was called, but no serried ranks of soldiers dined in this place where the pigs' mess was mixed in a timber tub with a long-handled shovel. Ration was shovelled out of jute bags, mixed with water to a sloppy consistency, and then taken in buckets to the pigs. Facing into a house full of hungry pigs required a certain amount of courage, brute force and timing, and the timing was the most important element. Hungry pigs shrieked and jumped at the door in waves, and the trick was to

get in the door and reach the trough while they were still between waves, building up for a renewed assault. If you did not
get your timing right they could take the legs from under you
and then you would emerge highly perfumed with a con-
centrated essence and pure toilet water. The home-coming
sows outside the gates were now screaming to high heaven
and trying to lift the gate out of the way with their snouts
while their bonhams, hearing them, squealed in hunger, but
once they were let in the noise died down.

The calves now provided the final chorus. An iron trough
set in a cement base was used to feed them and iron dividers
separated each head. The trough was filled with sour milk,
which had been brought home earlier from the creamery and
stored in two large tar-barrels in the corner of the yard. The
milk was drawn by bucket from the barrel until the trough was
full and then you opened the gate and stood well back to avoid
being knocked down in the ensuing stampede. Sometimes the
bigger calves were held back for a few minutes to give the
small ones a chance to get a head start. Once fed, the calves
went back to the fields.

The peace that descended on the farmyard when all the
demanding, clamouring animals had finally been fed was
emphasized by the volume of the noise that had preceded it. It
was such a relief to have them all quietened down that you
could almost feel the silence. This daily routine was called
simply 'doing the jobs' and in some ways was separate from
the milking which, because it involved so many more people,
was considered the biggest event of the day.

During the summer many of the farm buildings were empty
by night. The cows were 'out on grass' from early summer to
late autumn – how late depended on the weather – and the
horses only used the stables in the winter. The farmyard late
of a summer's evening had a whispering life. Swallows
swished in and out through the open doors and the farm cats
stretched out in the mangers, where the horses would not
tolerate them during the winter. Pigs, normally curled up together for warmth, now lay far apart to keep cool in their
warm houses, giving little grunts and snorts as if reliving

memories of rolling in cool mud. An occasional muted quack came from the duck-house and even the troublesome turkeys chirped quietly to themselves. The hens, sitting in rows on their perches in the whitewashed hen-house, gave occasional clucks and gurgles before burying their heads under their wings. Even his majesty the cock was taking it easy, sitting on the top perch and keeping a beady eye on his rows of ladies-in-waiting.

The Missioners

The missioners who thundered into the parish church most summers were to us as exciting as a travelling roadshow. We loved these tall, graceful men in long, sweeping black gowns whose black, sectioned birettas clung precariously to their polls and whose giant wooden rosary beads clanked around them like horses' traces. They were larger than life and we saw them as visitors from another world – a world of incense, long, polished corridors and continuous prayer. To me the missioner on the altar provided a one-man entertainment, which was all the more exciting when he strode back and forth shouting; it was high drama, and better again when he thumped the altar. Usually coming in pairs, these missioners generally comprised one quiet, holy one and a cross, dramatic fellow. Different orders had different levels of ferocity but we preferred the fire and brimstone brigade.

There was a great sense of togetherness in the parish during the mission week. We all shared the same schedule, as farm activity had to be wound up early in the evening so that everybody could converge on the church. If you were late you might be left standing outside and miss some of the excitement or, worse still, the free missioner of the night might come around to the back door and march you up along the church until he found a seat for you. He pretended he was doing you a good turn but in actual fact both he and you knew he was not.

In backyards around the town ponies and traps were tied up and bicycles were lined against the church railings. Young children living near the church had great fun stealing rides at breakneck speed down the high hill on the bikes of mountainy bachelors who did not have the filling of a trap for the mission.

166

Up one side of the churchyard, against the iron railings, was a long row of mission stalls called 'standings', from which holy pictures, statues, holy-water fonts, rosary beads and a wide and varied selection of medals, some with encased relics, were sold. Anything thought to have the power to cultivate devotion was available and the items were international in origin but not, of course, interdenominational. We savoured our examination of everything on offer and adorned ourselves with anything that could be pinned or hung on. We hung brown and green scapulars around our necks, and Blessed Martin and Saint Jude competed with each other for pride of place on our woollen vests, but as Blessed Martin's was the first black face I have ever seen I felt protective towards him, in case he might feel lost in this strange place, so he was always first in to my safety-pin. The general favourite was St Christopher bearing the Child on his back, perhaps because everybody felt the need of a St Christopher to carry them over the rough patches of life.

The colourful statues stood in rows high on the back shelves of the stalls. We studied the different facial expressions: the soft, pleading eyes of Our Lady; the dark, inscrutable ones of St Theresa. But the cherub-faced Child of Prague was my favourite because I liked his happy look. Various statues of the Child of Prague came into our house over the years but always they lost their heads and we had all sorts of strange beliefs concerning him. We believed that it was lucky if his head fell off; also, that he liked a prominent position, being averse to hovering in the background; and if you wanted a fine day you put him out the night before. I believed that there was a logic of sorts to everything and supposed that the reason for this was that the draught would catch him when he was left out overnight and he would need the sun the following day. Anyway, all the sideshows and their attendant beliefs and stories had the welcoming effect of adding colour to the mission and enhancing our appreciation of it.

Like most children, I relished ideals, and the higher the better. So the mission to me was a big spiritual clean-up, a bit like getting the house ready for the Stations, only this time the house was within my mind's four walls. My heart bled at the sermon on the passion and I felt I could identify with Christ carrying his cross along the hot, dusty road to Calvary. I felt so sorry for Our Lady, pregnant and tired on that cold winter's night, riding on the donkey into Bethlehem. But the missioners lost me, when they came to the sins of the flesh and waxed eloquent in explaining the finer details of the sixth and ninth commandments. It was all so complicated that I wondered what on earth they were talking about.

One night, after a sermon distinguished by a tirade on sins in marriage which had me absolutely fascinated, trying to figure out how such sins could be achieved, we gave a lift home in the pony and trap to a woman who lived near us.

'That man tonight,' she announced, 'wants to take all the fun out of life.'

My mother at this point tried to change the subject surrounded as she was by children of varying ages, all of whom were listening with open mouths.

'For God's sake,' the neighbour continued blithely, 'what else have Mick and I to pass the long winter's nights.' She threw back her head and laughed heartily, slapping my father on the back, but this time my mother was determined that enough was enough and turned the conversation firmly in another direction.

The mission continued for a week, and to each of us it meant different things. My friend Ann spent the entire week sitting in the front seat of the upstairs gallery aiming spits on the bald heads of the men below. My father was once the victim of her marksmanship and threatened that he would dry her spit if she dared try again; religious toleration did not extend to wet insults landing on my father's bald head. Ann was full of bright ideas on how to make life more exciting. Long queues formed for confession, which was part of the spiritual clean-up operation of the mission. We young ones had a special time set aside for us and once when the missioner was late my friend decided that action was required to relieve the boredom. She posted a look-out at the door and sat into the confessional to hear our confessions herself. We took turns going in on either side and telling the most atrocious sins we could think of. Suddenly there was a warning call from the door and we all scattered – all but the girl on the right-hand side of the box who, because she was furthest from the door and the sound was deadened by the heavy baize cloth of the confessional, did not realize that the missioner had replaced Ann. When the grille of the confessional was drawn back, thinking in the dark that it was her friend, she stuck her finger into the missioner's eye. We discovered that day that even holy men knew how to use strong language.

The mission closed with a grand finale. It took place on a Sunday evening when, cows milked, calves and pigs fed and the resulting farmyard aromas eradicated, we all headed for the church. Women arrived laden with lumpy parcels almost as if they had done their Christmas shopping. The stalls did a roaring trade now as this was the last opportunity to get something and have it blessed by the missioners.

The church was thronged to the utmost because anybody who had not come voluntarily to the mission had been visited by the missioner and a speedy conversion had been effected, so tonight they were all in except those we considered the real lost causes. The main aisle, which was reserved for men, was packed to capacity, and some brave bodies overflowed into the mortuary, which was normally reserved for single, laid out occupancy but which now offered standing room only. The confession boxes provided more comfortable accommodation – too comfortable in some cases because a gentle snore could sometimes be heard from them when proceedings proved particularly lengthy. The women's aisles to the right and left of the altar were a sea of colour as many a devout woman overflowing with missionary fervour crowned it with a new hat or sometimes even a complete new outfit. Sexual segregation did not rise to the three galleries where the steps as well as the seats were lined with people. The less enthusiastic took refuge on the gallery stairs and it was not unknown for a game of cards to be quietly played.

Gleaming brass candelabras bore dozens of tall lighted candles, their heavy waxen odour blending with the spicy incence from the swinging thurible. Rows of altar boys in bright red soutanes flanked the two missionaries in their gathered white surplices. Children overflowed into the aisles and sat around the altar-rails while the choir in full volume filled the church with organ music and Latin hymns. We said the rosary and were given a mixed grill of a sermon which recapped on every aspect of the previous week, and then with everybody bearing a lighted candle, we renewed our baptismal vows. We drowned the devil in holy water and buried him in candle-grease, and evicted him out of sight back down into hell.

Mad Saints

The kitchen window was broken one night when my mother and father were at the mission. Nobody saw it happen and nobody in the house was at fault, and the lack of explanation annoyed my father more than if there had been a culprit on whom he could have vented his anger. To make matters worse, the mission already had him in a bad temper because it demanded of him for the sake of peace a shut mouth, and this he found difficult to maintain. He went and listened to the missioners but the wry, caustic comments which occasionally escaped from him made clear to us that he was not overly impressed by them and only the fact that my mother took the mission so seriously prevented him from giving full expression to his opinion.

Wet days not suitable for farm work were repair and maintenance days, and so it was raining when he arrived home from the creamery with a big new pane of glass wrapped in dripping newspapers. He propped the glass carefully against the kitchen press, voicing long, detailed ultimatums regarding the fate of anyone chancing to come within half a mile of it. Having lectured all of us about the seriousness and delicacy of the job in hand, he proceeded to remove the broken glass.

Our old friend Bill sat by the fire with a few of us balanced on each knee, telling us funny stories while the two sheepdogs lay stretched out drying themselves in front of the open fire. Normally dogs were not permitted this comfort but, as my mother had gone to the morning mission and must have been delayed, we had taken advantage of her absence and let them in. The sight of easy-going Bill, the dogs and the gang of noisy children cluttering up the kitchen did nothing to soothe my father's frayed nerves. We regularly told my mother that she should have married Bill instead of my father because then we could have done as we liked. As Bill did not believe in work my father's answer to this was, 'You'd all have died with hunger'.

Painstakingly he removed the broken glass from the lower pane of the window, just as he had done many times before, as this particular pane stood right in our favourite line of fire. Now we kept clear of his end of the kitchen lest we might trigger a calamity. Things proceeded calmly enough and, having removed the glass, my father kneaded the putty in his hands, which seemed to have a soothing effect on him.

A wet day in the country was conducive to visiting the neighbours, and restless spirits set to wandering. So it was that Dan could always be counted on to choose such a day on which to turn up. Knocking being a formality he never deemed necessary, he simply walked in the door accompanied, as usual, by his huge mongrel, an animal of such mixed ancestry that it scarcely merited the term dog. Our own dogs normally treated this excuse of a mutt with contempt and completely ignored him, but the sight of him strolling into the inner sanctum of the kitchen, where they themselves were seldom allowed to stretch before the fire, was more than they could tolerate. They shot into action and in the ensuing tangle of dogs, locked together in a vicious, snarling ball of legs, heads and tails, they careered around the kitchen scattering everything in sight including my father's carefully propped-up pane of glass. It broke into smithereens and sprayed around the floor in a thousand fragments like a shower of solid raindrops.

Fighting dogs are a danger to interfering hands and limbs but anger disperses all caution and my father, with a few well-placed kicks of his strong leather boot, evicted the scrapping dogs out through the gaping window. Into the aftermath of this chaos sailed my mother, who had just walked home from the mission. So imbued was she with religious zeal that she failed to register our situation. Without even taking time to remove her coat she announced in a surprised and wondering voice, 'The missioner this morning said a strange thing. He said that if our ignorance and insanity did not save us we would all be damned.'

'In that case,' thundered my father, 'there is no fear of us, because if it's ignorance and insanity that's necessary for salvation then this house is full of saints.' And, catching his cap, he made for the door saying, 'As a matter of fact, woman, you're standing on holy ground.'

The Eternal Flame

The very large open fire which stretched across one end of the kitchen was the central point of the life of our home, and our family activities and gatherings all revolved around it. At its base a deep ash hole in the floor was covered over by an iron grid shaped to fit into the top of the hole, and an underground tunnel ran from the hole to the base of an upright iron bellows which stood on the right of the fire. A person sitting beside it in a comfortable *súgán* chair could turn the handle of the bellows, sending a draught along the tunnel and under the fire. The faster the wheel was turned, the brighter the fire would glow, but if handled too roughly the strap around the wheel could slip off and bring the whole proceedings to a standstill. As children we hated being landed with this awkward job. If the bellows was out of balance the strap would slip continuously and become a source of great annoyance; indeed, one of our neighbours, who was not renowned for his patience, found this so frustrating that he hit his iron bellows a belt of a sledgehammer and broke it into smithereens.

Over the fire and extending a few feet on either side of it was a huge chimney, and if you leaned in over the bellows and looked up you could see the sky. Smaller chimneys from other rooms joined it as it rose towards the roof-top, like a big river being joined by tributaries. Directly behind the fire the wall was black from years of smoke but on either side of this black area the hob was pure white, because whitewashing the hob with lime was one of the regular Saturday jobs in the house. A black iron crane stood on one leg to the left of the fire, a long arm extending from it, and half-way along that arm another one hung down and curved to form a hook at the bottom. From this arm swung the hangers to hold the various pots and kettles over the flames. The crane was operated by a long handle which curved into a smooth knob and the hangers could be eased up and down or the whole crane, which was on a swivel, could be swung forward, leaving the heat behind it.

Two heavy iron kettles provided boiling water: the larger of the two was always called the tea kettle, while the smaller one was reserved for less prestigious uses. When a kettle was brought to the boil over the fire the cover would dance up and down giving out a whistling noise and we would call to our mother that the kettle was singing. She was very fussy when it came to making tea: she never took anybody's word that the kettle had actually boiled but had to see for herself; then, when she had made the tea, she set the teapot to draw on a few red coals known as *gríosach*.

Accompanying the two kettles was a large pair of black, three-legged iron pots. The larger one was used for boiling the potatoes and the smaller one for the meal and vegetables. They were hung from the crane by the pot-hangers which hooked into the iron ears beneath their protruding upper rim, and they were covered by a heavy iron lid with a raised handle on top. To lift off the lid when it was hot the long iron tongs was sometimes used and saved many a person from scalds or burns. These two pots were used daily but they had a bigger brother which was used for Monday's washing of clothes and for Saturday-night baths. The baby of the pot family was the skillet, in which the porridge or gruel was cooked overnight in gentle heat by the fire.

Another companion of this set of pots was the bastable, which was about one-third the depth of the others and had straight sides. Its design struck me as less interesting since it lacked the generous curves which had given rise to the descriptive term 'pot-bellied', but it played an important role in the house, being used for baking bread. When it had been nicely warmed it was either greased or floured and a large round cake of bread was laid to rest inside it; the cover was securely settled on top to keep out ashes and hot turf dust, and then on the outer circle of the cover a ring of red-hot coals or *cíoráns* were placed.

My mother, being a night person, was usually the last to leave the kitchen, and so it was she who generally 'kindled' the fire. She raked it out and put the red coals to the side, and then covered them with hot ashes. Without a draught beneath them the *gríosach* did not light up but kept the 'seed' of the fire alive so that in the morning they were still red. The first person up in the morning removed the cover from the ash hole, emptied out the ashes with a cracked cup, which gave a dull, hollow sound as it scraped off the fire bricks, and made sure that the small underground tunnel to the bellows was clear. Having raked out the still warm ashes at the side of the fire, the hot *gríosach* was put on top of the grid which had been replaced over the coal.

The materials for starting up the fire again were usually stored overnight in a box at a safe distance from the fire but drying out in its warmth. We children were often sent out to gather a *gabháil* of *cipíns* or of 'roots', which were not as defined in the dictionary but were rather what my mother termed 'the limbs of trees'. These we cracked across our knees or split with a hatchet to render them into more manageable proportions.

On top of the *gríosach* were placed balls of dry hay, then *cipíns*, then the previous day's cinders and finally *cíoráns*, which were broken sods of turf. Then the bellows was turned gently to fan the small red 'seed' of the fire and the hay gave off a rich aromatic smell as it smouldered into flame, filling the kitchen with its spicy essence. Once the fire got going sods of black turf were put standing up around it like a guard of honour and soon the yellow flames licked around them. Then the ashes from the previous day's fire were shovelled into an old tin bucket which had been retired from carrying liquids, and the area around the hearth was brushed clean. The fire was ready for another day.

The entire household revolved around the fire, which provided warmth, cooking facilities and a social centre around which we gathered at night to chat or to read. My father had his own particular chair to the right of the fire beside the bellows and it was his job to turn the wheel to keep the fire glowing. Behind the bellows a cricket often chirped, making its own contribution to our conversations. To my father's left and under the oil lamp sat my mother, usually darning or patching, for it was a continual struggle to keep six pairs of childish heels, knees and elbows from breaking out. To the left of the fire stretched a long timber stool or form on which we children sat in a row, feet swinging above the floor. The chair next to our form belonged to our nearest neighbour and daily visitor, Bill, and other chairs in the circle were occupied by older members of the family or other visiting neighbours. If the circle of people became too big and we ran out of chairs, another timber form, which seated three or four depending on their circumferences, was brought into service from inside the kitchen table.

Family hygiene also depended on the fire because every Saturday night the big twenty-gallon pot of boiling water bubbled over it and the washing commenced of an assortment of little bodies which were encased in the mud, grass, earth, hay dust and chaff that perfumed our daily lives like our own country version of *eau de cologne*. Our hair was fine-combed to evict the tenants of our time, for if this was not done on a regular basis then they established squatters' rights and proved highly undesirable lodgers. On Monday morning the big pot again came into action for the weekly wash-day, which took a full day's hard labour because keeping clean was no easy job in the country.

From the kitchen fire came the 'seeds' to light the other fires in the house. A big, battered farmyard shovel, minus the handle, was filled with blazing *gríosach* and carried, a whirl of smoke behind it, at a lively pace into the parlour. It was also used to carry the seeds to upstairs bedrooms and later I would lie in bed listening to the fire crackling and watching the figures of light and shade dancing up the walls and across the low ceiling.

The kitchen fire stood at the centre of our lives, an eternal flame never to be quenched. Only when houses were finally abandoned were their kitchen fires allowed to die, and when one of our neighbours built a new house he carried the seed of the fire across the haggard in a bucket from the old house to the new. The fire was the heart of every home and its warm glow was never extinguished while people still lived in the house.

Always On A Monday

An enormous woman – in circumference rather than height – Bridgie came every Monday to do the washing. Great rolls of flesh were restrained within her cross-over navy overall, the straps of which disappeared into deep furrows; safety-pins glinted in rows on her bosom like medals on a soldier's chest. So intense was the pressure on the overall to cover her vast higher regions that it could not succeed in reaching her knees. She never wore stockings and her heavy legs curved neither in nor out but seemed to have been poured straight down into her men's boots. Her too-tight jumper just covered her elbows, below which large hands brought everything and everybody surrounding her under her control, and often she caught me by the scruff of my neck to get me out of her way. The hair which inadequately covered her head defied restraint, sticking out like straw in a variety of colours induced by her habit of rinsing it regularly in cold tea.

Above all else Bridgie's teeth set her apart from ordinary mortals. Each tooth went its own way with no particular collective direction in mind, and the top row lacked any sense of togetherness at all. Her dental arrngements enabled Bridgie to accomplish something which would otherwise have been impossible: both a non-stop talker and a chain smoker, she was able to park a cigarette between two top teeth and continue talking without a break. There it remained smouldering away until Bridgie remembered it and it flared back into life again as she gave it a gigantic pull. Sometimes, however, she forgot the parked cigarette and lit another one: then we would dance around her shouting with delight, 'Bridgie, Bridgie, you've two chimneys smoking!' Her answer to this was to snort 'Shit!'

179

in frustration and fling the old butt into the fire. My mother forbade us to adopt Bridgie's rough vocabulary but she dared not try to curtail Bridgie's own colourful flow of words, for the vibrations of her wrath could shake the very foundations of the house.

Early on Monday morning the big twenty-gallon pot was hung over the fire and filled with water and by the time Bridgie arrived it was sending steam signals up the chimney. Seasonal weather variations had no effect on her outfit and the only concession she made to extreme cold was to don a pair of hand-knitted grey socks that she turned down over the tops of her black boots. She threw a well-worn tweed coat over her shoulders; as it fell short of the overall it afforded scant shelter, but she maintained that 'only the too thin and the too lazy feel the cold'.

On arrival she made a pot of black tea and had a fag before commencing operations, sorting out the clothes into different heaps. As she sorted she gave a running commentary on the clothes – though it could equally have been on their owners. Catching up a very dirty pair of pants she would exclaim, 'Ah, you dirty bastard!' and coming to the whites she might hold up a nightdress and declare 'You little strap: another wear would do you no harm'.

She would grasp one of the strong timber *súgán* chairs and slap it face downwards on its front legs with its top-wedged against the table and lift the big timber wash-tub on to its back. Sometimes she placed two chairs facing each other and put the tub on their laps. With a tin gallon she ladled steaming water from the black pot into an iron bucket which she carried across the kitchen and poured into the tub; then she added cold water which she drew in buckets from the stream at the end of the garden, where water ran through a pipe we called the spout. When she was satisfied that the temperature was right she put on her bag apron and set to work on the clothes. She caught up one of the bundles, threw it into the tub and rammed the clothes down under the water with the legs of the timber washboard. Not content merely to wash the clothes, she attacked them, banging them on to the ridged washboard and plastering them on to it with a large block of red or white carbolic soap; then she scrubbed each offending garment up and down with great ferocity. And while she worked she would talk, sing or curse, depending on her prevailing humour.

As she washed the clothes over the ridged surface of the washboard clouds of steam enveloped Bridgie and the glow of her cigarette was like a beacon in the misty kitchen. She squeezed the clothes by hand, rinsed and squeezed again. Meanwhile, the pot was kept full and boiling over the fire as tub after tub of washing was piled high on the table. Sheets and whites got an extra final rinse in blue, which came in a little round solid block in a muslin bag, to give them the blue-white look.

Wash-day took over the entire kitchen, filling it with a soapy, steamy smell. Sometimes some of the whites were boiled in the big black pot and as they were lifted out with the handle of a brush they sent steam billowing upwards and turned the kitchen into a danger-zone of fog from which Bridgie barred children and males alike, considering both species to lack sufficient intelligence to avoid being scalded alive. To us the kitchen at this point offered the delight of paddling around barefoot in the copious water on the floor but Bridgie always saw us off declaring, 'Get out of my way or I'll catch you by the hasp of your arse and hang you off the clothes-line with the washing'. Her knowledge of the human anatomy sometimes sent us off to our mother to enquire the meaning of new words, and my mother often had a hard time trying to come up with explanations.

When early summer came Bridgie found a use for us: we became the agitators and danced barefoot on the blankets when she gave them all a lukewarm tub wash. The heavy, pure wool Foxford and Dripsey blankets harboured many a flea in comfortable conditions until evil-smelling yellow Keating's powder put a stop to their jump. Bridgie traced the genealogy of the flea back to the fact that 'Adam had 'em', and she taught us a little verse which we chanted together as we danced up and down in her tub of warm, soapy blankets:

181

> Big fleas
> Have little fleas
> Upon their backs
> To bite them
> And little fleas
> Have littler fleas
> And so ad infinitum.

Summer washing was done out in the garden near the spout where there was a plentiful supply of cold water, and then it was the hot water that had to be drawn from the kitchen. Bridgie ordered us to keep away from the wash-tub when it was full of water, but we had a game we played in the tub when her back was turned which we called 'doggie sail away': we floated two bits of stick across the tub and the first stick to reach the other side was the winner. One day while Bridgie was in the kitchen my sister Clare and I leaned across the raised tub urging our contestants. Suddenly Clare lost her balance and went head first under the water, legs waving over the edge of the tub. I was so shocked that when I opened my mouth to scream no sound came out. I ran towards the kitchen, and when Bridgie saw my ashen face she made immediately for the tub, cursing and praying at the same time as she manoeuvered her considerable bulk as fast as she could down the garden. At the tub she quickly hauled out Clare who, after a certain amount of coughing and spluttering, soon recovered. For weeks after this episode Bridgie kept us at a safe distance from her tub and warned us, 'Don't come within a donkey's roar of me ye bloody little brats!'

In time she forgave us for the fright we have given her and allowed us back around her tub, where I could watch again the soapy bubbles and the delicate colours they made. Sometimes Bridgie gave us an enamel jug full of hot soapy water. Then we broke a bit of stick off an elder branch in the grove, scooped a hollow in the middle to make a bubble stick, and stood it into the jug and blew until we had a jug full of bubbles. We sat on the warm grass and blew the bubbles into the air, watching them float away in their gorgeous, transparent colours and dissolve into nothingness. Fascinated by colours, on one occasion I watched intently a wasp which had landed on the edge of the tub, his bright yellow stripes contrasting vividly with the dark brown timber of the rub. Unfortunately, I was not satisfied merely to watch but put out my finger to test if the wasp was real and he proved in no uncertain terms that he was.

Blankets washed, Bridgie turned her attention to the other parts of the beds. On top of the wire spring came the horsehair mattress and the tick filled with feathers and down from the farm pluckings. Both the mattresses and the ticks she threw out of the bedroom windows or down the stairs and then she draped them across the hedges in the garden to give them 'a good soak of sunshine'. She rounded up my father to get him to help her stretch wire springs; such maintenance was vital as sagging springs were bad for the back and might slip off the iron frame of the bed pitching the unwary sleeper head downwards and legs in the air.

The padded and multi-coloured patchwork quilts awoke a poetry in Bridgie's soul. She washed them with soap and water blended with tender appreciation for the hours of concentration that had gone into their creation. But it was the heavy lace bedspreads that brought out the best in her. These were not for ordinary sleepers but were reserved for honeymoons, childbirth and death, for the grandeur of lace was appropriate to grace all of the most important occasions in life. Bridgie turned the washing of one of these special bedspreads into an act of reverence: running her fingers gently over the intricate design she would talk softly to this family heirloom. 'What beauty! How many did you breed? How many did you born? How many did you bury? All life had passed beneath you from the beginning to the end.' Washing the bedspread she became a different person as her face lit up and filled with joy.

She rinsed the bedspread and squeezed it gently and then took it to the little meadow below the house where she spread it out on the young grass and wild flowers. The rest of the washing she pegged on the wire clothes line or spread across the hedges, but the lace bedspread got special treatment.

Finally she brought it in and folded it carefully, placing moth-balls between its creases, and laid it, wrapped in tissue paper, in the old trunk where my mother stored family treasures.

If the day's washing finished early Bridgie would draw buckets of warm soapy water from the wash-tub and scrub down the upstairs bedrooms. Then she emptied the timber tub on to the kitchen floor and scrubbed it out. From start to finish it was a heavy day's work but Bridgie was as full of bounce at the end as she had been at the beginning. She was never told what to do but worked at her own pace, treating our house and our washing as if they were her own.

When she had finished she had tea with my mother at the kitchen table where she aired all her family grievances. Her husband was in her opinion over-fond of his drink, and so she gave him 'a few belts' when she felt that he needed her to 'bate a bit of sense into him'. But the one great regret in her life was that, although she had four daughters, she had no son. As she sat after her hard day's work, swirling her tea around in her cup and puffing her fag, she would say, 'Four children, mis-sus, but not one little tassle in my house'. It was one of a num-ber of her phrases which confused me on first hearing, and to my mother fell the task of explaining it.

One thing that never changed about Bridgie was her fare-well to us children. As she went out the door she would call out to us, 'I'll be back, brats, on Monday; always on a Mon-day'.

Winter Journeys

The most awkward outdoor chores always seemed to arise on cold, snowy winter days, and few if any were more awkward than taking a turkey to the cock or a battery to town to be charged. The two batteries on which our large brown box radio relied bore little resemblance to their slimline descendants of today. For a start, one was dry, the other was wet and both were large and filled with acid. The radio itself sat on the base of the back window in the kitchen and, as the walls of the house were about three feet thick, the window-ledge had sufficient room for both the radio and, behind it, the two batteries, to which it was connected by leads with little brass claws that fitted under the black and red knobs on the tops of the batteries. Sometimes a green mould formed at the connection point and my father would scrape it away again. The dry battery lasted a long time but the wet one had to be charged more often, depending on how much the radio was used, and scarcely a day went by without one of us children being told, 'Turn off the radio and don't be wasting the batteries'.

One cold January day, after he had taken hay to the sheep down by the river, my father came in and, rubbing his hands together to improve the circulation, went straight to the radio, having as always arranged to finish his morning jobs in time to catch the news on either Radio Eireann or the BBC. But today Radio Eireann had been reduced by a fading battery to a whisper and the BBC was lost in the airwaves over the Irish sea. In summer batteries in need of recharging could be carried into town on the creamery cart, but in winter when the cows took their holidays the cart no longer made the journey, and so now I was dispatched to town.

Dressed in an extra layer of clothes I clutched the heavy glass battery with icy fingers. Some protection from the pressure of the handle was provided by a pair of furry mittens my godmother had sent from America, but nevertheless I shifted it frequently from one hand to the other to balance the wear and tear. Occasionally I rested, and where the snow was still on the ground I traced the bird- and rabbit-tracks that could be found along by the hedges. Animals that usually merged into the colours of the countryside now contrasted vividly with the snow, and my journey to town invariably took longer than necessary when there was so much along the way to side-track me.

Arriving in town I went straight to Jim's pub which, amongst its many other services, charged batteries. Midway in the long counter was a big brown cupboard where charging batteries fizzed and spluttered in harmony with the surrounding activities. Old men sat spitting and arguing around the fire, while on the high shelves bottles of amber liquid glinted richly in the firelight. If one of the customers recognized me I was called over and seated by the fire for a warm-up and treated to a glass of fizzy lemonade.

There was one old man, however, who had to be kept at a safe distance. He had earned the name 'Catch' on account of his tendency to grab at any female form from eight to eighty years of age which came within striking distance. He was a small man who flopped around inside an enormous pair of wellingtons that came up over his knees. He lurched from periods of absolute silence to bouts of frenzied conversation but, apart from the occasional grab at a passing female, he was harmless.

I loved the smell of the porter and whiskey and most of all the mixed tobacco smells off the old men who chewed on a varied assortment of clay, straight and giant turn-down pipes. Sometimes one of the old men in a burst of alcoholic exuberance would get up and do a little dance, to be told by one of his good companions that he had 'the makings of a great dancer' and by another that he should 'sit down and have a grain of sense'.

Finishing my lemonade and dodging 'Catch', I collected a fully charged battery in exchange for my run-down one and set out for home. On a lucky day a neighbour might come along in a horse and cart piled with bags of meal and flour. Having climbed up the spokes of the wheels I would clamber in over the sideboard and nestle down comfortably between the bags in the middle of the cart, while the battery was wedged firmly against the sideboard in case it leaked.

The drive shortened the journey home but I always called a halt in front of Mrs Casey's because we children simply never came home from town without calling to see her. She warmed many a cold winter's evening with a big bowl of steaming-hot bread-and-butter pudding, but most of all she warmed it with her welcome. She coaxed her huge, long-haired sheepdog, Bran, back from the fire to make way for me to get into the corner inside the belows where no draught could catch me. After the hot pudding she gave me sweet, strong tea and a boiled brown egg (she had no respect for white ones) from the red-combed hens which thronged her haggard. Fortified by her goodness I arrived home with the dark, and my father breathed freely again, saved from the awful prospect of a night without the radio.

The battery was carried to town by road, but taking the turkey to the cock was a cross-country marathon. Normally our turkey-cock made this journey unnecessary but one year the old boy decided that he needed a sabbatical. He paid a terrible price for his jaded sexual urges because my mother promptly pulled his neck and he became the following Sunday's dinner. This did not, however, solve the turkey-hen's problem: she wanted a turkey-cock and lay on the ground, wings fluffed out and neck stretched forward passively. 'The turkey is lying,' my mother said, and if our cock was in no condition to do the needful a couple of miles across the fields was one that could.

The turkey-hen was bundled into a coarse grey bag; the top was tied but a hole was made where she could put her head out for air, and my sister Clare and I set out with our captive companion. A live turkey in a bag makes an awkward parcel and we took it turns to carry her under our arms. With one arm firmly around her she was manageable but sometimes her legs got in the way and she dug her long claws into us. As we were leaving home my mother had advised us to keep her head out of the hole in the bag in case she might be stifled. The problem was, however, that when the turkey stretched out her long neck she was quite capable of testing your cheek or finger for flavour. Although she did it out of curiosity rather than aggression, her motivation did nothing to soften the peck, so as soon as we had home and my mother at a safe distance we shut the turkey's door to the outside world.

As we crossed the fields we discussed the complex question of sex and turkeys. The ground was covered with hard, frozen snow and when we came to a hilly field we skated down the icy slope. Abandoning the turkey with her head newly liberated and poking out of the bag we climbed back up the hill and skated down again and again, but when it started to snow we collected our turkey and moved on, once more shutting her door.

Entering the gap of a small field beside the wood, we saw under the total whiteness of the snow-draped trees a cock pheasant resplendent in his colourful coat of rich, vivid feathers. He was magnificent in his gorgeous plumage with his elegant neck stretched out questioningly at our intrusion into his domain. Accompanying him were two less colourful hens and then another cock came out from behind a clump of snow-covered bushes quite near us. They filled the little field with their presence and we stood holding our breath for fear we might frighten them away. Then Clare had a brainwave.

'Do you think,' she whispered, 'that if we let the turkey out of the bag the cock pheasants would solve the problem?'

But before we could try out her theory there was a sudden flutter of wings and they all disappeared into the wood.

The greatest obstacle to be overcome on our journey was the river but luckily the water was low and we wobbled over large crossing stones having first flung the turkey across to the opposite bank, where she landed with a loud squawk. We came to the top of the last hill and looked back along the valley. There, under the trees, striding along at his leisure, was a big tawney fox.

'That's the boy,' said Clare, 'that would solve all our turkey's problems.' We pulled her head out through the hole in the bag and directed her gaze towards the fox, who looked enquiringly across the river at us and then trotted off into the wood.

Finally we reached our destination and Mrs Cleary relieved us of our burden. As she saw to the turkey's needs we went into the warm kitchen where her daughter, who was about the same age as ourselves, gave us tea and buns she had just baked. As we had our tea Clare went to the back window of the kitchen, which overlooked the haggard, and gave us a running commentary on the turkey copulation outside. When Mrs Cleary was satisfied that all had been accomplished, our turkey was returned to us and we went home across the snow-covered fields, at a faster pace now as both the night and the snow were falling fast.

Capeen

Bill brought him late one winter's night, curled up asleep in his tweed cap. He was tiny: pure white with one black ear and a black stumpy tail, I had never seen a puppy so small. Reaching out a timid finger to test if he was real, I felt his downy puppy hair; then he opened one black eye flecked with gold and peered up at me. A tiny, petal-soft tongue curled around my finger. Then he stretched out full length in the comfort of Bill's cap but still he was not quite the length of it. Satisfied with his stretch, he sat up on his miniature hind legs and gave a cheeky little bark and I fell in love with him there and then. Bill handed him to me and he was mine, and I called him Capeen.

Numerous dogs rambled around the farmyard: greyhounds – five or six of them – and a couple of sheepdogs, and a black gun dog called Darkie who went fowling with my father. My mother had a golden rule that none of them were allowed in the house, but Capeen broke that rule on his very first night. He was too small, I maintained to go outside, and anyway the big dogs might attack him. He slept that night in a box of hay by the fire, where he was to remain for many nights, but when the weather got warmer in the summer I transferred him to a spare manger in the stable.

He was a beautiful little dog who never grew very big, but what he lacked in size he made up for in intelligence. He could do everything but talk, though in any case the two of us did not need conversation because we communicated perfectly without words. We went rambling together through the fields and he chased rabbits just for the fun of it because his legs were too short to catch them and even if he had he would have been more surprised than them. We had races up and down the meadows and when I buried him in hay he quickly burrowed out and cocked his perky little head sideways almost saying, 'You can't fool me, I'm too smart'.

When we children went swimming in the river Capeen came too and he loved coursing through the high rushes of the inches to dry himself after his swim. He ran home before us, his stubby black tail darting in and out around the thistles that grew in the wet fields by the river. He conveyed us towards school every morning but came no further than the crab-tree at the bottom of the first field, where he was waiting again every evening. In the mornings he looked sadly after us but in the evenings he went mad with delight at the sight of us. I scooped him up to hug him and he almost tore the hair off my head with his dancing paws and swept his moist tongue all over my face.

A great sense of adventure filled his heart and he loved investigating new places, which sometimes led him into corners from which he could not extricate himself. Once when peering curiously over the top of the deep lime-kiln he toppled in and my father had to put down the long hay-barn ladder to rescue him. On the way up the ladder my father scolded him for his stupidity but Capeen, who was always bubbling with fun, licked his face in thanksgiving and, as a final token of appreciation, knocked my father's cap off so that he had to go back down again to bring it up.

Capeen did not like the greyhounds and barked at them, teasing them to chase him; then he would run into some small corner which they could not fit into and from his safe bolt-hole he would growl out at them. Darkie, a gun dog trained to raise snipe and woodcock, was his friend and sometimes they went hunting together with my father. Capeen just went along for the fun of it but was smart enough to do exactly as he was told.

He and the cats waged continuous warfare; sometimes he chased them and sometimes they chased him, but one cat he never chased was old Minnie, because he had learnt the painful lesson that whenever she got her claws into action she would leave a mark. Some mornings he jumped into the creamery cart and went to the creamery with my father. He enjoyed the journey into town and sat imperiously on the setlock looking contemptuously down at the town dogs which snarled up at him. My father loved him because, as he said himself, he was 'a real smart little fellow'. But he was the bane of my mother's life and Bridgie threatened regularly to 'bate sense into him', because his one great weakness was for washing which was flapping in the breeze; sheets waving above his head provided sweet temptation which he could never resist. He swung back and forth on the washing until Bridgie, who was ever on the look out for him, brought him down to earth with a fine hard slap across the tail. He would then scamper off and hide under a bush at the bottom of the garden with only his nose in view, while he waited until such time as he judged it safe to make a comeback.

He broke all the rules of the house and got away with it. Some cold nights I sneaked him upstairs and he slept at the foot of my bed. When I estimated that my mother was about to come to say goodnight I covered him with a pillow and, smart fellow that he was, he never gave the game away. When we sat at the table for meals on a long stool that seated a row of us, Capeen sometimes lined up with the rest of us. When Bridgie saw this she would roll her eyes to heaven and declare, 'Glory be to God, where will I see that dog next? I know where I'll see him: kneeling on top of the altar-rails with his tongue out waiting to receive – there's nothing beyond that fellow. Ye should take him to school because he is wasting his time around here.'

One summer evening no Capeen waited at the crab-tree as I returned from school. We were puzzled but not unduly alarmed. It was a Monday, so he could have been under his bush doing penance; or he could have gone hunting with Darkie, as sometimes they went off on their own. However, on investigation we found that he was not under his bush and Darkie was lying by the front door, so after a hurried dinner we began to search the hay barn, the stables, the stalls, but there was no trace of him. We went out into the fields and called but no answering bark came. The search went on for hours and after the cows had been milked the adults joined in and even Bridgie, her bag apron wrapped around her head, helped in the search.

That night when I said the rosary I begged God to mind Capeen because I did not like the idea of him being alone in the dark wherever he was. I went to bed with a heavy heart but deep down hope still flickered. I tried not to cry because that would have been to give in and abandon hope, and that was too terrible to think about. But when I moved my leg under the spot where Capeen sometimes sneaked in to sleep it was hard to hold back the tears.

When I woke the next morning it took a few seconds for the previous evenings' happenings to flood back to me. I jumped out of bed hoping to see that he was running around in the yard, but only Darkie was out there, sleeping in their usual corner. That day in school passed like a nightmare, and coming home that evening and arriving at the crab-tree to find no Capeen dancing in delight was worse. My father was waiting for me at the gate.

'We found him,' he called, and for a second my heart was bursting with joy. 'He's dead,' he said simply. 'He got caught under the gate in the bottom meadow and the gate must have slipped and killed him.'

I could not believe it; it was just too much to take in. How could such a stupid thing have happened? There was a pain inside me and a hard lump in my throat and I squeezed my eyes to blink back the tears.

'Where is he?' I whispered.

'He's in his manger,' Dad said.

He lay stretched out cold and rigid on the hay with blood at the corner of his mouth. My tears ran down on top of him.

That evening we dug his grave in the animal graveyard under the old apple-tree at the bottom of the orchard, and Darkie and Minnie came with us. I hated Darkie then because he was alive and Capeen was dead and I felt that in some way he should have looked after Capeen better. I blamed myself, too, for not having found him the night before when perhaps he had still been alive.

We lined a timber apple box with one of Bridgie's torn sheets and placed him in it; in death he seemed bigger than he had been alive. We eased his coffin down into the ground and covered him with soft brown earth. The apple-tree stood at the head of the grave with leafy arms outstretched in the shape of a cross. On its bark with hammer and chisel we carved his epitaph in letters as large as the trunk could accommodate: GOOD BYE CAPEEN.

If Ever A Man Suffered

Licences were required for dogs, bulls and guns, yet my fathers' cut-throat razor was covered by no such permit and lay in a harmless-looking slim black box on top of the tall press in the kitchen. It had a six inch long, paper-thin blade that curved off at one end and hooked into a white bone handle at the other, and it folded back into this handle when not in use.

Every Sunday morning after breakfast my father reached up to the top of the high press, took down the black box and placed it on the ledge inside the window. The front window of our kitchen was set in a recess with a deep ledge running all around it, and this was the altar of his weekly shaving ritual. He transferred a black leather strap from the side of the press to a rusty hook beneath the window-ledge before demanding, 'Where's my shaving mug?' It was always in the same place, on the top shelf of the press beside the big meat-dish, but it seemed he could never find it without being told. Inside the mug was shaving soap and a soft bristle brush in a bone base.

Having lined up his equipment on the ledge he lifted down a small mirror that hung beside the clock and asked, 'Is that bloody kettle boiling yet?' The kettle was, of course, always boiling at this point in his preparations, but because he could never fill the shaving mug without the kettle spout overshooting the top of the mug and causing him to be blinded in a shower of ashes when the water hit the fire, my mother intervened and placed the mug of boiling water on the ledge with the rest of his accoutrements where it promptly fogged up the mirror.

'How the blazes can I shave when I can't even see my cursed

195

face?' he said in eloquent thanks for her help.

Off came his cap and coat and, reduced to his striped shirt and waistcoat, he pulled a creaking *súgán* chair up in front of the window and commenced the operation. His cap hung off one corner of the back of the chair and over the other corner my mother placed a small towel. The biggest towel in the house she spread across his knees. He reached down for the leather strap and, finding himself too close to the window, he jolted the *súgán* backwards, knocking his cap on to the floor. He then stretched the strap to its full length and moistened it with a thumb dipped in the bowl of water; if the water was too hot he spat on the leather instead. When he judged the strap to be just right he opened the black box and unfolded the cut-throat. Catching it by its delicate bone handle he lightly flicked it up and down the ebony strap; the silver blade of the razor gave a soft, swishing, sensuous hiss as it glinted in the morning light.

To judge whether the blade had reached the necessary sharpness he required a hair, with which his own head could not oblige him as he was completely bald. So I dangled in front of him a long, light hair which I had eased from the top of my head and he lanced it with the razor, which was then pronounced ready for action. He dipped the bristle brush into the mug of warm water and sloshed its dripping head across the shaving soap. When he had worked up a fine white lather he brushed it all over the lower half of his face. This gave him a benevolent, Santa-Claus appearance but there the similarity ended because this Santa was volcanic and started to erupt as soon as he applied the razor to his face.

The razor took on the character of a deadly enemy as it moved across his chin, bringing lather and hair before it and and blood behind. He waved it in the air, viewed his ravaged visage in the foggy mirror and swore at it, 'You bloody bastard, are you trying to kill me?' A battle of sorts ensued and as my father's temper worsened so the razor became blunter and the floor around him disappeared under dollops of white shaving lather streaked with blood and speckled with hair. The towel that my mother had hung on the back of his chair to absorb this residue was long forgotten. After each fresh onslaught he ran his fingers along the blade and swished the lather on to the floor. Gradually his face emerged, pink and tender with bloody nicks which he patched with bits of newspaper.

Shaving and first aid completed, he folded up his razor carefully and wrapped it in its faded yellow tissue-paper before returning it to its box. The performance was over for another week but the leading man had no intention of cleaning the stage. Retrieving his cap from the snowy floor he went upstairs to get ready for Mass, leaving that end of the kitchen in a chaos of shaving soap, water, towels and bits of discarded newspaper.

Once and once only my sister Clare and I were foolish enough to disrupt his shaving routine. It was the first Christmas at which we had a really good-sized Christmas tree and we had acquired tinsel for it from the Miss Bowlers' shop and stood it into the window recess in a butter box filled with stones. That Christmas morning, coming home from early Mass, we were met by a strange sight. My father was pinned against the window with the Christmas tree on his back and tinsel hanging off his ears. In shifting it out of his way to give himself room he had unsettled the tree's temporary rooting system, and in the middle of his shaving session it had tilted forward on top of him, balloons bursting and the Christmas fairy taking a nosedive from the top into his shaving mug. When we ran to his rescue we were met with a stream of language which was hardly in keeping with the season of goodwill.

'Take that hoor's melt of a Christmas tree off my back.' he yelled.

We dragged the heavy, stone-filled box back and manoeuvered the tree into an upright position, thereby releasing him. But then we had to strip him of decorations which, in addition to tinsel, included a substance called angels' hair, which was meant to cover the tree in a shimmering flow but which was not to be touched once it was in position. And there and then we discovered why not. It had wrapped itself around my father to such an extent that the only way we could remove it was by unwinding it gently and methodically, but that proved impossible because he was dancing around the kitchen in a fit of jumping rage. Finally he tore upstairs, whipped off all his clothes and flung them down with instructions to 'Get that bloody muck off them'.

Whenever he recalled that episode afterwards he would raise his eyes to heaven and sigh, 'If ever a man suffered'.

Too Hot To Handle

Every Saturday evening the big old arm-chair just inside our parlour door was piled high with freshly washed clothes; not folded neatly but thrown there in big bundles which smelt of cool grass and fresh air. The clothes had been draped across bushes and hedges to dry, the sheets spread out on the green fields, and all came in smelling of wild flowers and the world outside, while some occasionally sported the evidence of a bird's blessing. By evening time the pyramid of clothes had reached the point of toppling over and my hour of reckoning had come.

I hated, abhorred and detested ironing. In our kitchen were two tables, one very large and the other of medium size; on this second table my mother baked and on Saturday it became the ironing-board. It was covered with an old, threadbare woollen blanket which was yellow with age, had three blue stripes at either end and was christened the ironing-blanket. Over it went two or three patched and holed sheets which had passed beyond further repair, and the aim was to get the holes of one to coincide with the sound parts of another.

The iron itself was hollow and made of iron with upright iron arms at both front and back which were bridged with a timber handle. Narrow at the front, it broadened towards the back where an opening was covered by a little door that slid up and down like a guillotine, and through this aperture heaters were slipped into the iron. These were the same shape as the iron and were made of pure, solid metal; they had been placed in the middle of the fire and left there until they had become so red hot that they were indistinguishable from the red sods of turf around them. It was torture to me to have to catch one of the heaters with log iron tongs and manoeuvre it into the opening in the iron. Any tilt in the wrong direction could have drastic consequences as I held the iron firmly in my left hand while the red-hot heater wobbled dangerously at the end of the tongs in my right.

Heater in and door closed, the iron was ready for action but at this point it was what my father aptly termed a 'burning bastard'. With no such thing as a control knob you could learn to match iron-heat to material only by trial and error. And what agonies I went through in those trials and errors! The ironing-sheets were the most immediate victims and quickly took on an auburn appearance. The tails of my father's shirts bore the evidence of many errors of judgement, for my mother always advocated testing the iron on shirt-tails first. Long, swallow-tailed and ample, the shirt-tails of the time were worn safely buried in the cavernous depths of trousers held up by braces. Even if one of the buttons which secured the braces popped, it was swiftly replaced by a nail, so there was never any chance of the shirt-tails making a public appearance and displaying iron-shaped scorches. Nevertheless, my father rained showers of curses on the offending iron whenever he was presented with yet another burnt offering.

The iron was a constant source of torment to me, and one of the problems it presented was that it could deposit soot and ashes on whatever you ironed if you did not take care when transferring the heater into it. A dirty iron placed on a damp, white table-cloth left an ashy or sooty mark buried deep in the fabric. Another common hazard was, of course, scorched fingers or wrists; the arms of the handle heated up as well, so the whole contraption radiated heat. As the heat of the iron cooled, seeming by this time to have transferred itself into my face and temper, it became comfortable enough to hold, but that meant that it was no longer warm enough to be effective so its companion was brought forth from the flames and the fiery agony was repeated.

Sheets, pillow-cases and table-cloths had all to be ironed, as well as everything we wore, so the ironing was no small job. Some of the dresses were starched, and the collars of the men's shirts were starched cardboard-stiff. If too dry, starched items were impossible to iron; if too wet, the iron clung to the damp starch. One of our neighbours, the redoubtable Mrs Casey, was an expert at starching and her husband's shirt-collar with its pristine white rigidity was always a source of wonder to me. Old Dan paid homage to this skill with a saying he had to describe a woman of exceptional efficiency: 'Jakus me, she'd starch the tail of your shirt!'

The Burial Bonnet

No one loved hardship like Bessie-Babe. She preferred other people's hardship but if none was available she could always be relied upon to come up with some of her own. The way Dan put it was that she had never heard of the resurrection because she had got stuck at the crucifixion, and she was the only person he knew who would have enjoyed the agony in the garden. She was an enthusiastic and appreciative attender at every funeral in the parish, and whenever we saw her wearing her special burial bonnet we knew that someone was either dead or on their last legs. Standing at the graveside she could turn on tears like a waterfall and for months afterwards if she met the mourners she liked nothing so much as to join them in a good cry. Indeed, she became a by-word in our house: if anyone cried over something and my father felt they were overdoing it he would say, 'Don't be doing Bessie-Babe on it'.

Once she fell seriously ill and it was agreed amongst the neighbours that hers could be the next funeral, but when another neighbour died the prospect of attending a funeral soon lifted her out of her sick-bed. As she stood at the graveside watching the coffin being lowered she remarked with a sob to Dan, who happened to be standing beside her, that she supposed she'd be next.

'That's what they're all saying anyway,' he assured her.

Bessie-Babe had a farm back the valley and sometimes Dan worked with her but declared that he could not stay too long or he would die from hunger. She was a widow woman and Dan firmly believed that she had starved her husband to death.

'That woman,' he would say, 'was born in a grumbling month and is the manest woman who ever wore shoe leather; as a matter of fact, she is the tightest and most miserable strap under the canopy of heaven, and that's a wide territory.'

Another of Dan's pronouncements about her was that she was 'too clane to be dacent', and her house was indeed spotless. 'A place for everything and everything in its place' was her motto, and whenever I was in her house I was always afraid to sit down in case I would upset something. She believed so strongly in keeping everying in its place that she would not allow Dan into her own kitchen but fed him in the scullery where she kept her pots and pans. We were not sure whether she did this out of an over-enthusiastic concern for hygiene, which she certainly possessed, or notions of grandeur. She undoubtedly considered herself a touch smarter than the rest of us, and Mrs Casey used to say of her, 'That one has high ideas, like Taylor's gander when he gets on top of the dunghill'.

Always looking for bargains, she kept the shopkeepers in town on their toes. Indeed, if Ned wanted to recommend something as representing great value he would say, 'Bessie-Babe bought this'. She bought, in fact, very little, being a devotee of patching patches and darning darns. She took large baskets of eggs into town where she bargained with the shopkeepers to get the best possible price for them. If she succeeded in extracting a high price then she would buy the neighbours' eggs at the old, lower price and resell them to the shop. Rabbits could also be sold to shops, and young fellows would often be seen cycling into town with rows of them hanging off the crossbars of their bikes. The rabbits provided them with good pocket-money but Bessie-Babe moved in on their territory for if there was money to be made she wanted to be in on it, and she became the only woman around who dealt in rabbits.

Every conversation with her opened with the same words: 'Whisper here a minute', and then she would deliver herself of an endless litany of complaints. My father dreaded an encounter with her and would run a mile to avoid it; he used to say that she put years on him. One day, after having been cornered by her for a long session, he came in home and threw himself into the chair, quite exhausted.

'That woman,' he declared, 'is like a waxy hen's shit: there's no getting rid of her, she just clings on.'

At a ripe old age she finally died and, having enjoyed burying so many, it was only right that she had a huge funeral herself. Dan was there, of course, and delivered the opinion that her burial bonnet should have been placed on top of her coffin like a soldier's cap.

Anyone For Pandy?

My mother boiled a big, black pot of potatoes for the dinner every day except Sunday. Whether there were to be ten or twenty for the dinner, the same big pot was hung over the fire; the dangling pot-hangers were threaded through its ears while flames licked around its black bottom. A tin bucketful of purple potatoes was then poured in, thumping off the bottom and sides before being packed down under the iron cover. These spuds came straight from the bosom of mother earth and there was no need to limit the supply as there were plenty more where they came from. Another reason why so many went into the pot was because hungry spud-consumers came in five successive categories: human beings, cats, dogs, fowl and pigs. We, as befitted the supposedly most civilized of the five species, got the first bite.

The flowery spuds were judged ready for removal when they started to smile across the top of the pot. A huge ware dish, reminiscent of a feast Henry VIII might have held, was then placed in the centre of the kitchen table and potatoes were poured into it until there was a mountain of them. Smaller, younger members of the household facing each other across the table had to wait for the mountain to be demolished before they could gain sight of each other again. As the potato mountain diminished small hills of skins arose, until all were satisfied.

Jacket potatoes were the order of the day, but occasionally the luxury of pandy came our way. You were not judged worthy of pandy unless you were very young, very ill or 'feeling delicate', as my father termed the state of being out of harmony with the world. Today pandy might be called mashed potato by the unenlightened, but it was not quite the same thing.

Pandy first required a big, soft, flowery spud with a long smile across its face. Starting at the smile, the skin was eased off gently and the naked spud, almost too hot to handle, was transferred fast by hand into another plate, leaving its clothes in a heap behind it. Next a lump of yellow butter was placed on top, from where it ran in little yellow streams down the sides. A gentle little poke with a fork opened up a cavity into which went a drop of milk or a spoon of cream skimmed off the top of the bucket, followed by a shake of salt. Finally, the entire slushy combination was lightly whipped together and frequently tasted to ascertain that the correct balance was being achieved. It took great care and a discerning palate to make really good pandy; it had to be yellow, soft, delicately flavoured, and as light as thistledown on the tongue. When you were sick or not feeling happy you judged how much yor mother and the world loved you by the quality of her pandy. It was our antibiotic, our tranquilizer and our sleeping potion.

The royal spud ruled in the kitchen, but the king was also democratic, for he came down a step from the kitchen table into the dogs' bucket, where he was joined by surplus cabbage and turnips – the regular vegetables on our unvaried menu – and bits of bacon which were too fat or grizzly for us to eat. The various leftovers were hand-mixed to a gooey mess with the aid of vegetable water and fed in disused churn covers or rusty pans to a motley collection of cats and dogs. The dogs got the first round, starting with the biggest because all dogs, like most humans, believe in the survival of the fittest. When the little dogs had finished the cats came into their own, daintily licking around the edges and picking up delicate morsels that the slashing dogs' tongues had missed. Any leftover pandy was saved for the cats as they were considered discerning enough in their tastes to appreciate it. The pandy was placed in a saucer and surrouded by a river of milk, so the cats had eating and drinking in it.

The fowl tucked in next and the leftover potatoes with their jackets still on them were hand-mashed, oozing stickily between bruising fingers which crushed them out through their skins. This was then mixed with crushed oats and produced a grainy, substantial meal which the hens gobbled down appreciatively. The remaining pandy was reserved for the chickens whose taste-buds and beaks had not yet been coarsened by the pickings of the great outdoors; they pecked timidly at the fluffy pandy, its delicate consistency ideal for their baby stomachs. The tiny young chicks and the pandy blended together in a soft yellow colour combination.

Pigs provided the final destination of the potatoes. In the centre of their house was a circular iron trough, its base curled up saucer-like, with iron dividers to keep hungry heads apart and prevent bad manners in the trough. All surviving leftovers from the kitchen table were indiscriminately dumped in here, where they were wolfed down with total disregard for either flavour or finesse. Pigs were certainly not numbered amongst the connoisseurs of pandy, which provided comfort and sustenance to delicate humans, cats and, especially, the female of the species.

Molly's Cottage

On Tuesday evenings we cleaned the eggs with damp cloths and bread soda, and the following morning we took a big basket of them down to Molly's, because Wednesday was the day the egg-lorry came to her cottage. I always looked forward avidly to what was for me one of the highlights of the week: the visit to Molly's cottage.

There was no gate between the road and her garden, only a gap in the mossy ditch which in the spring was covered with daffodils and in the summer was smothered with buttercups. Despite her goat's best efforts to devour everything in sight, Molly's flowers tumbled and climbed over the low stony ditch that surrounded her cobbled yard. The orange shafts of her donkey cart in the open shed contrasted with the black rick of turf. Often there was a bicycle or two in the shed which had been left by neighbours because behind Molly's cottage was a hill road which was easier to walk up without the encumbrance of a bike.

When we visited her on Wednesday mornings I always ran ahead as soon as her thatched roof came into view in order to get a few extra minutes to peer in over her half-door. The stillness of the shadowy kitchen reached out to me over the half-door and never failed to intrigue me. At first I could see nothing but the glow of the turf fire; I could smell the fire's peaty fragrance, and I could hear the ticking of her clock and the clicking of her knitting needles. But gradually my eyes adjusted to the dimness and the dark objects inside came into focus.

Directly opposite the door her dresser displayed all Molly's ware, and I was familiar with every item. Blue saucers stood proudly on the top shelf, matching bread-plates beneath, and cups hung off the hooks on the edge of each shelf. Below them were her dinner plates and, at the base, her big meat-dishes. At the corner of one of the shelves was a special set of ware which she never used. Her mother had given it to her as a wedding present, having received it from her own mother. The cups were paper-thin china with pale pink roses and the whole set was Molly's pride and joy. It was seldom taken down but sometimes she allowed me to hold a cup just to feel how delicate and beautiful it was. In the open section at the bottom were stacked her kettles and pots.

She had a wonderful pair of hands that embroidered, knitted and sewed, but most beautiful of all was her lace. It covered a little table under the small, deep-set window and on the table was a brass lamp, her spare glasses, and whatever she happened to be working on at the time. The shelf over the fire which she called the 'clevy' had a lace runner over an edged oilcloth; a pair of glass dogs sat there beside her clock, in front of which I used to sit waiting for its lovely, mellow chime. Every chair in the room was softened with plump feather cushions in embroidered and lace covers.

Much of her time she spent sitting beside her glowing turf fire, always busy with her hands, the clicking of needles often the only sound apart from the ticking of the clock and the clucking of the hens outside. A knitted shawl curved around her shoulders, and over her long, black, satin skirt a white, lace-edged apron rested when she was sewing. Peeping from beneath her long skirt her kid-leather shoes glinted in the fire-light; a small, dainty figure, she seemed almost like a doll and was the first adult whom I was tall enough to look down on.

She was always delighted to see us and when she wrapped her arms around us in welcome she was as soft as a ball of her own knitting wool and smelt of lavender. As soon as she had us seated by the fire she hung the kettle over it; nobody ever called to her without getting a cup of tea coloured with rich goat's milk and a slice of the delicious cream-cake which she baked in a very small bastable.

Molly was the same age as my grandmother but I never

thought of her as old, only as kind and rather frail. Her face was wrinkled with smiles and her brown eyes twinkled with humour. The biggest treat she could give me was to let me into her bedroom where her lacemaking really came into its own, edging the pillow-cases and draping down over the bed in the most gorgeous bedspread. Her dressing-table, chest of drawers and window-sill all had lace cloths, and on a whatnot in the corner lace cloths peeped over the edge of the little shelves on which family photographs stood in silver frames. Beside the bedroom fireplace was a clock with weights and chains and if the weights were far enough down she would allow me to pull the chains.

It was an entirely feminine house lacking any trace of male influence. As a young girl Molly had spent many years in America where she had married a man 'with wanderlust in his legs', as she said herself. When she had returned to the home cottage he had stayed there with her for a few months but soon became restless and set off on his travels again, coming and going several times but never remaining long. And then one day she had received a telegram informing her that he had been killed in an accident. She brought him home and buried him in the graveyard overlooking the river. One day she gave me a present of a little white china jug with a gold rim, saying 'Pray that my wanderer is at peace'. I took her at her word: I called it my praying jug and kept holy water in it.

I often thought that heaven could well be Molly's cottage on a larger scale. One evening my father called to visit her and found her asleep in her chair, as it seemed; Molly had left her cottage and had gone, undoubtedly, to the real heaven. When next I entered the house, for once I did not pause at the half-door but went instead directly through the kitchen to her bedroom where she had been laid out in her lovely bed of lace with her crochet shawl around her shoulders. All her clocks had stopped and I thought that my heart would break, knowing that I would never again sit with her waiting for them to chime.

The Second Step

I left the old stone school across the fields and moved on to the local secondary school in the nearby town; I left my childhood behind and stepped into adolescence. My new school was three miles from the main road entrance to our farm, and our house was almost another half-mile back from the road. Every morning we walked to school, leaving the house at about half past eight, and every evening we started the return journey at about four, arriving home at around five. In the half-light of winter mornings we dragged ourselves out of bed and gathered together some kind of packed lunch while eating our breakfast. There was no question of my mother preparing lunches as she was already out milking the cows, so self reliance came early to us.

I was definitely not a morning person and it took the three and more miles into school to bring me gradually into touch with the world around me. As we walked down the road we drove the cows of one of the neighbouring farmers back to the fields after milking. When we reached a field further down the road they turned in at a gap, and sometimes I was so far removed from reality that I drifted in amongst them. Occasionally, a slash of a tail across my face shocked me into sudden wakefulness and I came to my senses only to find that I was wedged between two large, round-bellied cows and it would take a good thump on the rump of one of them to open the trap I had entered.

Horses and carts with tall milk churns trundled by and sometimes, if we were few in number, might give us a spin. If we got a lift on a cold winter's morning we could warm ourselves then against the warm milk churns, standing between them or sitting on top. If, however, the cart jolted going over a stone or because the horses suddenly quickened at a slap of the reins, this could bring a spray of milk out from under the churn covers, resulting in a warm footbath. Or, if you were sitting in comfort on a piece of hay or a coarse bag on the setlock, you could enjoy the doubtful privilege of receiving this shower of milk down the back of your neck. By evening, in summer at least, the milk would have dried to a tacky and uncomfortable consistency and would be exuding a strong sour smell, causing others to do their best to avoid you.

When there was a pig market in town we drove the pigs before us on the way to school. But on arrival at the edge of the town we abandoned them to the adult in charge as we felt it beneath our dignity to be seen chasing pigs along the streets. Thick-skinned, stubborn animals, the pigs often created chaos by paying unwelcome visits through open shop-doors. Their baby bonhams were brought to market in a pony crib where they squealed in protest when jobbers poked amongst them testing their potential for developing into grade A bacon. The pig market filled the early morning air of the town with grunts and squeals and perfumed it with pungent farm smells. As the bonhams were confined to cribs and the sows were usually restrained by reins, only a small number of pigs actually ran around disrupting the normal life of the town, but even these few could make a mighty contribution to the general mayhem.

The fair days when calves and cows poured into the town created real havoc. On our way to school we would meet jobbers out on the road waiting to catch an unwary farmer and secure a bargain. These jobbers, wily operators who were well versed in the skills of bargaining and who moved from fair to fair trading livestock, were different in their appearance from farmers; they always seemed to wear fawn overcoats and brown leather boots, they generally had slick, suave appearances, and they were smooth talkers. Bargaining could go on all day with much toing and froing, and often a middle-man called a tangler clinched the deal and took his own reward from it.

I would watch the varieties of men at the fair as they struck the poses that seemed an essential part of their business, never quite getting used to their habit of spitting on to their hand before offering it for the final handshake to seal their agreement. Despite all the spitting and handshakes, arguments about luck money usually ensued; the man who had sold was expected to return some token amount to the buyer to give him luck with the animal, but this luck money could often be the cause of another protracted argument. The entire bargaining session, which often lasted many hours, was an exercise in debating skill, oratory and one-upmanship, all occasioned by the simple necessity of selling a cow. The grand finale of the whole performance could take place in the middle of an admiring circle of onlookers, all of whom felt free to voice their own opinions on the deal. Sometimes hidden within the ranks of the onlookers might be a 'puffer', whose function it was to raise the price despite having no intention of buying.

The best of all the fairs was the horsefair which took place only twice a year, in spring and autumn, and at which the amounts of money involved were much greater. Most farmers had two horses, and sometimes a pony for doing handy jobs like going to the creamery; donkeys, too, were very plentiful. All the farmers from the surrounding countryside came into town and were joined there by hordes of tinkers from all over the country who brought colour and excitement with them. Often, after many hours of drinking, they would finish off the day with a big fight, either between themselves or by taking on a few locals who were brave enough or, more likely, drunk enough to get involved. Sometimes a fight that had started between a tinker man and his wife could gather momentum and participants as it went on, and then the women would be likely to turn and throw in their lot with their men folk. Sometimes, too, those who had started as opponents could join forces against locals who had perhaps gone to the assistance of one of them who had seemed to be losing the battle.

All in all the horse fair was an occasion of much commotion in the town when hard bargaining and great drinking combined as old friends put the world to rights over big, frothy pints. Sawdust and straw was thrown on the pub floors to absorb the muck coming in on the farmers' boots. At one of these fairs my father met an old friend down from the hills and they went for a pint where the old man smoked a pipe and spat continuously into the sawdust. The lady of the house was fussier than most and viewed old Jack with growing contempt until finally she brought from behind the counter a large spit-toon, an item designed for such occasions and the likes of Jack. But Jack had never before seen a spittoon, and so ignored it completely and continued to spit on the floor, though she moved it around many times trying to place it in the most stra-tegic position to serve its purpose. Finally old Jack, in a fit of annoyance at her antics, shouted at her, 'Woman, if you don't take that blasted thing out of my way I'll spit into it!'

At the end of the town was Kate Brady's doss-house, where anybody who had no bed to go to, or who was unable to make it back to his home, found refuge. Kate had one enormous room with a wooden floor free of the clutter of furniture. She had a stick of white chalk with which she drew out each per-son's allotment, and she maintained law and order with a blackthorn crop. On a quiet night sleeping space was ample and guests could stretch out in comfort, but when times were busy things tightened up as the night progressed.

Our journey to and from the local secondary school helped us absorb many aspects of the life of the town. The school had been set up by a young graduate whose father had taught in our old national school in the fields. He and his wife and sister rented an old house and two rooms in a local hall. These two buildings – their house and the school – were around the corner from each other and there was much running back and forth past the Catholic church, which stood on the corner. Usually we had about four teachers and our number must have been around a hundred, so we all knew each other pretty well.

Academic achievement was not high on our list of priorities and, though the teachers applied as much pressure as they thought necessary, I never regarded exams as something to get excited about. For some strange reason I enjoyed doing them and felt that I could always do better when there was just the challenge of the paper and myself. My father was not greatly interested in examination results, and that took pressure off us. There was one boy in our class who had a father who was very anxious that he do well and I felt quite sympathetic towards him as not only had he the exam to contend with but a father looking over his shoulder as well.

We covered all the usual subjects, but Latin and Maths were my two heartbreakers. 'Mensa' and 'agricola' had no magic for me and I got thoroughly fed up translating Virgil back and forth. As for algebra and the mystery of how A plus B equalled C, it was like the Blessed Trinity to me and beyond human comprehension. I came to the conclusion that when God had created my brain he had omitted the mathematical department, and the only interest I ever had in Einstein was when I heard that he, too, had found school difficult. True or not, it at least brought a human dimension to him.

English was my special love and I was fortunate enough to have a teacher blessed with both brilliance and impatience; her love of English and her striving for perfection triggered her annoyance at the struggle she encountered in trying to drag us to some kind of literary heights. She put everything she possessed into teaching, but it was not until years later that any of us appreciated her efforts.

Christian Doctrine was the subject of a novel approach, in which one teacher brought a dozen songbooks into class and for half an hour every day we raised the roof with a mixture of rebel songs and hymns. Whatever about the religious content of the class we certainly associated it with zest and enjoyment.

Our school being so convenient to the church, we were roped in to contribute long Latin chants whenever there was a High Mass for the dead. We made an enthusiastic group of mourners in our enjoyment at the thought of the classes we were missing. On 2 November we did rounds for the Holy Souls, a custom which consisted of going into the church, saying a prescribed number of prayers, coming out and going back in again to repeat the performance. Our religious fervour increased as lunch-hour extended into school-time, and we hailed souls out of purgatory by the dozen. My father was always very sceptical about these rounds: when I came home from school and announced to him that I had so many rounds under my belt, he would give a wry smile at what he called 'the whole crazy carry-on'.

However, I had great faith in the power of novenas and prayer, and exam time was when I sought divine intervention most intensely. I had a novena for each subject, and St Patrick was the man in charge of Latin; someone had informed me that he had found Latin very difficult and had promised to help anyone with similar difficulties. My prayers were not motivated by any ambition to become a Latin scholar, but the idea of a silent army of saints waiting to be called into action appealed greatly to me. So, St Patrick was appointed Dean of Languages and in the event he came up trumps.

'Alice Taylor,' my teacher asked, 'how did you get honours in Latin? There must be some mistake.'

But there was no mistake and it did not surprise me one bit, because my mother had always believed that prayer could move mountains, not to mind conquering Virgil.

The supervisor for our Inter Cert exam, which was conducted in the local dance-hall, was an old dragon who had me terrified but who failed to intimidate one of the boys sitting next to me. As the exam progressed he constantly checked his facts from a book which he drew from inside his coat. When I challenged him outside about the risk he was taking he just laughed and said, 'Sure, I didn't give a damn whether she caught me or not'.

The last subject in the exam was drawing from natural form. A more lenient supervisor would have told us the subject matter beforehand, but our dragon remained tight-lipped. She had reckoned, however, without the resourcefulness of my cool copying friend. He went into the garage underneath the hall and persuaded one of the mechanics to reverse a car under the trap-door in the floor. Standing on top of the car he was able to get into the hall through the trap-door and he reappeared moments later with the news that a wall-flower standing in a vase was all set up for the next sitting. At that stage the knowledge was unlikely to benefit us but we did feel a delightful sense of victory over our rigid lady supervisor.

Half-way through my secondary education a new school was acquired when an old Church of Ireland church became available. This was divided up into classrooms and for the first time we were all accommodated under one roof. Here the partition walls reached a height of only about twelve feet – far short of the ceiling – so the hum from the other classes could be heard in each classroom; we were able to gauge the tempers of all the teachers from the tones coming over the partition. Oak rafters arched high above our heads and sunken windows in thick, ancient walls gave the church a special atmosphere. Our nearest neighbours were the Protestants, including Sarah Curran, who had worshipped here and who now rested eternally beneath the trees beside the church. While they might have regarded learning as a suitable replacement for praying, they must surely have turned in their graves at the din created by scores of boisterous youngsters now stampeding around their once quiet and hallowed corner.

For five years we walked the hilly road into secondary school, carrying our books in sacks on our backs or by hand in cases, and we got to know the people in the houses along the way. In the main street of the town was a little bakery where fresh doughnuts were baked every Thursday and the smell, which met us as we came down the street, set our mouths watering. Later, on a winter's evening we might sink our teeth into warm sugary doughnuts, and the eating of them shortened our journey.

When we arrived home one of us would dish up the dinner my mother had left warming by the fire and another would light the tilly heater to heat the large upstairs bedroom set aside for study. After dinner we tidied up and lit the tall tilly lamp which stood on the dressing-table in the study bedroom. In the light from the lamp the brass knobs of the two iron beds glinted in the corner of the room. The table at which we laboured wobbled and groaned with books, and often its wood-worm tracks developed many and varied expressions as idle pencils investigated hidden tunnels rather than explore the books on its surface.

We studied here until supper-time at about seven o'clock taking it in turns to go down and set the table and have things ready for the adults when they came in from milking the cows. And then, for the first time in the day, we all came together and discussed over supper the day's happenings. Afterwards we returned upstairs, though occasionally a good programme on the radio might draw our attention, and usually we finished our day at about ten o'clock when we came downstairs for cocoa and a chat. The rovers, as we called visiting neighbours, would be sitting around the fire, from which my father was often missing, having himself gone roving to another house. Soon, however, everyone returned to their own homes and then my mother got us all on our knees for the rosary.

Quench The Lamp

Τhe pace of life was slow for those who grew up with oil lamps and candles. It was not advisable to go rushing around in candle-light as the way forward was not brightly lit and you could easily bump into various shadowy objects which would suddenly bring you to a painful standstill. Candle-light was kind, however, to ageing faces, cobwebs and bad housekeeping, its soft, flickering glow casting gentle shadows over many a blemish, human and otherwise. Old Tom, one of our neighbours, always advised against buying a horse or choosing a wife in candle-light, for they were the two principal occasions of life on which he felt you needed the harsh reality of daylight to guide you.

He never chose a wife himself and his reason for not doing so was a trifle unusual. Females, he said, were either Sunday girls or Monday girls. Sunday girls looked good but Monday girls were good, and the bonus in life was to get a Monday girl who looked like a Sunday girl. He never succeeded himself so he remained a bachelor, and because he was of my father's generation he declared that the tide had now gone out for him. He was an only son with seven sisters so the female of the species held no mystery for him. All his sisters had long gone from his home and he came visiting to our house most nights. Tom liked female company and perhaps our house, with so many girls in it, reminded him of his childhood.

As we grew older we began to be trusted with candles in our rooms and we fastened them to the iron bedheads with pools of hot candle-grease. One of the greatest disadvantages of candles was the candle-grease that inevitably flowed freely on to everything in the house but mostly on to floors. Once a

219

week we young ones were dispatched upstairs with blunt knives to scrape the candle-grease off the bedroom floors. It was a tedious job but for some strange reason it did not make us any more careful not to spill grease back on the same floors the following week. Maybe we were slow learners.

Often we read late into the night by candle-light, which bathed the bed in a soft yellow light and left the rest of the room full of flickering shadows. One night my sister Clare fell asleep with the candle alight on her bedside table, to be awakened hours later by the heat of a blaze beside her. She quenched the leaping flames quickly by smothering them in the heavy quilt off her bed, and luckily the result was nothing more serious than a burnt-up table-top and a scorched foot caused when she stepped on a red-hot scissors that had fallen through the table.

My father was never told about such calamities, because any such news would trigger off such a litany of his cruc-ifixions that it was simpler and more desirable to keep him in the dark. How he and his easy-going wife had finished up with five daughters hell-bent on cracking his nerves was one of the mysteries of life which he would often ponder. If rein-carnation had been on his list of beliefs and if choice had been involved, there were days on which he would gladly have opted for the life of a monk, the more silent and enclosed the order and the more distant from us the better.

As dusk gathered into the kitchen on a winter's evening, we would ask mother, 'Is it time to light the lamp yet?' Earlier in the day the globe of the lamp had been washed with luke-warm soapy water and polished with a soft cloth or news-paper. The base had been filled with paraffin oil and the wick had been trimmed. All was done in readiness for the night because leaving these jobs till the natural light had gone could lead to breakages in the dusk, to overflowing oil and to frayed tempers as a consequence. The top of the wick, which had been burned black the night before, was trimmed off with a sharp scissors, and if the wick had burned out the new one had to have time to soak up the oil before being lit. Sometimes it was put down into the bowl of the lamp on the last night of the old wick. The paraffin oil itself was brought regularly in an oil can from town, and if it was forgotten the neighbours could always be depended on to come to the rescue.

At first the wick was kept down low after lighting to give the globe a chance to warm slowly, because sudden heat could crack it. A hairpin was sometimes hung on top of the globe to prevent this happening. Gradually the wick could be turned up, changing the soft yellow to a white glow, and then the shade was put on, softening the glow and diffusing the light evenly around the room from its position in an iron basket attached to the wall. When the large open fire was built up with logs and turf its leaping flames added to the lamp-light. Before going to bed, if some of her household were still abroad, my mother turned the lamp down low and left it to provide a soft welcome home to the latecomer.

A second oil lamp was kept in the parlour, and this was a rich relation of the kitchen model. It had a heavy, cream-coloured glass bowl embossed with green and pink flowers, and an elegant brass stand. The pink colour of the lampshade matched the base and was delicately fluted around the top in a way that always made me think of a ballerina doing a head-stand.

When the lamp was lit it bathed our parlor in a muted pink light, warming up the old bog-oak sideboard with its varied assortment of family treasures on top, including the gramo-phone. The dark marble fireplace shone in the lamp-light, which was reflected in the mirror above the mantlepiece. On either side of the mirror stood two ebony, semi-nude male figures which had been brought back from foreign parts by someone in an earlier generation of our family. My mother was not particularly partial to displaying semi-nude males in her parlour, but their antiquity gave them a metaphorical clothing of respectability and so she tolerated their presence. On the mantelpiece, too, were a little silver lady's shoe and two pink-and-white china ones.

The floorboards in the parlour were polished around a central square of lino decorated with roses, which was almost obscured by an enormous oak table which matched the sideboard. The walls were distempering in a pale pink colour and white, lace curtains hung from a long pole over the single window. The curtains were mostly for decorative purposes as you could see in through them if you so desired, and the cream, tasselled blind that hung in the recess of the window was seldom drawn. The table dominated the room and was surrounded by curved-back chairs with black leather seats. On the end wall, opposite the fireplace, hung a painting of my paternal grandmother, a smiling-faced woman with bobbed white hair who looked down on us with smiling eyes from a serenely beautiful face. A portrait of her husband, a tall, stern-looking bearded gentleman, hung on the wall beside the window, while a painting of my parents on their wedding day hung over the sideboard. Beside the fireplace and sunk into the deep wall was my mother's ware press, from which I often stole lump sugar, the presence of which was supposed to be known to her alone.

Between the press and the fireplace stood the rocking-chair: comfortable and ample, it was my idea of heaven to cuddle up in its many feather cushions, rocking back and forth, watching the fire casting shadows along the ceiling. I always felt that the pictures on the walls came alive then and no matter where I hid in the room my father's eyes seemed to follow me, for even on his wedding day he had apparently been alert for impending disaster. But my favourite picture was the one of my grandmother, who seemed to smile kindly on me. When I asked my father once how such a calm-looking woman had had such a temperamental son, he smiled and said, 'the balance of nature: don't ever marry somebody of the same temperament as yourself – the blend of opposites is a better combination.' I concluded from that that he took after his father. A great admirer of fine trees, fine horses and fine-looking women, he was inclined to be blunt. Once when a neighbour married a very plain-looking man my father sighed and said, 'My God, they'll have to put all their daughters under the table'.

The parlour was used for the Stations and visitors, and I loved it when the fire was lit there, awaiting family gatherings of one kind and another. When my older sisters left home and brought back friends to stay, they ate in the parlour and I alway acted as parlour-maid because then I could listen in to fascinating grown-up conversations about boyfriends and falling in love. Until then I had only come across such things in books, but in the parlour I encountered them in real life, though at second hand. When my sisters graduated to bringing home boyfriends it was better again because then I cold enjoy a close-up view of the real thing. The parlour was thus my first step towards the world outside or, rather, it was when the world outside began to come in under my curious gaze.

Having lived with the candle and the oil lamp for so long, we experienced the tilly lamp as a big break-through into a world of light in about 1950. It was a simple invention, still fed on oil but with a mantle replacing the wick and giving a much stronger light. It worked on the same principle as the gas lamps used now for camping, but with oil instead of gas as the source of power. Hot on the heels of the tilly lamp came the tilly heater, which brought warmth to rooms without fireplaces, a function that had previously been performed by cumbersome, evil-smelling oil heaters. For most of my secondary-school days my studying was done by the light of a tilly lamp in an upstairs bedroom heated by a tilly heater. Only necessities were catered for, and it was not deemed necessary to get a tilly lamp for the parlour, where bright light was less important.

Soon after the advent of the tilly lamp to our home canvassing started for the Shannon Scheme, which was to bring about a much greater change in our lives. This rural electrification scheme had to be canvassed for because, strange as it may seem now, some people were reluctant to accept electricity into their homes. One of our neighbours hesitated to take it, but when he discovered that we could not get it unless he did he decided to give his approval rather than inconvenience us. Another old friend absolutely refused despite all kinds of persuasions, declaring that it could not be safe to boil a kettle from a hole in the wall.

Teams of men went all over the countryside, digging holes

for ESB poles which were dragged into position by horses. Electrical contractors came and helped people plan their house lighting, but it was all so new and difficult to get accustomed to that most people did not put in sufficient sockets. The light switches and sockets, a far cry from the sleek models of today, stood out on walls like ugly brown warts. Wires were not tucked away inside walls and above ceilings but could be traced all over the house as they crept around skirting boards like raised varicose veins, drawing their power from the heart of the big black meter above the kitchen door. Even before the power was connected I was afraid that if I touched anything electrical I might drop down stone dead.

Many were cautious, too, about the way in which they installed and used the unfamiliar electricity. One man installed just one light on the upstairs landing of his house and told all his children to leave their doors open so that the light could shine in. When my father suggested to him that it would be bad for their eyes if they wanted to read in bed, he was told that they went to bed to go to sleep, not to read. Cost-cutting influenced people's approach to installation. One thrifty individual, with a view to cutting down on initial expenses, installed just one light-switch, so that when he turned this on the whole house lit up like a Christmas tree.

One of the things which electricity did away with was the primus, a little gadget fuelled by paraffin oil and lit by methylated spirits, which had to be kept clean with a primus needle to prevent it from shooting into yellow flames and sending smelly smoke signals all around the kitchen. The electric kettle was a great improvement and was the first electrical item to enter most houses, bringing the ease of a quick cup of tea without first having to light the fire or the primus. In its early years it was not, however, plugged in freely as that would have been considered the height of extravagance. A toaster soon followed the kettle into our house as my mother was always partial to toast. There were no pop-up toasters then, and the early days of electricity in our house were flavoured by the smell of burnt toast filling the kitchen and a fog of smoke billowing out from the toaster.

The concept of labour-saving devices such as washing-machines and fridges was too strange for us to swallow quickly. The one luxury my father did indulge in was a mains radio, and he was delighted not to be at the mercy of run-down batteries, but he refused to buy an electric razor and still used his old cut-throat monster. However, first we had to get accustomed to the bright light that flooded the entire house, and one thing to be said in its favour was that it made the journey upstairs to bed much less frightening; it was now no longer necessary to check under beds for lurking spooks or to peer through shadowy doorways for silent figures waiting to pounce. The magic of touching a switch and the whole room filling with instant light was thrilling for the first few weeks, and I went up and down stairs for no reason other than to experience the joy of turning on lights. Nevertheless, there was no question of lights being left on when nobody was in the room, because my father had a new headache, the electricity bill, and soon we were constantly being reminded that he had no shares in the ESB.

Out in the farmyard the electricity lit up the old cobweb-draped rafters of the stables and stalls and threw light on gynaecological interventions during calving time. It extended the working day, for jobs that had previously had to be completed before darkness fell could now be continued under artificial light. And although it made our working day longer it also made our lives easier in many ways. One thing was certain: it had changed our lives and changed them utterly, carrying us into a new world and leaving the old one behind.

The Gladioli Man

Being the youngest of five sisters had its disadvantages because it meant obeying many mistresses: they were all chiefs and I was the only Indian. As a consequence I spent more time and energy trying to avoid carrying out the instructions of older sisters than actually doing as I was told. My mother never dished out jobs because she worked on the principle that everything got done eventually: that when we got tired of looking at unwashed ware on the table we would get around to washing it; and that as we were sleeping in the beds it was up to us to make them, and to tidy our rooms. Never lecturing or nagging, she just left things undone while my older sisters took over and delegated household duties down along the line.

This weekly rota of jobs varied but one to which I strongly objected was the daily brushing of the upstairs floors and stairs. In performing this hated job I took regular rest periods and sat into a window-seat of one of the rooms to read a book, but when the sound of my busy footsteps ceased the silence told Sarah, my supervising sister below, that I was after taking one of my many breaks. She then took the handle of a brush and hammered on the kitchen ceiling to signal that progress should resume. But I figured out a plan to out manoeuvre her. Instead of sitting down to read my book I walked back and forth producing the required noise and at the same time was able to enjoy my reading. It worked for a while until Sarah, wondering how it could take so long to do so little, crept up quietly one day, caught me unawares and discovered my ploy.

My soul rebelled against the boring, repetitive jobs around

the house, but no matter how good an argument I put up as to the futility of certain tasks – and I was better at arguing than working – no argument stood a chance against my sisters' determination, so in the end they always won. Strangely enough, one of the weekly jobs from which I derived great satisfaction was cleaning the windows. This was done with newspaper and paraffin oil: the window was cleaned down first with an oil-soaked paper and then polished off with a dry one until it shone and I could see my reflection in it. The open fire accounted for much of the dirt on the windows and if the wind was in the wrong direction it might blow the smoke down the chimney, filling the kitchen. Then on the smoky panes of glass I would draw strange designs and create imagined scenes. I thought of the windows as the eyes of the house and that was probably why I felt such a sense of achievement.

Every Saturday there were plenty of jobs on the agenda in preparation for Sunday. The hob was white-washed; all the *súgán* timber chairs and the two timber tables were scrubbed white; finally, the kitchen was scrubbed out with buckets of water drawn from the spout at the end of the garden. If the voluntary workforce started to protest we were coaxed along by our shrewd older sister,Sarah, with promises of a big, juicy apple cake for tea, and, like the donkey and the carrot, we kept going. She always lived up to her promises, well aware that next Saturday's tasks were only around the corner of another week. We often sang as we worked together; we laughed a lot and, like all *gearrcaigh* in the nest, we squabbled a lot as well.

The first to fly from the nest of our home was my sister Lucy, who went nursing to London. My mother was very reluctant to let her first chick head away, but my father's criterion was always: if they want to fly, let them go. Every week I wrote her long letters full of every detail of what had happened at home, and probably I wrote as much for my own satisfaction as for hers. All our lives had been so intertwined that I could not bear to think that she, who had been part of it all, should now miss out on anything. Caught up in her new life in London she must often have smiled at the letters of a twelve-year-old with their vivid descriptions of how many chickens each hen had hatched out and the colours of the new calves.

She came home on holidays with suitcases full of lovely clothes and, oh, the heavenly smell of rare perfume! Sometimes friends came with her, speaking in strange accents, who had never been on a farm before. I loved escorting them out around the animals and watching the reaction on their faces, especially if they stood on what they thought was firm ground but which turned out to be otherwise. One girl who visited on several occasions had the unusual name of Joy Love, and it was a name which suited her wonderfully because she was full of gaiety and her Scottish accent was music to the ear. She and my brother spent a lot of time talking together because they were both interested in poetry, and she sent him a book of the complete works of Robbie Burns which I came to treasure myself. It had a deep red, soft padded cover with gold lettering and gilt-edged leaves, and it slipped into its own matching holder. The pages inside were thin and flimsy with beautiful red and gold lettering at the top of every page. It gave pleasure and satisfaction before a word was ever read, and I spent many hours trying to decipher the Scottish dialect without always succeeding.

When home on holidays Lucy, who was very pretty, was never short of admirers eager to escort her. During one of these trips, in the course of which she had gone out several times with a local lad who was also home on holidays, she coolly announced that a boyfriend from London was coming to stay. Almost as an afterthought she added that she was thinking of getting engaged to him. This, as far as my mother was concerned, was completely out of line. In her reckoning, if you were that serious about one man you cleared the field of all other contenders. But her oldest daughter had other ideas, so a long argument commenced.

'We know nothing about this fellow,' said my mother, with the implication in her voice that, since we did not, there might be something wrong with him.

'Well, what do you want to know?' came the reply.

'What does he do? What are his family like? What religion is he?'

When my mother stopped to draw breath Lucy chimed in, 'He's a medical student in the hospital where I work; he has one brother and his parents are very nice; and he doesn't believe in anything.'

'Holy mother of divine God!' my father exclaimed as he grabbed his cap and made for the kitchen door to go out to his animals, which he found a lot easier to understand than his daughters.

My mother was determined to get to the root of the matter. 'How do you mean he doesn't believe in anything? Where does he think he came from?' she demanded.

My sister was too smart to get caught in a theological debate with my mother, so she soothed her down by asking her to re-serve judgement until the subject of their argument appeared on the scene. An uneasy truce was agreed, which Lucy did nothing to cement when she went dancing again with her local friend at night.

A few days later our man from London arrived and revealed himself to be a very precise, English gentleman of few words, who had probably never seen a cow in his life before. I was fascinated by him. Anybody who did not believe in God was a great novelty and it was rather disappointing to find that he looked ordinary enough, except for his well-cut country tweeds, which might have been very suitable for an English hunt but not for Irish country roads. After a few days he began to thaw out and we discovered a very charming young man beneath his crisp, correct exterior.

When he returned to London he sent my mother a huge box of flowers. They were the first she ever got that she had not grown herself, as my father had never been inclined to say it with flowers. Their arrival at the local bus-stop created a bit of excitement. There was a pub at the bus-stop where the kindly publican, Jim, looked after all sorts of miscellaneous objects, from parts of ploughs to bundles of blankets, but a box of fresh flowers added a new dimension to his responsibilities for, while most things could be left there indefinitely without creating a problem, these had to be shifted before they started to wilt. Another difficulty was that most merchandise arriving by bus had been sent for and the person who had ordered it would come and collect it. The arrival of the flowers, however, had no precedent and was totally unexpected. But we, like everyone in rural Ireland, possessed a local communication system which soon solved the problem. Jim sent a message to Pat in the Post Office to tell Martin the postman to call to us the following morning to let us know that the flowers were lying in state on the pub counter. It probably took the flowers longer to get to our home from the bus-stop than it took them to come from London, but we got them in the end.

My father collected them on his way from the creamery the following day and the huge oblong box stretched like a cardboard coffin across the three churns of milk. On his arrival home the box was borne aloft into the parlour, where it was laid out on the big oak table. The entire household, including visiting cousins and helpers, gathered to witness the opening ceremony. My mother untied the ribbons with the air of reverence she normally reserved for her rosary beads. She gently folded back the layers and layers of soft, white tissue-paper and there they were, rows and rows of the most gorgeous gladioli. My sister Phil spoke all our thoughts when she breathed, 'That guy certainly knows how to impress!'

For days afterwards we had gladioli standing upright in every vase and jug, filling the parlour and kitchen. In later years whenever I saw gladioli I remembered the man my sister might have married.

The Royal Wee

T he miracle of modern plumbing is difficult
to appreciate for those who have never known its predeces-
sors, but for those of us who grew up with the chamber-pot
and po for companions the flush toilet came as a modern mar-
vel. Indeed, if there had been an award for the invention that
best filled a gap in the market it should surely have gone to the
man or woman who invented the flush toilet.

One came into our house shortly after the advent of electricity when my father harnessed a free-flowing spring that
poured down the hill behind the house and put it to a more
practical use. Old Tom, when he viewed it in action, declared,
'Be the hokey but that's a mighty yoke when you can flush
everything down a hole. That could give a man the idea that
he is no longer responsible for his actions.'

When Jim in the local pub installed an outdoor model that
operated by pulling a chain it created great excitement. One
old man sat on it for the first time and pulled the dangling
chain, quite unprepared for the consequences; in his ensuing
panic he ran into the pub, his trousers at half mast, shouting
that the whole place was going to be flooded.

Its ancestor, the humble po, led a sheltered existence in
obscure corners and shadowy places. It was seldom mentioned in polite society, yet it was the one household item that
straddled all social barriers and was essential in every dwell-
ing, from the humble cottage to the royal palace. But even
within the po democracy there were different social layers. At
the bottom of the ladder came the humble white enamel
model with a navy blue or red rim and matching handle. This
was the poor man's po. They could be stacked on top of each

other and could withstand rough treatment, though when this happened and the enamel got chipped care had to be taken lest adjoining enamel become embedded in vital points of the anatomy, causing a certain amount of discomfort. Next on the social ladder came the plain white ware model, but in recognition of its middle-class status its title changed from plain 'po' to rather more euphonious 'chamber-pot'. The chamber-pot was a fine, solid, serviceable job. It had no tendency to chip and only if you dropped it on the hard stone floor did it crack. My grandmother opted for one of these, but because the ordinary po position was beneath her dignity she ensconced it in a mahogany chair called a commode, which had a false bottom into which the chamber-pot withdrew.

The chamber-pot had as working companions a large ware jug and a basin. Because there was no water on tap this jug was filled from the rain-water barrel daily and the water was then poured into the large bowl for washing when necessary. You washed in cold water unless you had a retinue of servants to draw hot water for you. After washing, the water was poured into a white enamel bucket and later taken out and emptied.

All this action took place at the dressing-table, which might have a circular hole on top into which the basin fitted or, more commonly, it might have a marble top and a colourfully tiled back. Underneath some dressing-tables was a closed-off section with a little door, inside which the chamber-pot lived in seclusion. Beside the jug and bowl on top there were usually a matching soap dish and shaving mug, and sometimes a bone container for the male's studs.

At the top of the market a high-class chamber-pot blossomed into flowers, usually pink roses or blue forget-me-nots. Its bedroom companions sported the same colours and were quite decorative; some were colour co-ordinated with paint-work as well. Some boasted embossed flowers and were works of art in the variety and intricacy of their design and colour. In some houses a special chamber-pot, ornate and not intended for ordinary bottoms, was reserved for visitors.

Emptying the po was an exercise that had to be carried out

daily and this delicate operation was performed by the senior females of the household after they had first established that no unexpected visitors were within the precincts. My grandmother, if she had misjudged the situation and found herself approached by someone who was where he should not have been, whipped her long black apron into action, covering all before her. The fact that at seventy-five this gave her a decidedly pregnant look did not disturb her in the least.

When she had visitors and wanted to know if they needed to avail of her chamber-pot facilities she asked, 'Would you like to sit down?' and 'Would you like to tidy yourself?' On first hearing this politely worded invitation I was somewhat confused, as I observed that the lady to whom my grandmother had addressed her questions was already sitting down and looked quite tidy. However, I knew my grandmother well enough not to question the appropriateness of her terminology and after a while I managed to figure out her meaning.

One neighbour had occasion to use her chamber-pot to dampen unwelcome male ardour. A drunken visitor refused to stop knocking on her front door in the small hours of the morning. After repeated attempts to persuade him to depart she finally, in a fit of temper, opened a window above the front door and baptised his head with a mixed blessing, which proved most effective in speeding him on his way. Another old neighbour, when the handle fell off his ware chamber-pot, used it as a money box and still kept it under the bed.

The same old man used a new chamber-pot he had in reserve to solve the problem of some unwelcome visitors. They had invited themselves to stay with him and he was at his wits' end as to how he could shift them when he got a brainwave. He brought out the new chamber-pot, but pretended that it was the one from under his bed. Then he placed it on the kitchen table and proceeded to wash the ware in it. His visitors made a hasty exit.

The po might have many titles: those with a musical bent called it 'the piano', those with literary notions 'the Edgar Allan' and those with medical inclinations 'the vessel'. We children called it 'the jerry-pot' and those with no respect at all called it 'the piss-pot'. But the title that appealed most to me was that given to it by my dear old friend Molly who termed it 'the goesees-under'.

The once-humble chamber-pot has since climbed into the exalted realms of the world of antiques, which it graces as a collectors' item. At an auction recently a Wedgewood model fetched a handsome price and I smiled, thinking of its late owner, an eccentric old gentleman who had refused to transport his fragile anatomy to the modern wonder of the flush toilet, maintaining that the po position kept things properly in motion. Now his precious po was destined to become an expensive flower-pot, and I had no doubt he would have considered it a fitting end for so serviceable an item.

Home Drama

A trip to Cork City assumed for me as a child the momentous importance of a journey to a foreign country, and it was on one of these rare and wonderful excursions that I discovered books. A collection of hardback classics which I found on the shelves of Woolworths provided me with a passport to another world. I drew my books home from the city one by one and, if funds were unusually plentiful, I might sometimes stretch my haul to two. I cried at the hungry plight of poor Oliver Twist and rejoiced at his final escape into a better life. I moved enthusiastically on through other books by Dickens, relishing his characters, but all of these paled into insignificance when the territory of my reading shifted northwards; I came across the brooding Brontës and was drawn into the absorbing tension between the correct behaviour of their time and the powerful undercurrents of dark wild passion which was embodied in their writing. I read and re-read their books until I felt I had a personal relationship with the entire family and believed that I could easily find my way around their isolated house and across the lonely moors. The only respect in which the world of the Brontës disappointed me was in its cold, detached father who failed to match up, I felt, to our colourful and dramatic man, who sometimes stretched our patience to the limit but around whom there was never a dull moment.

These popular classics had cream-coloured covers, were printed on soft cream paper and were well bound so that they did not fall apart. Their smell when new was of another world, a world of the imagination, and I loved it so much I would run my nose up and down the pages to inhale their essence. I found that just as some gardens offered welcomes with their fragrances and some houses had their special atmospheres, the feel and smell of a new book was an indication of the life within. The books in Woolworths cost three shillings each, an amount which was hard to come by, and my appetite for reading seemed always to outstrip my supply of coins, so I was constantly in search of opportunities to earn some pay for special jobs at home.

We children bargained with my father for so much per drill for thinning turnips and picking potatoes, and sometimes we had to threaten strike action to extract our earnings. If a calf, a bonham or a lamb was sickly – an *íochtar* – we became foster-parents and staked our claim for a share of the price when they were sold. Another source of revenue was 'stands', as we called them: visiting friends and relations often put their hands in their pockets and withdrew a brown or silver coin. Brown was the usual story but occasionally we might get silver and then we struck oil, for a shilling had a lot of spending in it and a half-crown was riches indeed. A friend of my father's, who was having a pint with him one fair day, gave me a half-crown and I could hardly believe my eyes. I never forgot his kindness and the way he smiled and said 'enjoy spending it', and I did indeed because it became the down payment on my much-prized copy of *Little Women*. Years later I travelled many miles to be at the funeral of the man who gave me the key to the world of Louisa May Alcott.

We did not own a car, and neither did any of our neighbours, but there was a hackney-man in town who went to Cork weekly or sometimes even twice weekly if he had a load. There was also a bus, and this set out early each morning, returning late at night, but its route wound through a wide swathe of surrounding countryside, so the hackney-car was first choice for comfort and convenience. Jim the hackney-man was also the publican, so we waited on high bar stools for him to drive us to Cork, sipping fizzy brown lemonade and watching the old men drinking their frothy black pints as we waited. Like most pubs it did not restrict itself to selling drinks, and this was also the place to buy needles, hairpins and elastic. Jim was very much a part of our lives, as well as of our neighbours'; unfailingly patient and pleasant, he was a storyteller who could shorten any journey. He was involved in most of the important events in the lives of the people of the neighbourhood because he drove us to and from weddings, funerals, christenings and other family occasions. During his years as hackney-driver he had witnessed the life stories of many families, but he treated every family as his own and was never known to divulge a confidence. Being so aware of the goings-on in families and being so understanding with it, he was often called upon to sort out family tangles. Once when Lucy, home on holidays, was complaining about her earnings as a newly qualified nurse he asked her how much she was being paid; she told him and he just said quietly, 'Many a man is keeping a wife and children on that'. She was glad later that he had put matters in perspective for her.

With every trip in the hackney-car to Cork my collection of books grew and soon I felt the need for a special corner for them. At the top of the house was an old attic which we called the black loft because it was poorly lit by one small dormer window and a tiny deep one in the gable-end overlooking the grove. When we were small we sometimes squeezed through this window, which led on to the roof of the old stone turf-house and from there down into the grove, but later we out-grew its miniature proportions. The dormer window was the better of the two because it had a view out over the fields: from here I could see the old stone school – from a safe distance – and the little bridge over the river that crept along between high banks, forming a natural boundary between neighbour-ing farms.

The black loft was my retreat corner and I created a world of my own there amongst the relics of the past: the family cradle and the brass cot, both of which I, as the youngest in the family, had been the last to occupy; the butter churns and the horse tackling – too far gone for use but awaiting repair some wet day unless it might find its way eventually to the harness-maker. The plaster on the walls was crumbling and rafters bared themselves under the roof; the floorboards sagged, re-vealing the ceiling of the room below and making it essential to step gently to avoid a hasty and unpremeditated exit to the lower regions.

Three steps led down to the black loft from my parents' bedroom, which was in a newer part of the house which had been built above the level of the old house. Just inside the door of the loft a sagging rafter could catch unwary visitors and easily render them unconscious. At the far end stairs led down into a room below the parlour, which was used as a spare room and had bay windows opening into the garden. Thus I had more than one exit when seeking to escape from undesirable chores, even though the stairs at the far end were officially closed due to their dangerous condition. I loved the thrill of using it as an emergency exit; swinging past the gaps I relished the excitement of knowing that if I fell into one of the black holes beneath me I might never be seen again.

Mice had made the place their own, so when I was about to enter I always gave them prior notice by flinging one of my father's boots in before me, and they duly scattered in all directions and out of respect for my presence never invaded my privacy. They were less considerate, however, in their habit of leaving evidence of their visitations. Also, they had an unfortunate appetite for our home-made glue, a paste of flour and water which they seemed to regard not at all as an adhesive but as a heaven-sent source of sustenance. Had it not been for impenetrable iron trunks, many a scrapbook and home-made picture would have been destroyed by them.

Scrapbooks provided the perfect medium for paying private homage to the glamorous film stars of the time, and one of my hobbies was collecting movie magazines and compiling scrapbooks about my favourite stars. Elizabeth Taylor, Ava Gardner and Rita Hayworth shone as foremost beauties while Stewart Grainger, Montgomery Clift and Clark Gable were the dashing male heroes. Sometimes on summer evenings after the cows had been milked we walked to the cinema in town to see some of the stars in action. My mother did not entirely approve of all these bare-breasted beauties, nor their frequent changing of husbands, but when I showed an interest in the

British royal family she was much more positive, feeling that even if they were rather far removed from us, at least their morals were above reproach.

I was denied the luxury of a bedroom of my own because demand exceeded availability, so I shared with my sisters and with many visiting cousins during the holidays, and this often led to chatting which continued far into the night until my father thumped on the timber partition and eventually silenced us. But nobody else bothered with the black loft and so it became my private domain. In the summer it was very hot and in the winter it was freezing, and because the window did not shut properly the weather outside sometimes found its way in. High winds sprayed raindrops in and blizzards whirled snowflakes through to fall like thistledown on the bare, dusty floor. The conditions, however, did not deter me, and it was here on a woodworm-eaten and wobbly table with one short leg that I wrote my first story.

My sisters and I underwent a phase of impromptu home drama. To begin with we used the kitchen as our stage, the room off it serving as our dressing-room, but as we progressed we found these arrangements too amateurish and so we moved to an empty loft over the stalls. This loft was normally used for storing straw but was empty between seasons. We put it to good use. Old curtains that belonged to the parlour were rigged up and props collected from all over the farm.

We lacked a script so we made it up as we went along, which often resulted in the cast becoming involved in long, heated arguments on stage because their dialogue was failing to coordinate. Then an intermission was called and the whole thing was gone through before we started in again. We were an ad lib, think-as-you-go-along theatre group, and as the audience for one show could be on stage for the following one we tended to restrain our criticisms. Sometimes we might purport to present a play that we had heard on the radio, but if the playwright had happened along he might not have recognized it as his work.

We whiled away many a wet day up in that loft until my mother decided to turn it into a hen-house, to which we strongly objected, but our needs were of no importance in comparison to the needs of the hens, so for the summer we moved out of doors and performed under the trees in the grove behind the house. The only constant supporter we had was our old friend Bill, who came up with helpful prompts when any actress ran out of lines. He was a most accommodating audience. My father refused to allow us to move our theatre group into the black loft, which was my suggestion, as he was afraid that in the excitement of high drama we might forget the sagging floorboards and one of us put our foot in the wrong place and come down through the parlour ceiling. So we remained a mobile theatre group and whichever stall, stable or pig-house was available, we moved in, though sometimes we had to put a lot of work into eradicating the aroma of the previous residents.

I made gallant efforts to provide plays for our performances but they were taken apart on stage and rewritten to suit individual performers. The cast was entirely female as my brother had set up his own boxing club which had declared an empty corner of the barn their boxing ring. Sometimes when there was no play on we became the ringside audience, shouting on whichever of the champions we favoured.

When I first saw boxing gloves I was intrigued by the size of them and sometimes when my brother needed a sparring partner I donned the gloves and learned to dance around and duck and weave. He usually used a punch-bag which hung off the rafters of the barn for practice but he assured me that I was slightly better. We developed an interest in boxing championships then and gathered around the radio to follow the fortunes of Joe Louis and Bruce Woodcock and other champions of the ring, especially the Irish ones. The night that Rinty Monaghan became world champion and sang 'When Irish Eyes Are Smiling' we all danced around the kitchen with glee, and we followed with the greatest of interest the career of our own local hero, Irish middle-weight champion Pat O'Connor.

The black loft remained the corner where I spent time on my own. In the spring when the swallows came they refurbished their old nests under the roof beside the window and I watched them swishing in and out. In the evenings during the summer months I might sit inside the little window to watch the shadows slanting across the fields and listen to the corn-crake playing the same tune non-stop like a record with the needle stuck. The monotonous regularity of his voice merged into the chorus of night voices so completely that sometimes I was quite unaware that he had stopped.

In our family we all felt the need for our own places to which we could retreat from time to time and often as I looked out from my perch at the top of the house in the quiet of the evening I would see my father walking down the fields to his own particular spot by the river. I liked to watch him saunter along with his hands in his pockets, his cap pushed to the back of his head and the dogs with him chasing rabbits, real and imaginary, through the bushes. That was his relaxation time when he went, the cares of the day behind him, down to his favourite place to watch the fish jump and to listen to the sounds of the countryside.

A Marriage of Convenience

Mike and Maud had a small farm on the hill across the river from our house. They were too far afield to be on my visiting list as a child but as I grew older the distance became shorter. Mike had been well into his fifties before he had decided that a wife might add to the flavour of his life, but because a do-it-youself effort had never appealed to him he had simply let it be known in the right places that he was available and hoped that somebody suitable would feel that he was just what she wanted. He was quite realistic about his requirements and about what he had to offer. As he described it later, he was not in the market for 'a flighty young one who would burn me out in no time at all'. What he wanted was companionship with a mild bit of excitement thrown in, and he was quite emphatic about the small measure of the excitement because he needed reserves for his greyhounds, who were the great love of his life. Indeed, the one essential qualification he did insist on was that his future wife should love his dogs as himself. In due course his greyhound contacts came up with the answer; being doggy people themselves they knew exactly what Mike was looking for, and thus Maud came into his life.

They had been married for over twenty years when I first started visiting them. Mike loved to tell the story of how Maud had come to be his wife. According to him Maud had a sister and it was she he had met first; they had decided to get married but she had had a cold on the morning of the wedding and so Maud had come instead. Maud for her part neither contradicted or confirmed his story, only shaking her head saying, 'We must listen to the wind that falls the houses', and maybe that was the secret of their happy marriage. Mike felt free to live like a bachelor while Maud ran the farm. He had never had any great interest in work, whereas she had shared the running of a small, mountain farm with a sister and two brothers and she had the desire and ability to carry far more responsibility. 'She likes to get her head,' Mike constantly remarked approvingly; being of a leisurely disposition himself, he had great admiration for industrious people, despite having no wish to imitate them. He was tolerant and Maud was pleasant and good-natured and, as Mike said, 'her heart was in the right place'.

Mike had received little formal education but he had a great interest in the wonders of nature and the movements of the planets. When one of our neighbour's sons qualified as a teacher he gave night classes in the local school for people such as Mike, who had missed out on schooling and were keen to broaden their fields of knowledge. An interested and interesting collection of students, young Dan the teacher must have found them quite a contrast to his day pupils. One night he was endeavouring to explain to them, with the help of a globe, about the world turning on its axis and the regularity with which this took place, but it was too much for Mike who slapped the bench with his hand.

'Will you for God's sake, Dan, talk a bit of sense. I'm over there on that farm with seventy-five years,' he exclaimed, pointing out of the school window in the direction of his own place, 'and the bloody ground never stirred an inch.'

When electricity came Mike was fascinated by all the gadgets that came with it, and his was the first electric blanket in our part of the country. He also purchased an electric clock and was delighted with the fact that it kept perfect time. For years he had been at the mercy of a temperamental alarm clock that, a little like himself, decided to take a rest every so often. The alarm clock had been used in both the kitchen and bedroom but now it was placed on permanent bedroom duty while the new electric clock took over in the kitchen. One wet day Mike decided to investigate the reason why the alarm clock kept such bad time. Maud had gone into town and he had the place to himself; he pulled the kitchen table up close to the fire, sat himself down in comfort and proceeded to dismantle the clock. Every little screw and wheel was taken apart and laid out on a newspaper on the table, and Mike passed an enjoyable few hours studying the intricacies of his timepiece. He had taken careful note of every piece in the process of dismantling, yet when he had put it all back together again he found that he was left with one spare part.

'Do you know something,' he said to Maud, 'it's no wonder that clock kept bad time: the fool that made it put in an extra wheel.' The clock, of course, never ticked again.

Mike and Maud had no children because, as he put it, time was against them, a fact for which he was eternally grateful. He suffered from no unfulfilled paternal longings, unlike his neighbour and friend Pat O'Shea, who lamented his lack of a son and heir in verse:

> Fine green fields
> And no one for them;
> She fooled poor Pat O'Shea:
> She said she was
> Twenty years and four
> But she was forty years
> And far more.
> She fooled poor Pat O'Shea:
> My fine green fields
> And no one for them.

Mike gave Pat very little sympathy and he always said that what Maud did with the land when he died was entirely up to her. And when he did die, his last words to Maud were to mind his greyhounds.

As with everything he did, Mike took death in his stride. One morning he was not feeling well so he stayed in bed, and at lunch-time he just closed his eyes and died. Maud was not one to panic, so in due course she sent for Mrs Casey to lay him out. As she was passing our house Mrs Casey called for my mother and when they arrived at Mike's my mother talked to Maud while Mrs Casey went into the bedroom. After a few more neighbours had arrived Mrs Casey beckoned my mother into the bedroom.

'There is something wrong here,' she announced. 'He is not cooling down.'

'What on earth do you mean?' my mother asked in surprise.

'Mike is dead long enough to be getting cold, but he's not. I've laid out many a dead man and I know how dead men act and Mike isn't acting like a dead man.'

'But he must be dead,' my mother insisted, not knowing quite how to handle this development. 'He looks dead anyway.'

'Well, he doesn't feel dead,' Mrs Casey said, putting her hand on Mike. As they pondered their dilemma Maud entered the room and saw the two of them looking at Mike.

'What's wrong?' she asked. 'Why are ye not laying him out?'

'The way it is, Maud,' Mrs Casey explained, 'Mike is hot and he should be cold.'

'Oh,' Maud said, looking puzzled and going towards the bed. She examined Mike and the bed and then her face cleared and she smiled. 'Well, the old devil,' she exclaimed, 'he had the electric blanket plugged in – he loved the comfort of it.' And going to the foot of the bed she unplugged Mike and Mrs Casey was able to get on with her job.

Maud died a few years after Mike and now their little house is in ruins. They had gone into marriage with no great expectations on either side, yet their home had always been full of contentment and good humour.

'Come Home Dacent'

Nothing could compete for excitement with the carnival, which came to town every year in June. We lined the street waiting eagerly for the fancy-dress parade, squealing with excitement when it came into view and straining our eyes to identify the mysterious locals dressed up in their costume disguises. The carnival queen, with her glittering tiara and her ladies-in-waiting dressed in frothy, full-length gowns, was the ultimate in glamour and the envy of all the little girls dressed, as we were, in our sun-bleached hand-me-downs. The parade over, we went to the 'merries', where we swung high in the swinging boats and chased each other around the big spinner, inside which dolls and sets of ware competed with each other to tempt mothers and fathers.

My father did not go to the carnival but sat at home and smoked his pipe by the kitchen fire, grateful for the rare pleasure of having the house to himself. On such occasions he never lit the lamp but sat in the gathering dusk, the only light being the yellow flicker of the turf fire and the red glow of his pipe. When we returned home at about midnight we burst into his silent domain, regaling him with stories of money lost and won on pongo, of rides on the merries, of the excitement of our day, and patiently he listened to us before seizing an opportunity to escape upstairs to bed.

We left the carnival field as night was falling, but before we headed for home we gathered around the door of the old ballroom which stood over a garage in a field. The field was hilly and the garage seemed to burrow into the hill at the rear while the dance-hall rode on its back, its doors opening on to the street. We watched open-mouthed while older sisters and neighbouring girls with curled hair went in, all dressed in swirling skirts. Curls were the fashion and nobody would admit to straight hair except the old ladies who caught their hair into a knot or 'cuck' at the base of the poll. How we envied those glamorous girls, and when the door opened and we caught a glimpse into the hall itself it was a sight from another world. Glittering balls hung from the ceiling, the floor shone with a maple sheen, and bursts of familiar tunes escaped with each swing of the door. We were well versed in the music of the day and the band was playing all our tunes; Guy Mitchell provided the foot-tapping numbers, while Frankie Lane and Nat King Cole slowed the tempo.

Finally we were dragged away by my mother or a neighbour, or else my sister Sarah came to the door of the dance-hall to dispatch us all off home. If we had any pennies left we called into a little shop that stayed open late for the carnival and pooled our resources to buy a bar of chocolate for the road home. A full bar of chocolate was an unheard-of luxury, so one bar was broken up into squares and shared around, and sometimes squares had to be further divided so that everyone could have a bit. The miracle of the loaves and fishes was no miracle to us.

We walked up the old road, as the road home was called, and the strains of the music became fainter, soon to be replaced by the call of the corncrake and the occasional crow of the cock pheasant. The moon shone down, lighting up the road ahead and throwing the hedges into shadow; we enjoyed imagining that all sorts of spooks lurked in these shadows, and this often triggered off an unplanned race along the road. When we ran out of breath we staggered to a halt and sat on a mossy ditch to recover; here we told each other stories or, if the girls outnumbered the boys, we planned what we would wear at our first dance when we were old enough. Starting off again we lapsed into silence for a few minutes and could hear the cows snorting and munching grass inside the ditches. We leaned against an iron gate and some of us climbed up to sit on top and watch the cows in the moonlight. We seldom saw the countryside this late at night and it had an eerie stillness under the moon, with the farmhouses huddled on the hills and trees crouched on the horizon like dark, shadowy figures.

*   *   *

And then the years had passed, the carnival was in town again and I was sixteen, quivering in anticipation of my first dance, waiting to take my first step into a new and exciting world. I was just finishing my Inter Cert exams and the last subjects received scant attention as the other girls and I planned our big night. We tried on each other's dresses, skirts and blouses, each seeking the magic combination which would show her off to her best advantage.

To me the unattainable dream was a low-cut dress with sufficient cleavage inside it to keep it afloat. But, at a time when fashion demanded round-bosomed, curvaceous female bodies, I suffered the pangs of adolescence, yearning to be other than I was, with my long legs and my body so thin that my grandmother had told me I was like the stroke of 1 on a sheet of paper.

One of my friends, on hearing of my fervent aspiration to display a plunging neckline, brought me a bright red, scanty dress which belonged to an aunt of hers who was home on holidays from London. It was the last word in sophistication: I was about to become a scarlet woman, the fulfilment of all my dreams. But when I waltzed into the kitchen with this flimsy model high above my knees and cut so low that it displayed what I had not got, my mother nearly had heart failure. My sister Sarah pronounced a sarcastic verdict of 'dressed-up tart', and my father, as he passed through the kitchen, scratched his head and muttered something about a 'hoor's top'. And it was there in the kitchen that my red dress was whipped off me, wrapped up in a brown paper bag and thrust back into my schoolbag beneath my books. I was sent off to school on the last day of my exams with my only hope of become a scarlet woman buried beneath Virgil and Shakespeare. I had always been impressed by the tragedy of Lady Macbeth, but that day her tragedy seemed pale by comparison with mine.

After trying on black taffeta skirts with white frilly blouses and miscellaneous dresses, all of us first-timers got ourselves sorted out. Ownership posed no problem: we pooled our resources and a democratic vote decided who looked best in what. It was unanimously decided that a white dress with a shower of pale pink roses looked best on me, and once the decision had been reached I resolved that if I could not be red and devastating then I would be pale and interesting. In fact, I was going to be the most pale and interesting girl who ever went to a dance, and so intent was I on creating this image that I refused to go out in the sun, hoping that my tan would fade and my freckles disappear. I had read in Sarah's copy of *Woman's Weekly* that a face-pack of flake meal whitened the skin and removed blemishes. The beauty expert who had written this sterling piece of advice had no doubt assumed that only normal people read her column, people who would be intelligent enough to carry out the operation just once a week. But she had not reckoned on an enthusiastic sixteen-year-old determined to become ashen-faced within a week.

I pursued my beautification programme under a tree, in the suitable seclusion of a grove behind the house. Here I wedged between the two lowest branches of a tree a jagged piece of broken mirror advertising Irish Whiskey and examined my appearance. I had to angle my face sideways in order to get a good view of it in between the R in Irish and the W in Whiskey below. As I tilted my head lumps of the caked flake meal that I had applied to my face fell to the ground and the hens from the nearby hen-house gratefully gobbled it up. My dedicated beauty therapy came to an abrupt end, however, when my mother decided to investigate the reason why her large jar of flake meal for the morning porridge had been reduced to such a low ebb. It seemed I was destined not to be pale and interesting either.

Everyone else was going into curls for the big night but my hair was too long so I had to opt for plaits. Until I had reached fourteen my hair had been pure blonde but when I needed it to look its best it decided to go a strange-looking brown. To remedy this for my dancing debut and to recover my former flaxen glory, I purchased a bottle of peroxide in the local chemist's shop but, before I could achieve my objective, my mother thwarted me again. I was striving desperately to make myself beautiful but my mother was equally determined to keep me the way I was. Quietly and firmly she outmanoeuvered me at all points and, despite my tantrums and tears, she never lost her cool. In the end the only course open to me was to plait my long hair and coil it around my head; at least that way there would not be too much of it on view.

Before venturing on to the dance-floor it was obviously necessary to learn to dance, and this responsibility my sisters undertook with determination and great insensitivity. Propelled around the kitchen, I was forced to reverse into complicated semi-circles that made me feel that my legs and head had suffered a breakdown of communications. No suitable records were available to play on the gramophone because my father's repertoire favoured John McCormack and Delia Murphy. 'The Old House' and 'If I Was A Blackbird' were not exactly ideal for the quick-steps and sambas that I was supposed to master. This left the radio as the sole source of our ballroom dancing music. Victor Sylvester on the BBC had a whole hour of ballroom dancing, but an hour was not enough so, when any suitable music came on, the sister on kitchen duty ran to the front door and blew the whistle that was normally used to summon men in from the fields for meals, thus sometimes creating a false alarm. I was expected to come running, even if the whistle sounded at the most inopportune moments, and on many occasions I left a half-fed calf bellowing in protest as I raced for the kitchen, casting wellingtons ahead of me so as to have my feet free for action. Often I would not make it in time: the dance music had died and my flight had been in vain. If my father happened to witness any of these performances, and especially if he had answered a false alarm, he would take off his cap, scratch his head, cast his eyes to heaven and exclaim: 'Lord, pity the man who has five daughters!'

The morning of the big event dawned at last. Those who

wanted to curl straight hair had had to commence operations the previous night, rolling their hair up in little tin curling pins called dinkies for the tight look or donning huge spiky rollers to achieve a softer effect. These devices were not, of course, conducive to sound sleep and those who used them paid a price for their curly looks; as my father remarked, it was like going to bed with their heads in barbed wire. Some brave individuals went to Mass without taking out their rollers but wrapped scarves around their swollen, lumpy heads. Older people disapproved of this and peers, especially those of the opposite sex, often passed caustic remarks, leading the unfortunate girls to find out how difficult it was to treat a comment with contempt when your head was twice its normal size.

After the last Mass that Sunday the troops gathered when pals came together as much for the shared anticipation as for the final dress-rehearsal. But first body reclamation began: under-arm fuzz was mowed down with a safety razor stolen from my brother while he was out; we passed it around and it soon lost its edge but one resourceful young lady had a packet of blades which allowed us to continue the hair eradication programme. Legs were inspected, some were declared ripe for harvesting, and once we got started nothing was safe. Eyebrows were trimmed to near-extinction and some hairstyles deemed to be not quite right came under attack from scissors, often with disastrous results.

Next we turned to underwear. We had recently discovered the wonderful world of the bra: some because they were too richly endowed, others because they sought to give themselves what God had not, by recourse to 'falsies' or by stuffing their bras with hankies. Our inexperienced manouevres with our bras provoked high entertainment and we spent more time laughing than fitting them on. Stockings were even more novel, for up to now we had always gone bare-legged about the farm, and when I saw my first suspender-belt it reminded me immediately of a pony's tackling.

The long-legged knickers my mother favoured were cast aside for flimsy silk panties, very brief, with lace edging around the ends. Not quite trusting the delicate elastic, I got a good firm type from my mother's work box and with a safety-pin re-threaded the band; I was determined to avoid the experience of an older friend who one night had suddenly felt that what should have been around her hips were now down around her ankles. The dance-floor had been crowded and nobody had noticed, so she had smartly stepped out of them and whipped them up, slipping them unobtrusively into the jacket pocket of her dancing partner, who later had quite a surprise when he reached for his cigarettes.

Our activities were brought to an abrupt end when my father banged on the kitchen ceiling with the handle of a brush and demanded to know if there was anyone to bring in the cows for milking, to feed the hens and the calves, or had we all taken leave of our senses and did we want him to sell out the whole place and buy a dance-hall. A mad scramble ensued and we all scattered in different directions to get the various jobs done while neighbouring pals ran home across the ditches to do likewise. The cows were galloped home across the fields; buckets of milk were slapped under calves' heads, and hens and chickens were rounded up to be fed. The jobs completed in record time, we gathered in the kitchen for supper, which had been hastily prepared by the sister on duty there. Supper finished and ware washed, we resumed the real business of the evening: getting ready for the dance. Dress-rehearsal over, the live show was about to begin.

In various corners of the house we scrubbed ourselves down over enamel dishes and buckets. Then we gathered in the upstairs front bedroom where the beds were buried deep beneath our dresses, skirts, blouses and frilly underskirts. First bras and suspender belts were fastened, and those who wanted to look thinner than they were squeezed themselves into corsets with much gasping and breathing in. Next came the delicate operation of easing fine nylons over our legs, while avoiding the tragedy of a ladder, before hitching them to suspenders. Then we drew on our panties, about which old Tom aptly remarked that they did not provide much shelter.

The next garment under the dress was a slip. An interlock

one served the purpose and a silk one was the last word in elegance, but without a slip one was considered not quite respectable. It was the style of the times that every dress should billow forth, and so over the slip went an underskirt of stiff, white net to provide the necessary support. Then came the dress, about which so much agonizing had gone on for days, and the sandals, which were usually white. All that remained to be attended to was the face, and the secret here was to put on enough make-up to erase the scrubbed and shiny look but little enough to escape my mother's inspection. One stick of pancake make-up, one box of face-powder and one tube of lipstick covered all shapes and shades of faces. An imaginative friend discovered that the red cover of her father's creamery book, in which butter and milk sales were recorded, could be dampened and used as rouge, but my mother promptly made her wash it off. My dreams were of the full scarlet mouth of Ava Gardner and the smouldering, black-lined eyes of Joan Crawford, but my mother made sure that they remained just dreams. Cussons talcum powder, in a little orange-and-white box, was as near as we came to perfume, so we shook it in all corners.

Finally, leaving the bedroom in chaos, we trooped downstairs into the kitchen where my parents and a few of the neighbours, including Tom, waited to put us through a passing-out parade. Many good-humoured comments were passed and we girls gave as good as we got. But old Tom remained silent, puffing his pipe in a cloud of smoke until we were going out the door. Then he delivered a parting shot: 'Come home dacent,' was all he said.

We walked the three miles into town, joining up with other young people along the way, singing and practising our steps as we went. At that stage I had an attack of first-night nerves. What if my legs refused to keep time to the music? What if nobody asked me to dance? What if my panties fell down? The possibilities of disaster seemed endless and I almost envied the children buying chocolate for the road home, but not quite, because just then we came within range of the sound of music and my heart started to beat with a fierce new excitement.

Sarah had appointed herself cashier, so she went to buy the tickets and the rest of us queued up behind her like ducks going to a pond. As I waited in line I thought of all the instructions that had been hammered into me by my sisters and their friends: Don't get stuck with one fellow for the night; avoid drunks by keeping a weather eye out for them and getting lost in the crowd when you saw one coming; dance with everyone but if somebody turned up who was beyond endurance say you had the dance promised to someone else. I was beginning to feel that the Inter Cert had been a walkover compared with this test of diplomatic skills.

Sarah, having procured the tickets, propelled us forward and, once inside the door, we were soon enfolded in a warm world full of swirling couples, coloured lights, pulsating music and the smell of paraffin oil and sawdust. We made our way to the cloakroom, where we hung up our coats. Here older girls preened themselves in front of cracked mirrors and straightened the seams in their stockings. Comments like 'God, he nearly crippled me' and 'Hope he'll ask me to dance again' floated through the powdered air and a feeling of gaiety and sisterhood prevailed. We first-timers were welcomed and cautioned about 'the octopus', 'the prancing jennet' and the handsome 'scalp collector'; the research team was voluntary, caring and anxious that we young ones should enjoy ourselves and avoid the tried and tested male hazards.

Outside the cloakroom was a sea of girls and I wondered where the men were hiding, until I made my way out to the front, and there across the hall were rows of men, a bewildering array of them. Before I could decide who I hoped would ask me to dance a schoolfriend came over as the band started up, saying, 'Come on and I'll see if your dancing is better than your algebra'. The dance-hall floor was a great improvement on the stone floor of the kitchen, and with the live music and a partner who obviously knew what to do with his legs my dancing problem faded fast as the music went in through my ears and out through my toes. I was sorry when that first dance was over because this lad who but a few weeks previously had been just a classroom companion was now a smiling entertaining young man. The atmosphere of soft lights and soothing music put our friendship on a new and altogether more interesting footing, and I decided that after the holidays school would never be as boring again.

After a few dances I realized that most of our school was there and also many of the neighbours, so I relaxed and felt that if this was what dancing was all about it was great fun. Then a blond, very handsome man in his twenties asked me to dance. This guy was a different model from the others and when the dance was over he did not move away but waited for the next dance, which he seemed to assume was what I wanted, and indeed it was because he was good-looking, charming and flattering. The next number was slow and dreamy, but as I felt his arms tenderly wrap themselves around me I had the unholy thought that perhaps this was the octopus. I was soon distracted, however, by another problem as the strong elastic with which I had reinforced my panties began to cut into me like a strand of wire. When the music stopped I excused myself hurriedly and headed for the cloakroom. My friend Ann followed me to know what was happening. I exclaimed about my panties.

'Take them off,' she said, 'and put them into the pocket of your coat.'

'I can't go back out there with no panties on!' I gasped in horror.

'You've three choices,' she declared, 'go home, suffer on, or take them off.'

'Put like that there seems to be no choice,' I said, 'but old Tom would say that it wasn't dacent.'

The two of us were still laughing when one of my sisters came in to check up on how things were going for us and to issue half-time instructions. She soon solved the problem of the tight elastic with a nail-scissors and a safety-pin.

'Now,' she instructed, 'keep away from that blond guy.'

'Why?' I asked, disappointed.

'He's a real Duffy's Circus operator: different venue every night.'

'There had to be a catch,' I said regretfully.

'Just make sure that you are not his catch for tonight,' she warned, adding, 'keep away from the back of the hall now as all the old reserves are in from the pub and you'll be like a red rag to a bull to them.'

My friend and I thought this very funny; nevertheless, when we went back into the hall we headed up to the area near the stage from which the band, who were also local, had a bird's eye view of the whole scene. One of them bent down to us to enquire, 'Are ye steering clear of the old reserves?'

My handsome blond was back for the next dance and I wondered to myself how I was to shake off someone I really did not want to shake off. Ann had advised ignoring older sisters but I knew that home would be a very uncomfortable place if I did that and a curfew might even be imposed. So I lost myself in the crowd and the problem solved itself as school-pals gathered around and the rest of the night sped by. My handsome admirer soon replaced me with a blond nearer his own age who was the proud possessor of a plunging neckline, which further convinced me of the desirability of a cleavage.

When the dance was over we spilled out on to the street, glad of the cool night air. At the end of the town we waited for the crowd from our road to gather together. Some were later than others coming back as they had gone walking with fellows or girls they had met at the dance, but all the first-nighters were present.

We all walked home singing and laughing and never noticed the length of our journey. When we arrived we found that my mother had left the fire stacked up to boil the kettle; we made tea quietly and went back over the events of the night in loud whispers. Then someone got the notion to fry rashers and sausages and while we waited for the fry to be ready we threshed out the night, sometimes going into fits of suppressed laughter when we recalled some incident. Finally we dragged ourselves up the stairs and, after clearing paths to our beds, fell in, exhausted.

It was midday when the warm sun pouring in the window woke me the next day. My head was slightly muzzy from the

throbbing sound of the band and the smoky atmosphere in the hall. Other heads were in worse condition to judge by the groaning and complaining that accompanied their getting up, while toes and shin-bones were examined for signs of wear and tear. A subdued crew, we all traipsed downstairs where my father had just arrived home from the creamery; he viewed us with an unsympathetic eye and announced in verse:
'There is no time for joy or laughter
In the cold grey dawn of the morning after.'

This unwelcome shower of wisdom he followed with even more unwelcome instructions to get moving because the hay in the meadows by the river was ready for saving.

Making hay on a hot summer's day after a night spent dancing is not the easiest job in the world and we were a reluctant *meitheal*, but as the day wore on our youthful exuberance came to the surface and while we worked we discussed and relived yet again the momentous events of the previous night.

Little Bits Of Darning

Peter was born with a romantic heart, filled with the love of music, song and women, and as his life went on it was the women who came to occupy the greatest share. He loved all women; his life and thoughts revolved around them: women he should have married, women he could have married, and even women he considered himself lucky not to have married. They were a constant source of entertainment to Peter and he was a constant source of entertainment to them.

Although he was of our parents' generation, that placed no barrier between Peter and young people. He could go to the pub with my father for a pint after Mass and yet come dancing with us that night, and he would be equally at home in both situations. He was a beautiful dancer and would glide the most awkward beginner around the dance-floor, making her feel as if all the dancing skills were hers. If a night was not going according to plan we would ask Peter to dance and he could be relied upon to help out at awkward moments. He even came dancing armed with a book to fill in the duller intervals.

Peter's origins were shrouded in romantic mystery: the way he put it himself was that he was the result of 'a little bit of darning'. He explained further that most families had a skeleton in the cupboard as a consequence of some member having deviated from the straight and narrow, and most families coped with these upsets and drew both erring one and consequence back into the fold. Peter termed the process of recovery from these upheavals as 'little bits of darning'. His own parents had had no children when his father had come home

258

one night from a horse fair with a bouncing baby under his arm which he had presented to his wife. My mother expressed her doubts about this story but Peter swore that it was true and, true or otherwise, we found it intriguing.

He would describe his first experience of falling in love in great detail. Just sixteen, he had fallen head over heels for the daughter of a family down the road. So besotted was he that he sat all day on a stone wall opposite her house waiting to catch a glimpse of her. Finally her mother came out.

'Tell me, Peter,' she enquired, 'is it your first time?'

'Yes, mam,' he answered respectfully and added, 'It's killing me.'

'Well now, Peter,' she told him, 'I'll give you a cure.'

'Will you?' he asked eagerly.

'Yes indeed, Peter,' she said consolingly. 'Go home now like a good boy and take a fine dose of salts.'

Peter would laugh heartily when telling this story and add, 'Wasn't she a sound woman?'

He lived on a small farm, but didn't put much work into it, and when he got a legacy from America the first thing he did was buy a piano. He had no idea how to play it so, to give himself time to learn, he rented out the farm. It being the first piano to come to our district, we all called to see Peter's unusual investment: it was a beauty with two brass candleholders and every night he lit his candles and practised his playing. Sometimes, to take a rest from his piano practice, he picked up his fiddle, which he had played all his life as his father had taught him when he had been only a child, and while he played he danced around the house in total enjoyment of the music.

When he had mastered the piano he invited us all to a performance and we proved an appreciative if not very discerning audience. He also sang songs he had written himself and put music to and he recited verses he had composed about various local happenings. Any evening in Peter's house was great fun. It was also a house for card games and players came there from miles around. However, on some nights that were meant for card playing, Peter would not be in the right mood and so would turn them into musical nights instead, much to the annoyance of the card enthusiasts. But Peter's violin poured forth music so sweet that the card players soon forgot their annoyance and danced off the floor with gusto.

Young and not-so-young lined up for half-sets and old men crippled with 'the pains' found new pep in their step and bounced on the floor like garsoons. On other nights a concert would evolve and then we were all expected to do our party pieces. Ability had little to do with performance and if you could not dance you had to sing or recite; if you foundered in mid-verse everybody else came to the rescue and joined in. Card playing, on the other hand, was a serious business which often led to frayed tempers and arguments, but when these occurred Peter was always quick to clear the house.

Sometimes he would get a notion and write to all his old girl-friends with extravagant declarations of love that he did not mean and they, from previous experience of him, were smart enough not to take seriously. Letters he received in answer to his bold assertions he would read out for the entertainment of Bill, who was a great friend of his. After reading out a sentence that pleased him particularly he would say to Bill, 'I will read that last sentence again for you so that you can feel the love expounding there'. In his own letters, one of his more dramatic conclusions was, 'If my pen were a pistol I'd blow out my brains for love of you,' and on one occasion this protestation blew up in his face.

Former girlfriends who were safely married posed no threat to his romantic meanderings, but when one wrote from America that she was now a widow and was coming home to claim him for her own, Peter was thrown into a complete panic. He calmed down after a while and trotted off to Bill to ask for help in solving his desperate problem, but Bill had read too many 'pen and pistol' letters to this same lady to have much sympathy with him, so he told Peter that the time had come to turn his pen into a pistol and blow his brains out, or else marry her.

Peter declared that he was caught on the horns of a dilemma and did not know which way to jump. In one way he was apprehensive at the prospect of her arrival, but in another way he was fascinated by the thought of meeting her again, and he mused about how things might develop. And when he had recovered from the initial shock he appeared to become quite philosophical about the whole affair.

It did seem to set him back a bit when he discovered that the gentle, soft-spoken slip of a girl with long blonde hair who had lived in his memory for twenty years had turned into a busty matron with brassy hair and a strident voice. But he recovered his composure and soon seemed to be enjoying escorting around his colourful Yank, as he called her. She was flamboyant and good humoured, which was very important to Peter who had said that there was only one eventuality which he could not overcome and that was if she had grown dull and boring. So Peter sang for us all:

> 'And when you think you're past love
> It's then you find your last love
> And you'll love her
> As you never loved before.'

Now that Peter was happy with his lot we relaxed a little, but at the same time we felt that there was no guarantee that he would see the whole thing through.

When the shock came it came not from Peter but from the Yank. One day she packed her bags and told Peter that although he had not changed, she had, and somehow she just could not visualize herself living in the depths of rural Ireland.

We thought that Peter would be devastated, but not a bit of it. So immediate was his recovery that Bill concluded he must have pulled a stroke: the Yank had gone away thinking that she had changed her mind, but Bill was sure that Peter had changed it for her. Whatever the truth of the matter, Peter was smiling, and when we questioned him about it he would only say that fate had destined him to keep many women happy rather than make one woman miserable.

Faigh Do Cóta

The dances held on St Stephen's night, on Easter Sunday and at the summer carnival were gala occasions for me, not least because it was only during the holidays that I was allowed to go out dancing. Music was always provided by a local band whose members we all knew and whose repertoire was well tried and truly tested. So established were their routines that anyone who had been going to dances for a while could almost tell the time of night by the tune being played, and always before they played the national anthem they gave advance warning by playing 'When The Saints Go Marching In'. Anyone wanting to acquire a companion to walk her home needed to have sorted herself out by the time 'The Saints' started up.

A couple who were seen dancing together for more than two dances was considered to be entering into serious negotiations, and if they went together for a drink at the mineral bar it was then considered that negotiations had been completed. There was plenty of flirting and fun between us and we girls joked amongst ourselves about different male approaches, which varied from 'Can I see you home?' to 'Would you like an orange?' or 'Would you get your coat?', which last we termed a 'Faigh do cóta' operation.

Reluctant to leave the secure ground of platonic friendship for the quicksand of romantic encounters, I walked myself home for many months, much to the annoyance of my best friend Ann, who declared that if I did my Leaving Cert without having been kissed my education would not be complete. She brought great pressure to bear and, after having failed to persuade me for some time, she decided finally that on St Stephen's night of my last year at school I was to be introduced into the kissing world, under any circumstances.

In the course of that night I met a young lad who was also doing his Leaving Cert but was away at boarding school during term time. He was good fun and interesting, though he did not set my hair on fire, which the more experienced Ann had assured me was not necessary, though I had my doubts. After the dance we walked out along the road to the house where I was staying with friends. As we walked we chatted and it struck me that I would be feeling much more relaxed were it not for the prospect of the kissing which I expected was going to be part of the proceedings.

'Do you know something?' I said to him, 'I've never been kissed before and I'm not so sure that I'm going to like it.'

He stopped dead in his tracks and stared at me with such a shocked look on his face that I started laughing, and when he had recovered he joined in.

'God,' he said, 'you believe in the direct approach!'

'Well, it avoids complications,' I said, 'and I've got to start somewhere.'

'Do you thing we should start practising?' he asked, still laughing.

'Well, if we do, we'll wait until we get out under those trees further on,' I said, because I was definitely not going to start practising right there in front of Mrs Lane's house. A sufferer from insomnia, Mrs Lane was forever telling my mother about the hours she spent looking out of the window at night and how long and boring it was. I had no intention of shortening the night for her.

When we arrived beneath the trees he put his arm around me and, looking over his shoulder, I could see the moon through the trees. I wondered would the moon still be in the same place after my first kiss and would I still be the same person. It was a strange, mildly exciting experience but his nose was cold, which put a slight damper on the proceedings. The moon did not dance in the sky nor the earth shake beneath my feet, and I told my companion that while it was OK I felt that kissing was a bit overrated. He assured me laughingly that it could improve with repetition, but it was a bad night for practising as a freezing grey frost covered the countryside, so we soon parted company.

The following week he went back to school and shortly afterwards I received from him a letter telling me that we would have to get together again at Easter to put in more practice. It had been his first kiss as well. He had not told me at the time, he wrote, because he had not wanted to undermine my confidence in his ability.

'You Can't Beat The Nuns'

In my mother's book the nuns were without equal when it came to making a thorough job of anything. So she insisted that all her daughters spend time with them in a domestic-science school to learn the basic skills for survival and the social graces that the nuns alone could impart; to prepare us for life as she put it. I protested vigorously, as the last thing I wanted was to spend a year locked up with nuns. My mother, however, reckoned that if my older sisters had needed house-training I, because I was the youngest and most useless, was in even greater need of it. My protests went unheard; on occasions such as this when conflicting opinions clashed my mother always won: she became deaf and dumb and totally unmovable, and all arguments simply ground to a halt. A side of her that was seldom seen, this steely determination came to the surface when she deemed it necessary for the common good; if something was right then no amount of arguing would make it wrong, and vice versa, end of story.

So one September day I found myself in my late teens heading reluctantly towards Drishane Convent, some fifteen miles back the road from our home. In every brood ability may be unevenly distributed, and when domestic skills were allocated I was under the hen's wing. On my very first day in Drishane I blotted my copybook by telling the domestic-science teacher, Sister Benignus – or Benny as she was generally known to her respectful pupils – that rice pudding should be flavoured with pepper. She raised her eyes to heaven and announced in regretful tones, 'You do not appear to take after your sister Clare'. And from then on for the entire year I was to live in the shadow of my more accomplished sister.

The head nun was a chubby, chirpy, correct little person
with sparkling brown eyes and a wobbling chin. She always
reminded me of a sprightly robin, and this birdlike appearance was emphasized by the Drishane coif which was peaked
at the front. She was a stickler for correct behaviour and
demanded that we all walk tall, and when she entered the
dining-room she went around poking us between the
shoulder-blades and saying in her chirpy voice, 'Deportment,
girls, deportment: always sit up straight and do not slouch'.
She believed in decorum in all things, and in law and order,
and she ran her school on the well-oiled wheels of good planning and orderly routine. Her twenty-eight pupils were
divided into four groups and rotated between cookery, sewing, housecraft and poultry; she made it clear that in each
aspect this was to be a year of self-improvement for each of us,
in which everything, no matter how trivial, was to be done
well.

We were awakened at 7.30 every morning by Sister Ita clap-
ping her hands along the dormitory where we slept in cur-
tained cubicles; then she chanted 'Benedicamus Domino', to
which we were all supposed to answer 'Deo Gratias' and jump
out of bed. That was the theory; the reality, however, was that
most of us groaned and complained and did not feel in the
least like offering thanks. I would hang in there as long as I
possibly could, but Sister Ita kept on going up and down until
she had us all dug out of our beds. Beside each bed was a little
dressing-table with an earthenware basin and a jug of cold
water, with the aid of which we washed ourselves – upper half
first from top down; then lower half from bottom up.

We clattered along the polished wooden corridors and
down the wide stairs – using a different side each week to
balance the wear – and out into the grey dawn. On winter
mornings the old castle which stood beside the path through
the garden glistened with frost, while light poured out
through the stained-glass windows of the little chapel. If any
wisps of sleep still lingered in our brains the sharp air of early
morning soon cleared them away, and by the time we had
climbed the timber spiral stairs to the chapel our minds were

as alert and receptive as they would ever be. With the coming of spring this early morning walk was a lovely introduction to the day as the mist rose from the lake beyond the lawn that sloped away on the left-hand side of the path and the dew sparkled on the overhanging trees which surrounded the lake.

Some of the grounds around Drishane were landscaped but saved from monotony by the old castle and the hidden corners around the grey, stone buildings. The gardens and lawns extended to the playing pitches and the quiet fields of the convent farm stretched as far as the eye could see. It was a gracious, restful place and I passed a varied and interesting year there in blessedly tranquil surroundings. We were taught all aspects of cookery, household management and needlework; and although not naturally endowed with domestic skills, I learned that with good planning and organization the tedium of housework could be reduced to a minimum.

In the laundry the ironing of linen table-cloths and serviettes was carried out according to a set ritual. When it came to instructions on how to iron a man's shirt I expressed strenuous reservations but Sister Ita simply swept them aside. The laundry itself was a large, flag-stoned room with big earthenware sinks set against the walls all around, and there was a huge old iron pull-out clothes dryer for use in the winter months. The windows of the laundry looked out over the orchard where in summer the clothes fluttered on the line between the apple-trees.

While one group was busy in the laundry another prepared lunch in the kitchen, a big airy room with a red, quarry-tiled floor and tall windows which looked out over the sweeping driveway, playing pitches and farm fields. It was dominated by a huge Aga cooker. It was my first experience with an Aga and I decided that if in later years I should ever be confined to a kitchen an Aga would be my working companion. It was big, roomy, comfortable and tolerant, almost like a caring grandmother sitting in the corner. It had a big boiling ring that could carry many pots and a simmering ring of the same size, together with hot ovens and gentle warming ones.

Off the kitchen was a long pantry with a wire-mesh window and long, timber, glass-fronted presses. On a table under the window we made butter-rolls for the afternoon tea. If the cooking group were efficient we ate well and if not we suffered the consequences; as our own critics we were pretty effective. The test of a good cook, Sister Benignus told us, was to be able to recover from a kitchen disaster and present the meal at the dining-room table as a triumph. This was easier said than done and we ate a few kitchen disasters which were very recognizable as such, but as the year went on they became fewer and fewer.

'Up-house' the group learned all about waxing and polishing and were responsible for keeping the place spick and span. We made our own polish – two cups of turpentine and boiled oil and one cup of methylated spirits and vinegar – which fed as well as poslished the furniture. Amongst the other skills we acquired were how to pack a case efficiently and how to serve a meal to a VIP guest. And in all their teaching of us the nuns were pleasant and good-humoured, while letting us know that when in Rome you did as the Romans did.

Elsewhere in a much larger part of the school other pupils, in for a five-year stretch, were preoccupied with Inter and Leaving Certs, but we were blissfully free of exams. While others swotted we had an end-of-term concert and play, a humorous depiction of the lifestyle of the convent which the nuns laughed at as heartily as anyone. Having scripted and produced the entertainment, I was rewarded with a prize for my first exercise in the dramatic arts. Prizes were presented by the nun who was responsible for encouraging our spiritual and creative development; a very sensitive, holy nun, Sister Eithne possessed a quirky, wry sense of humour, and as my prize she ceremoniously presented me with a facecloth and a box of soap.

With me in Drishane was Ann who had been a fellow student at the old school across the fields and later at the secondary school in town. One evening before going to the chapel for night prayers she decided to pin her long hair in coils on the top of her head. She had not forseen how peculiar it would look when her school beret was perched on top; but the operation had taken longer than anticipated and there was no time to take her hair down as we were late already. We ran breathlessly down the path and up the long, spiral stairs to the chapel. As we ran I got a fit of laughing every time I looked at the creation on the top of her head, and then we scurried at last into our seats just as the Reverend Mother started the rosary. Kneeling beside Ann I tried hard to suppress the urge to giggle, but while I had some success the girls in the seats behind had none. Gasps of suppressed laughter burst from the rows of girls behind us and those in front, when they heard the noise, looked back and beheld the amazing hairstyle with the beret perched so precariously on top, and then they started shaking with amusement. Nothing induces laughter as much as the knowledge that one should not, especially when everyone else is trying to stop laughing as well. Even the sobering thought that behind us were rows of demurely praying nuns did nothing to control the situation. It was a great relief when night prayers ended and we could escape from the church but first we had to walk down the aisle past rows of serene-faced nuns. As I passed the final row I shot a quick glance at the head nun; she caught my eye and gave a knowing smile, and the incident was never mentioned afterwards.

Young novices entered the Drishane order in October and March and watching these black-garbed figures in the chapel I was impressed by their courage. Of course, some found that the religious life was not for them and left, but amongst those who stayed the one who impressed me most of all was Sister Gemma. A pretty girl, bubbling with good humour and gaiety, she seemed even as she walked to bounce off the ground almost as if earth had no claim on her. Some years later, while she was still quite young, she died of cancer, but at her funeral I felt no sadness, sure that she had gone to where all her thoughts and motivations had had their origin.

My year spent at the convent gave me my first experience of nuns and I observed their lifestyle with fascination. In many ways I found it intriguing and attractive though I was shocked by their lack of personal freedom. The fact that so many women lived together under one roof in apparent harmony impressed me as a tribute to their self-discipline and tolerance, and although there must inevitably have been moments of friction between them we never witnessed them. United in religious zeal, their community was cemented together by their love of God and their interest in their pupils. The School of Housecraft there has been closed for many years now, but although I had argued with my mother that a year spent there would be a year wasted, I have always been glad since then that she got the better of me in that argument.

Back Across The Fields

Danny looked at the world through eyes that saw the beauties of the countryside which we usually ran past as we played. Because he was less robust than other children he walked more slowly, and often he called us back to look at what he had discovered. Ours was a mixed school in which girls and boys treated each other as equals, and if a row broke out we girls kicked shins and pulled hair to assert ourselves. In the classroom the boys stuck our long hair into inkwells and used the nibs of pens to inject their venom into our bare necks and elbows whenever the opportunity arose. But while Danny played football with the boys at lunch-time he never took part in the ink-dipping and nib-prodding skulduggery that the others engaged in. Those who sat in front of him had no need to fear attack from the rear, for Danny was too gentle to inflict hardship on anyone.

It was he who introduced me to my first telephone. It was a stone. In the morning if he had passed to school ahead of me he placed a stone on top of the old bridge. Soon the children of each family had their own stone and on arrival at the bridge in the morning we could see by the stones who had gone before us; if it was early and we had time to spare we might sit on the bridge and wait for the others.

Our schoolbags, made from a strong, green material, we called 'purses' and they needed to be strong for they were battered, bruised and dirtied through encounters with hedges and muddy gaps. Some had two armbands through which we looped our hands so that they could hang off our backs. Danny's, however, hung off a long strap that swung around his neck and knocked off his boney knees. He always had more in his bag than the rest of us because he never tidied it out but simply carried his books forward from year to year.

The hands of all the children going to our school were brown and mostly muddy; all, that is, except Danny's, which were pale and blue-veined with long, tapering, sensitive fingers. And on these fingers pet birds perched, quite unafraid, when he stretched out his delicate hands to them. The rest of us stood back and watched him do this because if we moved close the frightened birds flew away. His relationship with the birds placed Danny a cut above the rest of us in my book, but he never thought himself superior on this account and he was simply surprised that we could not also do what came to him so naturally.

He spent much of the day looking up at the sky and watching the clouds, and he had names for the different cloud formations. Sometimes on a summer evening he persuaded us all to lie down on the grass and look up at the sky with him, and when we did this we became aware, ironically, of the world at our feet. Here in the grass were ladybirds, grasshoppers and ants, which we called pismires, and all the teeming insect life that we normally walked over unseeing. My sister Clare pulled the long blades of grass and persuaded us that she could play music through them, and sometimes she succeeded though her audience was not always entirely appreciative. We pulled the long-stemmed dandelions and blew away their soft, fluffy hats to tell the time: one o'clock, two o'clock – each puff an hour. Not as accurate as Greenwich Mean Time but more enjoyable. If a tall foxglove with its cascading purple flowers happened to be growing near us, we went through a routine of cracking the bells, or 'fairy thimbles' as we called them, making sure first that there were no wasps visiting inside. We also used some unfortunate flowers – usually marguerites or other large daisies – for games of 'he loves me, he loves me not'.

Danny conveyed to us some of his awareness and appreciation of life. Looking at life from soft, brown, moist eyes, he saw more than the rest of us and coaxed us to see it too. When he put his mind to his studies, he was the star pupil, but learning enjoyed no great priority in his life and some mornings he arrived in school with his sack unopened since leaving the previous evening. If the master was suspected to be on a rampage Danny would sit on a stone in the last field before the school and run off his exercise or lessons. He had a nose that dried up in the summer like the hill streams, but in winter the sleeve of his jumper was in constant use as an emergency handkerchief. Tissues, of course, were unheard of and the torn-up sheets that we were supposed to use as hankies often wound up being used as sails for boats in the *glaise* or for other more necessary pursuits.

Danny's hair had a mind of its own and stuck out in all directions. His mother used laughingly to say that a scrubbing brush was necessary to subdue it every morning, but before long it would again resemble a furze bush.

After leaving school he remained on the home farm and when his parents died he lived a contented bachelor existence on his own. Many years later, on a cold January day when the ground was covered with snow, I called to his house; he was not at home but I finally ran him to earth in a neighbour's field where he stood surrounded by neighbouring children. The years had brought touches of premature grey to his wayward hair but his brown eyes held the same trusting, merry look. As we walked together down towards his house I told him that I intended walking back across the fields to the old school and asked him to come with me. I could see that he felt that the journey might be too much for him but as always his spirit was willing, so we set out to retrace our footsteps for the first time since we had gone to school together.

The paths were now overgrown and the hedges had closed in over the stepping stones that spanned the ditches, but we burrowed our way through as snow tumbled down on top of us from high branches. At the old school we found that the trees had grown in and around it and grass had grown up to the window-sills; it stood huddled in the arms of nature which now claimed it for its own as ivy trailed across its gaping windows. Where once children had laughed and shouted, now the cawing of crows from the tree-tops was the only sound.

There was about it a peacefulness, as if the years of learning had blended into the walls and the grey stones were now sheltered by the overhanging branches.

We went around the back to inspect the old dry toilets: now they were crumbling with age and we laughed as we recalled the request of 'Bhfuil cead agam dul amach'. Leaning over the rusty gate beside the school we looked up at the sky and started to talk about the clouds and it was as if time had stood still.

When we arrived back at Danny's thatched cottage the snow had started to come down again and we were glad to poke up the fire and make the tea. As I sat beside the fire I looked around his large kitchen, which bore all the signs of the freedom of bachelor living; no 'fussy woman' disturbed the leisurely pace of Danny's life. He had plans for a new house and he spread them out on the table and we studied them. It would have amenities that this old one lacked, including central heating, but I wondered if Danny might find it difficult to leave his old house. He took me into a room off the kitchen to show me a magnificent oil painting and large mahogany sideboard that would have been a collector's dream. We talked about his love of birds and I promised to paint a picture of pheasants for his new house.

As I walked out the long yard I turned to wave to Danny, who was framed in the doorway of his long, low, thatched house. With the snow on the thatch and the light from the deep-set window cutting into the darkness, it was like a scene from a Christmas card. I walked home across the fields, memories churning around in my mind. The moon had risen high in the sky and the snow-covered countryside stretched out around me, while the frosty grass crunched beneath my feet. When I saw the lights of our own house I slowed my footsteps, reluctant to leave behind this outdoor calmness that enfolded me.

During the summer that followed I painted the picture for Danny's new house, but it was destined never to hang there. One day in early autumn a phone call came to say that he had died, quietly, just as he had lived. At his funeral I met many of our old school friends and we shared a feeling of vulnerability brought about by the fact that he was the first of our class to go. Some of them I had not met since leaving the old school-house in the fields, so on an occasion which combined both happiness and sadness there was much reminiscing. And as I drove back past his silent house that night I stopped and got out to lean on his rusty gate, and I felt glad that he had never left his old home that was somehow where he belonged, and where his spirit would always be at peace.